Date Due

DEC 11 2000			
NOV 3 0 2002			
AUG 19 2010			

SATISFACTION SURVEYS IN LONG-TERM CARE

About the Editors

Jiska Cohen-Mansfield, Ph.D., is the director of the Research Institute of the Hebrew Home of Greater Washington and a Professor of Health Care Sciences at George Washington University Medical Center. Dr. Cohen-Mansfield received her Ph.D. in clinical psychology from the State University of New York at Stony Brook, and completed a post-doctoral fellowship at New York University, Institute of Rehabilitation Medicine. Dr. Cohen-Mansfield also has a master's degree in statistics from the Hebrew University in Jerusalem. She has published numerous articles on the topic of agitation in persons suffering from dementia, as well as addressing important issues for the frail elderly, such as sleep, religious beliefs, decisions regarding the use of life-sustaining treatments, physical restraints, vision problems, depression, autonomy, and stress in nursing home caregivers. Dr. Cohen-Mansfield has expertise in the development of assessment instruments and working with multi-site studies concerning geriatric services. Dr. Cohen-Mansfield is a Fellow of the American Psychological Association and of the Gerontological Society of America. Dr. Cohen-Mansfield is the recipient of grants from various institutions including: the National Institute of Mental Health, National Institute on Aging, the Agency for Healthcare Policy and Research, the National Institute for Nursing Research, and the Alzheimers Association. Dr. Cohen-Mansfield is the recipient of several awards, including the International Psychogeriatrics Association Outstanding Selected Submissions Award, the International Busse Research Award in Social/Behavioral Sciences, and the Recognition Award for Outstanding Contributions in Gerontological Research of the Maryland Gerontological Association.

Farida K. Ejaz, Ph.D., L.I.S.W., is the Senior Coordinator for Residential Care Research at The Margaret Blenkner Research Center of The Benjamin Rose Institute. She has over 12 years of experience in gerontological research and has published numerous articles on issues related to long-term care. She has also served as an adjunct faculty member at the Mandel School of Applied Social Sciences at Case Western Reserve University since 1991.

Perla Werner, Ph.D., is a Senior Lecturer at the Faculty of Social Welfare and Health Studies at the University of Haifa, Israel. Dr. Werner has been involved for many years in the research of behavioral problems accompanying dementia and care needs and treatment issues in frail elderly persons. Her current interests include the psychosocial and economic aspects of decision making processes involved in the care and provision of services for elderly persons suffering from dementia and other chronic diseases such as osteoporosis. Dr. Werner serves as an Observer in the Israeli National Council for Geriatrics and as a Member in the Israeli National Council for Hip Fractures.

SATISFACTION SURVEYS IN LONG-TERM CARE

Jiska Cohen-Mansfield, PhD
Farida K. Ejaz, PhD
Perla Werner, PhD
Editors

 Springer Publishing Company

Springer Publishing Company, Inc.
536 Broadway
New York, NY 10012-3955

Acquisitions Editor: Bill Tucker
Production Editor: Maxine Langweil
Cover design by James Scotto-Lavino

99 00 01 02 03 / 5 4 3 2 1

Library of Congress Cataloging-in-Publication Data

Satisfaction surveys in long-term care / Jiska Cohen-Mansfield,
    Farida K. Ejaz, and Perla Werner, editors.
        p. cm.
    Includes bibliographical references and index.
    ISBN 0-8261-1284-6 (hbk.)
    1. Nursing home care—Evaluation.   2. Long-term care of the
sick—Evaluation.   3. Patient satisfaction—Evaluation. 4. Medical
care surveys.   I. Cohen-Mansfield, Jiska. II. Ejaz, Farida K.
III. Werner, Perla.
RA997.S248   1999
362.1'6'068—dc21   99-15736
                                                                  CIP

Printed in the United States of America

CONTENTS

Section II Practice

CONTRIBUTORS*

Jiska Cohen-Mansfield, Ph.D.
Professor, George Washington
 University Medical Center
Director, Research Institute
Hebrew Home of Greater Washington
6121 Montrose Road
Rockville, MD 20852
Phone: (301) 770-8449
Fax: (301) 770-8455
e-mail: mansfield@hebrew-home.org

Farida Ejaz, Ph.D.
Coordinator for Residential Care
 Research
The Benjamin Rose Institute
Citizens Building
850 Euclid Avenue, Suite 1100
Cleveland, OH 44114
Phone: (216) 621-7201
Fax: (216) 621-3505
e-mail: farida@apk.net

Perla Werner, Ph.D.
Yehuda Hanasi 29, Apt. 9
Neve Avivim
Tel Aviv 69206
Israel
Phone: 0011-972-3-642-1849
Fax: 0011-972-3-640-9496
e-mail: wernerp@netvision.net.il

Barbara J. Bowers, Ph.D., R.N.
University of Wisconsin-Madison
Madison, Wisconsin

Pat Carter
The Hebrew Home of Greater
 Washington
Rockville, Maryland

J. Mac Crawford, R.N., Ph.D.
Ohio State University
School of Public Health
Columbus, Ohio

* Please address correspondence to Dr. Jiska Cohen-Mansfield.

Maureen Hirsch, R.N., M.N.
Vital Research, LLC
Los Angeles, California

Dennis Hocevar, Ph.D.
Rossier School of Education
University of Southern California
Los Angeles, California

Susan Kohler, M.S., CCC-SP/L
Glendale Adventist Medical Center
Rehabilitation Services Dept.
Los Angeles, California

Jean M. Kruzich, Ph.D.
School of Social Work
University of Washington
Seattle, Washington

Michael Murray, Ph.D.
Department of Health Administration
University of Toronto, Canada
Toronto, Ontario

Linda Noelker, Ph.D.
The Margaret Blenker Research Center
The Benjamin Rose Institute
Cleveland, Ohio

Peter G. Norton, M.D., Ph.D.
Department of Family Medicine
University of Calgary, Canada
Calgary, Canada

Robert L. Rubinstein, Ph.D.
Department of Sociology and
  Anthropology
University of Maryland Baltimore
  County
Baltimore, Maryland

Dorothy Schur
The Margaret Blenker Research Center
The Benjamin Rose Institute
Cleveland, Ohio

Warren Slavin, M.B.A.
The Hebrew Home of Greater
  Washington
Rockville, Maryland

Liane R. Soberman, M.A.
Department of Health Administration
University of Toronto, Canada
Toronto, Canada

Gwen C. Uman, R.N., Ph.D.
Vital Research , LLC
Los Angeles, California

Harold Urman, Ph.D.
Vital Research, LLC
Los Angeles, California

Barbara van Maris, MSc
Smaller World Communications,
Toronto, Canada

Gwenn Voelckers
The Wesley Group
Rochester, New York

Roy Young, MBA
Vital Research, LLC
Los Angeles, California

Jon R. Zemans
The Wesley Group
Rochester, New York

David R. Zimmerman, Ph.D.
University of Wisconsin-Madison
Madison, Wisconsin

Chapter 1

INTRODUCTION

Jiska Cohen-Mansfield

W ith the growth of the elderly population, there has been a parallel increase in long-term care facilities. Concurrently, the costs of care have been escalating, resulting in government and market limits on expenses. In order to reduce costs, tighter entry criteria have been established, thereby increasing the level of disability among long-term care residents, and raising the demands on staff. The decreased access to nursing homes has increased competition for patients, which, together with a growing older population in long-term care, has resulted in increased attention to performance and quality, leading the industry toward utilization of various methods of quality improvement, including the use of satisfaction surveys. Similarly, OBRA 87 and the resident rights movement have focused attention to the "voice of the consumer." Hence the increased interest in and use of satisfaction surveys in long-term care.

CRITIQUE OF SATISFACTION SURVEYS USE IN LONG-TERM CARE

Satisfaction surveys present a potent tool to improve long-term care services. Their primary significance lies in their capacity to utilize the point of view of the people for whom long-term care services are created in the first place. Satisfaction surveys are subjective measures that rely on the perceptions of the recipients of care. This is in contrast to more objective indicators, such as number of falls or rate of mortality. Because most people who reside in long-term care institutions are frail, suffer from multiple chronic illnesses in addition to dementia, and have a limited life expectancy, the objective criteria may not be the most meaningful indicator of quality. Indeed, two recent studies have demonstrated the limitations of objective quality indicators in long-term care (Mukamel & Brower, 1998; Porell & Caro, 1998). Rather, the subjective sense of quality of life, or level of comfort, may take precedence over more objective indicators of care.

A second consideration supporting the use of satisfaction surveys in long-term care relates to their traditional focus on empowering consumers of care. Because of their frailty, nursing home residents are less likely to initiate complaints or organize an improvement process on their own. A satisfaction survey is an avenue for procuring the residents' input. Thus, it offers a way to give voice to those who are otherwise easily side-stepped when care-related decisions are being made.

Another important strength of satisfaction surveys lies in the opportunity they provide to integrate and utilize the diverse outlook of all those who are involved in long-term care. Long-term care is comprised of a tightly knit group of interactions among residents, staff, and relatives wherein the well-being of each component is intrinsically related to that of the others (see Fig. 1.1). Although a long-term care facility provides a home for residents, a place of employment for staff, and a place to visit relatives for caregivers, it is not simply any one of these. Rather, it is a place to live the rest of life, a place to provide care in its deepest sense, and a place to which relatives entrust the care of their loved one. Furthermore, it is a place to deal with suffering and decline, it is about caring and giving even under the most difficult circumstances, and thereby it is a place filled with emotions and value-laden moral judgments for all involved. In long-term care facilities, the activity which is merely doing a "job" for one person can make a tremendous difference in the experience of "quality of life" for the other. In making it possible for "work" to encompass the emotional aspects of caring, the worker needs to be cared for as well. Indeed, it is this interconnectedness among those involved that prompted us to include materials concerning satisfaction for residents, family, and staff members of nursing homes in this book.

Despite the many strengths of satisfaction surveys and despite the rapid increase in the use of satisfaction surveys in long-term care, they are also the target of much controversy. They have been termed invalid, unscientific, mere promotional tools, misdirected, and not targeting quality of care. Of course satisfaction surveys are tools, and as such can be used well

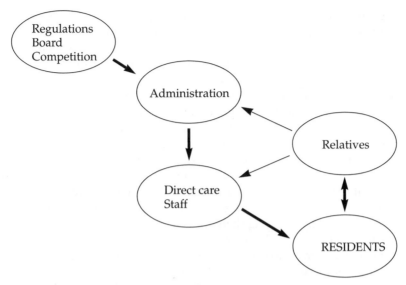

Figure 1.1 The nursing home—a schematic view.

or can be misused. Therefore, it is important to recognize and understand the criticisms which have been leveled at the use of satisfaction surveys. Some misuse can be attributed to the pressures of working or living in long-term care environments, which may limit the proper utilization of surveys or the provision of resources needed to effectively address survey results. Other issues in the use of satisfaction surveys in long-term care are more generic, and generally fall into one of two categories: those relating to their general use , and those pertaining to their use in long-term care specifically. With this book, we hope to help nursing home staff members and related professionals, researchers, consultants, and educators to evaluate these issues in order to maximize the potential of conducting satisfaction surveys which can be used for the improvement of long-term care services.

In considering the critique of satisfaction surveys in long-term care, it is clear that a number of objections hold true for any satisfaction survey, regardless of setting. First, there are situations in which the expressed subjective opinion of a consumer may run counter to what is believed by most to be quality care. For example, when a resident requests a medical treatment that is known to be futile and causes significant negative side effects, the satisfaction of the resident may be low when staff do not adhere to the request, whereas quality may be compromised if the staff fulfills the request. Although this conflict between quality and satisfaction is a justified concern, it does not reflect the majority of issues usually raised by satisfaction surveys.

Another type of objection which holds true for satisfaction surveys regardless of setting is the dichotomy of goals for the institution and the individual. Primary objectives of the institution are fiscal management and growth (each of which relate to public relations and quality of care), whereas the resident's primary objective is to live life in the most comfortable, happy, and meaningful manner. While these goals can coexist harmoniously, there are invariably many situations in which conflict can occur. Related to this issue is the fact that when residents, relatives, and staff are assessed for satisfaction, the needs of each group can be quite diverse. Given limited resources, this could lead to competing agendas, despite their interconnectedness . As with the previous critique of satisfaction surveys, conflicting goals and needs are an integral part of any medical care setting. Satisfaction surveys merely tap into and highlight these longstanding issues. By bringing them into clearer focus, satisfaction surveys have the potential to lead to creative problem solving .

Other objections raised in relation to satisfaction surveys relate specifically to the long-term care environment as the setting in which such surveys are implemented. The fact that most nursing home residents suffer from cognitive impairment provides a major barrier to the use of satisfaction surveys with them. Many residents are compromised in their verbal ability, such that some cannot be interviewed. Even for those who can communicate, cognitive impairment may interfere with their ability to provide valid answers which reflect their overall experience, rather than merely reflecting their mood at the specific time when an interview was conducted.

Another objection relates to the artificial nature of satisfaction surveys. According to this critique, because the long-term care facility is home to the residents who live there, a home model, rather than an institutional model for assessing a resident's level of satisfaction, would be more appropriate. In a home model, for example, ongoing discussions about the resident's well-being would be an integral part of informal communication during staff-resident interactions. Adjustments in routine or in care activities would naturally follow. While this sort of quality improvement process is a worthy goal for long-term care in the future, it is very distant from the institutional model of long-term care which currently pervades the industry. Optimizing the use of satisfaction surveys is probably the best option for the near future.

DEVELOPMENT OF THE BOOK

The idea for this book developed from discussions and a 1996 preconference workshop of the "Researchers Based in Long-term Care" Interest Group within the Gerontological Society of America. In this setting, we realized that while satisfaction surveys were increasingly being used in long-term care, knowledge about them was not readily available. In generating this book, we hope to offer this knowledge to a wider audience, and to promote further investigation to optimize the use of such tools. We would like to thank the Society and Interest Group members for their contributions in promoting the discussion on satisfaction surveys in long-term care.

In assembling this book, we set out to include authors who represent the wide range of players involved with satisfaction surveys in long-term care: researchers based inside and outside long-term care facilities, nursing home administrators, consulting firms, and others. The heterogeneity in these chapters therefore reflects both the diversity of authors and their backgrounds , and the variability in the availability of literature on the different topics.

DESCRIPTION OF BOOK CONTENTS

The first part of the book explores theoretical issues related to satisfaction surveys. More specifically, this section addresses what the focus of satisfaction surveys should be; what domains are investigated and how they are determined (see also Appendixes for a summary of domains tapped in published instruments); and how personal and institutional characteristics correlate with satisfaction. This section also examines the evolution of satisfaction surveys, who currently conducts them in nursing homes, the types of nursing homes that utilize them, and the obstacles faced in their conduct. This section therefore provides the context in which satisfaction surveys can be initiated, and the background information needed for the proper interpretation of data gathered from such surveys.

The second section of the book describes the practice of utilizing satisfaction surveys. This section was designed to aid those involved with long-term care with the difficult decisions needed for planning a satisfaction survey—from setting the goals for the survey (quality improvement, providing a vehicle for the input of consumers and staff, providing an atmosphere of caring, marketing, public relations), to deciding who will be surveyed, when, and how (who will conduct the survey, preparing and administrating the survey), to collecting and utilizing data (including both interpretation of data and development of action plans). The chapters describe how satisfaction surveys are conducted with residents, both the cognitively intact and the cognitively impaired, their surrogates, and the staff members who provide the care. These chapters are augmented by summaries of the characteristics of currently published satisfaction surveys and a summary of the main dimensions for comparing these instruments to enable one to make appropriate decisions when starting a survey (see appendixes of the book.) Whereas the technology for developing and conducting a survey, though complex, is relatively straightforward and well-known, the methodology for actual utilization of those surveys to improve quality is only beginning to be understood. Although a survey should not be conducted unless it is put to good use, the literature of how to do so is very limited. In the second section of the book, several chapters explore how results are to be used to improve care, one utilizing quality improvement processes, and another exploring the integration of satisfaction surveys with other quality indicators. The last chapter in this section addresses ethical issues in satisfaction surveys. Table 1.1 summarizes some of the process issues involved in the survey from the decision concerning who should conduct the survey to the decisions involved in implementing an action plan on the basis of the survey.

The appendix provides the reader with examples of surveys, norms, and supporting documents needed to conduct satisfaction surveys. It begins with tables summarizing published satisfaction surveys of residents, relatives, and staff members. Specific examples of published and unpublished instruments are also provided. These examples are intended to clarify the process and to provide options in the conduct of satisfaction surveys. Any actual use of these surveys requires permission from the authors.

CHALLENGES POSED BY SATISFACTION SURVEYS IN LONG-TERM CARE

This book represents an initial effort to explore and describe the use of satisfaction surveys in long-term care which we hope will serve as a catalyst for the improvement of satisfaction survey use. With the growth in use of satisfaction surveys in long-term care, there has been a corresponding awareness of the difficulties of their use with this population, spurring new investigations of satisfaction surveys in long-term care. Much of the investigation is forthcoming, and thus the sense that this is a field under current development and exploration is very obvious in the book. Some chapters present case examples, because empirical research information is very limited or nonexistent. Other chapters describe ideas under development, or what has yet to be developed. Indeed, nearly every chapter in this book could serve as the basis for further research and inquiry. Examples of issues requiring further study include the following:

- How does one capture the life experience of the nursing home resident and the needs arising from this experience? (see Chapter 2)

Table 1.1 The process of satisfaction survey—an overview

Goals

- ❏ Quality improvement
- ❏ Providing a sense of caring
- ❏ Marketing
- ❏ Public relations

Initial decisions: Who, when, how

- ❏ Who should be surveyed?
  - • Residents, surrogates, staff
  - • Current, past
  - • Total population, a subgroup, a stratified representative sample
- ❏ When should surveys be conducted?
  - • Annually, biannually
  - • Up on a rotating basis by unit
  - • Event-related: after admission, discharge, prior to making budgetary decisions.
- ❏ How should surveys be conducted?
  - • Focus groups
  - • Personal interview
  - • Phone interview
  - • Mail survey
  - • Combination
- ❏ Who will conduct the survey? (Examine issues such as: expertise in survey administration and utilization, experience in long-term care, prior response rate, cost, time frame)
  - • In house
  - • Outside firm
  - • Combination

Preparing for the survey

- ❏ Buying into the concept
- ❏ Allaying fears regarding confidentiality, retribution

Administering the survey

- ❏ Who will administer it? Regular staff, contracted company, volunteers.
- ❏ Handling missing data
- ❏ Confidentiality measures
  - • Nonuse of names/departments
  - • Editing out of names
  - • Data analysis only in the aggregate

Table 1.1 *Continued*

Summarizing the data

- ❏ Type of data provided:
  - Report
  - Database
  - Presentation: to whom? when? by whom?
  - Recommendations
  - Combination
- ❏ Content of data provided:
  - Raw data
  - Frequencies of satisfaction
  - Correlates of total satisfaction/importance of areas assessed
  - Frequencies of extreme dissatisfaction
  - Open ended comments requiring action
  - Correlations among different customers, e.g., family and resident responses, staff and family responses
  - Comparisons to the industry (benchmarking of the data)
  - Plans of action
- ❏ Interpretation
  - Which types of complaints/dissatisfaction are realistic (for purposes of implementing change)
  - Which complaints need to be taken at face value?
  - Which complaints may be indicating a need or problem different than the one expressed?
  - What is the response rate and how does it affect the results?
  - Environmental and external factors that might affect ratings

Moving data to action

- ❏ Which aspects of care need to be improved?
- ❏ Which aspects of care can be improved?
- ❏ What additional information is needed to develop an improvement plan?
- ❏ Which systems are in place to initiate and monitor change?
- ❏ How is change to be evaluated?

- To what extent are reports by cognitively impaired residents sufficiently valid to warrant intervention efforts? How do we determine the level or types of cognitively impaired residents who can contribute to a valid and reliable survey?
- What are the most effective ways to institute positive change in response to a survey?
- Which types of change can be achieved with relative ease, and which are difficult to accomplish?
- With what other types of long-term care populations should surveys be used? For example, currently untapped potential users of satisfaction surveys such as the following:

  - Satisfaction surveys conducted with relatives after the death of the resident aimed at improving the care of the dying and the handling of death and grief;
  - Satisfaction surveys conducted with those discharged to the community, or to other facilities to improve continuity of care, and to access those who may have left the facility as a result of dissatisfaction;
  - Satisfaction surveys with facility volunteers to capture their perceptions of opportunities for improvement of care in the facility, as well as ways to enhance their satisfaction as volunteers.

In sum, satisfaction surveys offer a potent tool to enhance the lives of those in long-term care. The technology for their optimal use is still under development. We hope that this book will serve as a stepping stone for this development with the goal of improving the lives of residents in long-term care facilities.

REFERENCES

Mukamel, D. B., & Brower, C. A. (1998). The influence of risk adjustment methods on conclusions about quality of care in nursing homes based on outcome measures. *The Gerontologist, 38*(6), 695–703.

Porell, F., & Caro, F. G. (1998). Facility-level outcome performance measures for nursing homes. *The Gerontologist, 38*(6), 665–683.

PART **I**

THEORY

RESIDENT SATISFACTION, QUALITY OF LIFE, AND "LIVED EXPERIENCE" AS DOMAINS TO BE ASSESSED IN LONG-TERM CARE

Robert L. Rubinstein

RESIDENT SATISFACTION

The last decade has seen a huge growth in attention to quality of life issues in nursing homes. The passage of OBRA, the establishment of the MDS and related reporting structures, the growth of SCUs and special care of all sorts, and the availability of alternatives to nursing home residence have all played a role in helping nursing homes face quality of life and quality of care issues. In addition, many nursing homes have begun a shift from regarding residents and their families as more or less passive entities to establishing a more interactive and partnered relationship with them. Research into resident or consumer satisfaction has been an important part of this. Measuring consumer satisfaction in the nursing home, whether the consumer is the resident or the family member, is a very important tool in increasing the sensitivity of nursing homes to human needs.

It is important to state the central significance of resident satisfaction surveys in the nursing home. These should be regarded as vital, compelling and humane. As noted below, such consumer surveys are one of the few ways that medical settings have of finding out what's right and wrong and fixing or preserving it, as appropriate. There are few other, if any, systematic methods as effective.

Also, work needs to be done to improve the quality of residential satisfaction surveys. As we will discuss below, there are many challenges in the nursing home and to residential satisfaction surveys, not the least of which is dealing with dementia and related disorders.

This being said, it is also a challenge to think with a critical eye about residential satisfaction as a domain. Indeed, this essay began as an effort to conceptually think through and link resident satisfaction to quality of life issues in nursing homes. When one tries to think about the domain of resident satisfaction in the nursing home independently or as linked to quality of life, it is clear that the domain of "resident satisfaction" is limited. Most tellingly, it appears devoid of any explicit model or theory of the person. Rather, a generic portrait of "resident satisfaction" is a list of behaviors, events, or things that consumers of nursing home services and amenities like or dislike. The question of personhood—who the consumer is—is played down. This is not a trivial issue for a setting that provides full life care.

There is an obvious potential relationship between quality of life and residential satisfaction. This is that the more the residents like services in the nursing home—the better their quality of life—the happier they are or the less they might be depressed. Unfortunately, hard evidence for such a relationship is unclear as is the directionality so that the less depressed a person is, the more satisfied she might be rather than the other way around.

No explicit theory of the person is ever elaborated for these constructs. However, there is an implicit theory in the domain of resident satisfaction that suggests that one is an individual in the American cultural sense, a person with rationality and "say-so." We will make more of this observation below.

If we focus solely on studying resident satisfaction without reference to other domains, such as quality of life, one can do a good job of identifying a resident (or other "consumer," such as a family member or other proxy), establishing key domains of satisfaction, asking questions about these domains, and summarizing this data. This is greatly worth doing. The difficulties in this matter are largely technical, requiring some experimentation with what works best, and concern for a large number of technical issues. These include: identifying the focal "consumer" whose "satisfaction" is being gauged; identifying institutionally appropriate domains of "satisfaction"; establishing simple, understandable, and effective item wording for resident and family; determining what level of language complexity or style of wording should be utilized; finding how one might best include data (or exclude data) from residents with cognitive, neurological, or other communicative disorders (Lawton, in press); fixing an appropriate length for the instrument; setting rules about the use of proxies for responding to items; deciding about how best to include (or exclude) nondemented consumers with hearing or speech difficulties; meeting concerns about how responses from ethnic minorities might differ from those of nonminorities; determining the validity and replicability of the instrument; highlighting and assuaging any potential vulnerability of residents when reporting negative feelings or circumstances in a custodially scrutinized environment; and choosing appropriate data-analytic strategies. These are issues that are highly significant, are in the process of being determined and reported, through books such as this one, at paper sessions at professional meetings, at a series of workshops held at the annual meetings of the Gerontological Society of America, and finally in part through meetings sponsored by HCFA.

Generically, satisfaction surveys in nursing homes, at least those with which I am familiar, ask questions of residents and family that deal with many important domains regarding the perceived quality of care and services and amenities provided. These may include the following: overall or general satisfaction with the facility; estimations of value in regard to the price paid; social and emotional support from other residents and staff; perceptions of courteousness and respect in attitude from the staff; the perceived quality of content of programming and activities; success or lack of success in adaptation to the institutional environment; pleasantness of decor and environmental amenities and feelings of "home-likeness"; perceptions of food and meal quality; evaluations of the quality of health care and health-related services, including physicians, nurses, and CNAs; perceptions of the quality of help available (when it is needed) with ADLs and IADLs; feelings of safety and security; and the perceived ability to maintain one's independence, act with self-determination and proactivity, and receive respect.

A separate but related issue (and one which will not be developed here) is the significant question of what is to be done with the data once collected and analyzed. This is essentially a "political" or "strategic" or "administrative" question. The underlying agenda of surveys is two fold: to take a snapshot of how an institution is doing in terms of institutional constructs such as "quality" and "service," and to use such findings to improve institutional functioning with regard to those domains under scrutiny, be they clinical, maintenance tasks (food and laundry), psychosocial, or those directed to general resident well-being. Yet the satisfaction survey and the implementation of change are two very different things. I am familiar with some nursing homes that have engaged in involved consumer surveys, but have failed to systematically make any needed changes discovered through the consumer survey. Institutions may lack the will or needed resources to make such changes. They may be overwhelmed in a variety of ways.

These are some key issues in resident satisfaction surveys. Let us return for a moment to the question raised about how "resident satisfaction" relates to quality of life. As soon as one attempts to link these domains, a variety of conceptual and ideological issues about the person are thrown into relief in that each of these perspectives makes assumptions about the nature of personhood (that we will discuss below). In addition, these domains should logically overlap. Because quality of life contains both objective and subjective indicators, resident satisfaction should be an appropriate candidate for long-term care quality of life components. Thus, resident satisfaction and quality of life should in theory be positively correlated.

However, there are several reasons to go beyond these constructs. First, once analysis pushes outward beyond a central construct of resident satisfaction, one begins to see the larger cultural and ideological framework upon which this construct rests. Because of ideology hidden under the "presenting construct," one may either ignore this (as is usually done) or comment upon it. This larger framework must be attended to.

Second, linking any two constructs presupposes attention to their underlying "theories" or "the model of the person" they incorporate. As far as I am able to ascertain, and specifically with regard to life in nursing homes, neither resident satisfaction or quality of life is often linked to a model or theory of the person. Domains, scales, and items selected are chosen by a privileged researcher almost always without regard to an empirically based set of ideas—a theory or model—about the resident. Even in instances in which "satisfaction" or "quality of life" indicators are derived with resident input, they are constructed in such a way as to miss much of what is going on in the residents' lives (see below). Again, it is important to note that "resident satisfaction" has an implicit theory about the nature of the person.

Third, and most startlingly, when one begins to focus on resident satisfaction in nursing homes, and in respect to other key domains, such as quality of life, an important knowledge-based omission is highlighted. It is difficult to understand resident satisfaction in the nursing home when we may lack any systematic or particularized understanding of what nursing home residents believe themselves to be doing in the nursing homes. That is, what are their own explanations, understandings and evaluations of why they are there? What does nursing home residence mean in terms of each person's life history?

The widespread incidence of Alzheimer's disease and other neurobehavioral disorders in the nursing home may lead one to suggest that questions of meaning, life history, and personal explanation are of little practical importance because so much of the person is lost due to the dementing illness. Certainly, these are to be dealt with within "resident satisfaction" However, this is no excuse to systematically fail to attend to key aspects of personhood. Indeed, it is a compelling suggestion that the remaining components of personhood, and personal capacities, should be nurtured, with programs attending to complementing and enhancing the remaining capacities of the resident. Thus, what the person believes herself to be doing in the nursing home is a central and largely unasked and unanswered question. The implications of this observation for assessing resident satisfaction are profound.

Fourth, it is intuitively obvious that resident satisfaction in the nursing home must differ from other theories of "resident satisfaction" or "patient satisfaction" or "consumer satisfaction" in non-nursing home, inpatient or outpatient settings. However, lack of an explicit theory or relegation of "resident satisfaction" to some implicit or covert ideological construction sets an inadequate limit to such understanding. Unlike theories of satisfaction developed for the primary care or hospital context, long-term care is a permanent condition of a person's life. Because of the total institution nature of long-term care, the nursing home *conflates* health care with life in general and confuses "being a patient" or "being a consumer of services" with "living." Certainly, the consumer role enlarges and humanizes the patient role, but it may be considered a derivative version of it (see below).

Finally, a problem in relating resident satisfaction to quality of life is found in the increasing (and often hidden) equation of quality of life with health-related quality of life alone. While quality of life is often vague and complexly defined, many quality of life measures combine items about the life impacts of specific diseases or conditions with some global well-being or life satisfaction items higgledy-piggledy, and without regard to any conscious conceptual or theoretical underpinnings or the total person. The relevance of such an approach to nursing home residents, who may be demented, suffering from multiple physical and functional impairments, and living "in a last stop," remains to be seen.

I will focus next in part on the cultural ideological model I believe to underlie "resident satisfaction" in the nursing home and related work on "patient satisfaction" (rather than on satisfaction and quality of life instruments, per se) before turning to another metric of "satisfaction." What I say is difficult to consider because nursing homes have become so institutionalized, medicalized, routinized, and reified that to think of them in different ways than they are currently construed is very difficult—almost unthinkable.

THE MODEL OF THE PERSON IN RESIDENT SATISFACTION

Thinking about resident satisfaction can be straightforward in that it includes (1) an agent (the resident consumer), (2) a producer or goods and services (the health care setting and its personnel), and (3) some set of values and evaluative processes brought to bear by the consumer on the domain of the produced. This simple model also assumes a rational, choice-making, conscious, jural individual. In this context, resident satisfaction becomes a measure of how well the individual believes services to have been provided.

In a focus on resident satisfaction in the nursing home, the construct "resident satisfaction" assumes a number of things about the person:

- "Resident satisfaction" assumes that the nursing home resident takes on the role of the consumer or actor in the world of goods and services in the form of the simple model described above. Other than through resident impressions about care and service, resident satisfaction does not seek to understand the experiential world of the resident, nor how the person's biography or life experience may affect her perceptions of life in the nursing home. Ultimately, the resident's sense of satisfaction is reducible to the action of a consumer, rather than to the action of a person who lives her life. Three roles, that of patient, resident, and consumer are conflated. Studies of satisfaction emphasize the patient/consumer/resident role rather than the person role.
- This construct also assumes the central relevance of the "consumer" role for the resident, who is now primarily a consumer of medical and medically oriented services.
- "Resident satisfaction" assumes that the standards or structures shaping everyday life are in effect in the nursing home. Resident satisfaction surveys may assume a world of empowered "say-so" for persons, when in fact any such authority may be strictly a tacit fiction used for the survey, rather than an entity in real life.

- Resident satisfaction surveys highlight only those topics under examination in the resident survey satisfaction process. For any number of purposes, this can administratively inflate that portion of the total person represented by the topics under investigation, at the expense of other aspects of human life that may be important to the resident, but are de-emphasized in the nursing home. For example, surveys may focus on the health-related aspects of nursing home life, at the expense of other domains such as "joy" or "how the nursing home experience fits into life at large" or "what I'm doing here" (see below).

- "Satisfaction surveys" may assume that events or conditions about which one may evaluatively have satisfaction are experienced in conventional ways, so that they can be generalized about. Thus a survey item such as "Are your nurses generally respectful?" cannot really be assessed in general when a resident has several nurses who may change over time and with differing and varying demeanors.

I argue that the "resident" role in nursing home resident satisfaction subsumes a more generic consumer role. In surveys, the patient/resident/consumer role remains dominant (in comparison to the person role). This removes much of the content area relevant to the full person. However, playing the consumer role may have little relevance for the nursing home resident, whose primary perspective is that she is just "living her life." It would appear that, unlike consumers in primary care or hospital settings, people who live in nursing homes are largely "living life." "Living one's life" is an activity that is based on personal meaning, experience, biography, and identity (see below). "Consumption" is the wrong entity for "living life."

To reiterate, it is true that resident satisfaction and quality of life both tap important domains and are certainly related in important ways. But at this point it is important to specify that these are professional's categories, and not the "natural" categories used by the person. Both "resident satisfaction" and "quality of life," as measured by professionals, exist in contrast to a set of categories that residents as persons might use "naturally" to give meaning to experience. A sense of personal identity, a biography, a set of social relationships, a set of key life experiences, and a system of personal meaning are the stuff of everyday life. These lead, within the person, to some understanding or explanation of why the person is in the nursing home and what she is doing there. This rich set of personal constructs forms the backdrop for the metric of resident satisfaction and quality of life. Seen in this way, resident satisfaction and quality of life measures transect this set of personal constructs in important but particular ways.

And we have little understanding of the perceived relevance or impact of residential satisfaction and quality of life measures on the person or this constellation of personal constructs, the essence of their lived experience. We will return to these issues again below.

In the next sections, we will turn to some consideration of related domains in resident satisfaction and attempt to show satisfaction in relation to quality of life and "lived experience."

RESIDENT OR PATIENT SATISFACTION IN RELATED DOMAINS: PRIMARY AND HOSPITAL CARE

Strasser, Aharony, and Greenburger (1993), have developed a comprehensive model of patient satisfaction which merits extended consideration here for its potential relation to resident satisfaction as well as its conceptual model. It is well-conceived and dynamic, but it unfortunately only partially relates to the world of long-term care. These authors describe six key principles that serve as guides to their model: (1) patient satisfaction is an affective and cognitive perceptual process; (2) patient satisfaction is multidimensional; (3) it is dynamic; (4) it reflects attitudinal reactance; (5) it must account for individual differences; and (6) it must frame the role of the patient as an activist and as a judge so that the patient becomes an endogenous variable in assessing the satisfaction process.

The model begins with cognitive and affective "stimuli." These are defined as "Information to which patients are exposed throughout their health care encounter" (1993:, p. 332). Stimuli can be human or nonhuman. Examples include "the tone of voice used by a health care provider, "a radiological technologist's assuring touch," or the impression on a patient made by the walls of a hospital room. In this model, stimuli are next subject to processes of screening and encoding (or internalization), this defined as "transferring an external stimulus into internal representation or meaning" (1993, p. 332). I would note that, in the context of the argument that I am developing here, this meaning component is potentially important. Through screening and encoding, patients may react to a stimulus and internalize it (perhaps providing a stimulus with important personal meanings). Alternatively, patients may "attend" to a stimulus, but give it little or no meaning at all. Finally, patients may simply ignore stimuli.

Next in the model, screening and encoding stimuli lead to "value judgments," or the personal evaluation of the stimuli that are internalized. This is one's recognition that one has internalized a stimulus. Next, this model describes a first level of attitudinal reactance which represents the position taken by the patient in responding to value judgments, or (put another way) their satisfaction or dissatisfaction with the internalized stimuli. These are in part based on a patient's own temperament, personal history, and life experiences. It should be noted that for all model elements, the authors suggest that a consideration of individual patient personality and life history is important, and the model includes feedback loops between such personal factors and all model elements. Finally, the model posits a second level of reactance, or "the patient's action designed to attain a desired outcome" (1993, p. 338). This is the component of the model that incorporates behavior and behavioral change over time.

As an exercise for relatively brief medical encounters, the model appears quite adequate. From a long-term care perspective, a difficulty in the model is the definition of the patient. Nursing home residents are not merely patients, and the vast ideological enterprise of long-term care is to publicly demedicalize nursing "homes." From this perspective, patients are residents who, as people, must have psychosocial needs met and who live their lives as best they can. The person is not a true patient (as in the sense of the model), but rather is a consumer and a resident, this a medicalized social role defined by the health care practitioners. For nursing home residents, the medical encounter may not be episodic, but is continuous. The model cannot deal well with this ambiguity of patient/person. The model provides the basis of a conceptual process for evaluating health care episodes. But a model more appropriate for the nursing home would require minimally the factoring in of nursing home elements as key features. For example, such a model must account for the continuous nature of health care episodes in long-term care; they must account for the conflation of person-identity with patient-identity that is at the heart of the "nursing home." Moreover, the model provides acknowledgment that personal meaning, personality, and life historical events can influence patient satisfaction. While this is acknowledged, no specific examples are given.

Strasser and colleagues outline some potential limitations to the proposed model. For example, they wonder to what extent the model they propose is "phenomenologically valid" (1993, p. 341). They also note that "the proposed model is a rational one." Yet patients may be quite irrational and may fail to "understand the consequences of their actions." However, this seeming problem is in fact an advantage. They note that when the rationality of the model is defined only with regard to the patient's sense of rationality, not that of the researcher or the health care provider, it is successful. Significantly, they write, "We suggest that if irrationality is perceived, it is fundamentally illusory since it is derived from the observer's perception, not the patient's. When the model is applied to observers, the model can ostensibly emerge as irrational. When the model is applied to patients, its rationality remains intact" (1993, p. 343). Thus to its credit, the locus of the model's action is in patient perceptions, regardless of what they are.

In a related paper, Aharony and Strasser (1993) note that there are many reasons to believe in a strong positive correlation between patient satisfaction and quality of care (at least in primary care or hospital settings). We would extend this possibility to quality of life as well. They note that studies show that satisfied patients will continue to avail themselves of services. Satisfied patients maintain relations with primary providers; they will be more proactive in participating in their own medical treatment; and they will be more open to informing the health care provider of symptoms and other health behavior information. Within the more severe constraints provided by the nursing home, we would expect that these points will also apply.

However, the underlying "model of the person" behind satisfaction studies is the jural individual portrayed as a consumer with choices. A nursing home resident may not be entirely free to choose her physician. Certainly, such a resident has little choice over the rest of the health care team or in how she maintains relations with this team.

Aharony and Strasser (1993) suggest that satisfaction surveys not only have an impact on quality of care in primary care and hospital settings, but that they are the major structural mechanism for facilitating this influence. They also suggest that satisfaction surveys may be incorporated in a total quality management (TQM) approach to health care. While it is of course unclear if the quality in a TQM approach can be equated to a resident's perception of quality of life, they note that almost nothing is known about the effect of satisfaction surveys on "patient care, services and organizations."

To extend their argument, they broach then a possible model of relationship that we may elaborate on here.

HCFA has defined quality of life and quality of care in its Resident Assessment Instrument User's Manual (HCFA, 1995) in the following way: "All necessary resources and disciplines must be used to insure that residents achieve the highest level of functioning possible (Quality of Care) and maintain their sense of individuality (Quality of Life)" (HCFA, 1995, 1-1) .

In Figure 2.1, satisfaction is depicted as directly shaping quality of care. The model also depicts satisfaction as both directly and indirectly shaping quality of life. However, all these model elements are situated upon what may be called "lived experience," or the seemingly natural personal organization of the meaningful, usually ranged around the constellation of identity, biography, personal meaning, and similar constructs. I am arguing that the upper part of the model, while potentially revealing powerful relationships, has reduced worth without a thorough consideration of the component subsumed in the bottom portion. In a sense, the questions can

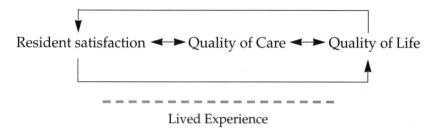

Figure 2.1 Total Quality Management Possible Model of Relationship

be posed as methodological ones. At what point can satisfaction data be aggregated? At what point can satisfaction data be removed from the deep personal context of the individual life? I am suggesting that the set point needs to be very close to the domain of lived experience, the "model" that should underlie the measurement of resident satisfaction. Before we get to a more detailed discussion of these elements, a brief introduction of some facilitating material is necessary.

The Explanatory Model

Let me put the last thought in another way. An additional of set of important ideas may be highlighted with reference to an important construct from medical anthropology, the explanatory model, which, while decades old, has yet to be utilized effectively in gerontology. The idea of the explanatory model comes from Arthur Kleinman's germinal analysis of patient and healer interaction in Taiwan (1981). Kleinman identifies the explanatory model as the perspective on the illness of each participant in the clinical setting, that is, the patient's or healer's or family's notions about what is happening with the illness, the cause of it, its sources, how it affects one, what might be done about it, and other such basic questions. Not surprisingly, in Kleinman's study, the explanatory models of the patient's and healers don't usually correspond, nor do they in most settings. He notes that the interaction between the explanatory models of the patient and the healer "is a central component of health care" (p. 105) methodologically or clinically. Kleinman (p. 106) suggests that explanatory models are accessible with a few questions including the following: "What do you call your problem? What name does it have? . . . What do you think caused your problem? . . . What kind of treatment do you think you should receive?" There are several others. Use of these questions aids a clinician (and others as well) in systematically assessing the patient's view of what is going on in the clinical encounter. Kleinman's goal is to legitimate the patient's perspective.

Clearly, the nursing home is quite different from a more standard clinical setting: patients have multiple, chronic, long-term illnesses from which they never recover. And unlike the medical situation described by Kleinman for his fieldwork, there is little in the way of medical pluralism in the nursing home. For better of worse, a single medical model orders the clinical world in long-term care.

Yet the reality that the patient has her own perspective on the nature of her illnesses and what is going on with them is of importance both clinically and in terms of assessing satisfaction. Absolutely critical here is what the nursing home resident (the patient) believes to be the explanation of why she is there in the first place!! It is hard to believe that such beliefs have no impact on "consumer" or "resident satisfaction." Equally as significant is the likelihood that there is a major discrepancy in explanatory models between staff and patient. It is likely that while staff believe they are "medically treating chronic illness," it is possible that residents may believe themselves to be "just living life" although they may acknowledge or understand the staff perspective.

A Few Words on Quality of Life

While it has become a central construct in gerontology and in the study of health and illness in later life, quality of life has been difficult to define. "Vague" and "hard to define" are phrases often associated with it. Attempts to define it are numerous. Increasingly, work in gerontology on quality of life measurement has conconceptualized it as a component of health. Core constructs of quality of life are evaluated with and eye to their relationship to health status and illness conditions.

For health-related quality of life (HRQOL), there is some consensus about core constructs. These may include social, psychological, occupational, and physical status (Fallowfield, 1990); functional ability, broader measures of health status, psychological well-being, social network and support, and life-satisfaction, morale, and self esteem (Bowling, 1992); physical status and functional ability, economic and vocational status, psychological status and well-being, social interactions, and religious and spiritual life (Spilker, 1996); physical and occupational functioning; psychological well-being, social interaction, and somatic sensation (Schipper, Clinch, & Olweny, 1996); and behavioral competence, domains of everyday life, environment, and generalized psychological well-being (Lawton, in press).

Quality of life is often used in a health-related context to assess both global health and disease specific impacts. Indeed, HRQOL and its representations in specific disease conditions (such as HIV, diabetes, hypertension, and cancer to name a few) are important areas of research and application (Dimsdale and Baum, 1995; Spilker, 1996). Schipper et al.(1996) note, "The quality of life rubric that has emerged . . . represents an attempt to quantitate . . . the net consequences of a disease and its treatment on the patient's perception of his ability to live a useful and fulfilling life" (p. 15).

The focus on the health measurement component of quality of life has examined health issues at the expense of other issues. In an important chapter, Spilker (1996) has suggested that "health quality of life" and "nonhealth quality of life" exist in inverse proportion depending on the health status of the individual measured. For well individuals, nonhealth quality of life factors overshadow health quality of life factors. In contrast, for individuals with chronic illness, the health quality of life factors are disproportionately more significant than the nonhealth quality of life factors.

Even in quality of life measurement, there is a tension between health and nonhealth-related quality of life components. Nonhealth quality of life includes factors such as "values and beliefs, desires and goals, personality attributes, coping strategies, spiritual status . . . social networks, family structure, social group, financial status, vocational status" (Spilker, 1996) and many others.

The tension between a health focus and a nonhealth focus that is revealed in quality of life measurements mimics a larger tension that cuts through this chapter as a whole, namely that between the resident/patient/consumer and the person. Table 2.1 lists some of these tensions as they have been reported in the different segments of this chapter.

RESIDENT SATISFACTION AND THE PERSPECTIVE OF "LIVED EXPERIENCE"

Recalling again the Model presented in Figure 2.1, and the argument laid out in the chapter, Table 2.2 presents a list of elements of lived experience that must implicitly and explicitly provide a foundation for understanding resident satisfaction in the nursing home.

Identity refers to the core sense of who the person is, the distillate of both past social roles that are and have been meaningful and the current sense of whom one is in the world. "Satisfaction" of some sort can often be found in relating present activities and events to key elements of personal identity. With dementia and similar disorders, responsibility for the

Table 2.1 List of conceptual constructs in patient or resident health care roles in long-term care

Patient as resident	Patient as person
Resident as consumer	Resident as person
Care staff's explanatory model	Resident's explanatory model
Processor of cognitive and affective stimuli	Evaluator of stimuli in reference to life events and personal meaning
Health-related QOL	Nonhealth-related QOL

Table 2.2 Key Elements in Assessing the Nursing Home from a "Lived Experience" Perspective

Identity: The core sense of who a person is and has been, held by that person. These may change over time, but many core senses of identity are stable. Maintenance of identity may involve the participation of a *cobiographer*, that is someone whose own "story" is linked to that of the resident.

Lived experience: The experience of everyday life, which often seems natural and unquestioned, and is shaped by one's sense of identity, system of personal meaning, and similar constructs.

Personal meaning: The constellation of personal meanings, values and beliefs used to identify, interpret and judge ongoing events and qualities of life. Personal meaning is derived both from shared cultural norms as well as personal interpretations of these and of one's own experiences.

Biography: One's own sense of both the content and structure of one's own life.

Personal safety: The degree of freedom from assault or insult to personhood and identity. Can include both physical safety as well as verbal insult, infantilizing, or other forms of disrespect.

Social relationships: Essential to personhood, social relationships can often serve as endorsements of the self.

Personhood: The status of being a full person. Personhood incorporates the above components, and others as well. It exists in contrast with other roles developed for residents of nursing homes.

resident's identity is turned over to family and professional carers. The nursing home bears primary responsibility for a person's identity and for mobilizing resources to retain as much of that identity and remaining capacities as is possible. This identity maintenance task force may also contain a cobiographer, often a spouse, daughter, or other relative who has a primary responsibility for upholding a resident's biography, in part because their own biography or story is linked to it.

While also a generic term for all the components discussed in the table, lived experience refers to the seemingly natural flow of everyday life. Personal meaning refers to the subjectively significant events, feelings, understandings and beliefs held by the person. Personal meaning is often contextualized in the subjectively defined life course, that is, in a person's sense of their own biography. Personal safety refers to the sense of personal intactness and comfort held by the person. Thus while resident satisfaction instruments may tap whether residents feel they are treated with respect by staff, such issues as verbal and interpersonal respect can provide a level of perceived safety, comfort, and intactness. Similarly, thefts of personal property against impaired elders may be incrementally more damaging, not only because they are additive to the entire parcel of assaults experienced in the nursing home, but also because they mar the sense of safety and intactness of the person. Finally, social relationships are also important ways in which the person is positively reflected.

Collectively, these elements compose a domain of personhood upon which any attempt to evaluate resident satisfaction must rest. This observation refers back to the dichotomy between the person and the medicalized social roles presented in Table 2.1. I am suggesting that resident satisfaction should be calibrated in terms of aspects of personhood.

REFERENCES

Aharony, L., & S. Strasser, (1993). Patient satisfaction: What we know about and what we still need to explore. *Medical Care Review, 50*(1), 352–385.

Bowling, A. (1992). Measuring health: A review of quality of life measurement scales. Philadelphia: Open University Press.

Dimsdale, J. E., & Baum, A. (1995). *Quality of life in behavioral medicine.* Hillsdale, NJ: Erlbaum.

Fallowfield, L. (1990). *The quality of life: The missing measurement in health care.* London: Souvenir Press.

Health Care Financing Administration (1995) *Resident Assessment Instrument. User's Manual.* Baltimore, MD: HCFA.

Kleinman, A. (1981). *Patients and healers in the context of culture: An exploration of the borderland between anthropology, medicine and psychiatry.* Berkeley: University of California Press.

Lawton, M. P. (In press). Assessing quality of life. *Alzheimer's Disease and Related Disorders.*

Schipper, H., Clinch, J. J., & Olweny, C. L. M. (1996). Quality of life studies: Definition and conceptual issues. In B. Spilker (Ed.), *Quality of life and pharmacoeconomics in clinical trials* (pp. 11–23). Philadelphia: Lippincott-Raven.

Spilker, B. (Ed.) (1996). *Quality of life and pharmacoeconomics in clinical trials.* Philadelphia: Lippincott-Raven.

Strasser, A., Aharony, L., & Greenburger, D., (1993). The patient satisfaction process: Moving towards a comprehensive model. *Medical Care Review, 50,* 322–382.

Chapter 3

THE DOMAINS OF SATISFACTION IN LONG-TERM CARE*

Liane R. Soberman, Michael Murray,
Peter G. Norton, and Barbara van Maris

INTRODUCTION

Since the early 1980s, organizations have become increasingly focused on quality issues. In the late 1990s, the ideas of Deming (1986) and Juran (1988) had an effect on the philosophy and culture of most health care organizations. According to Deming (1986), one of the five hallmarks of a quality organization is knowing your customer's needs and expectations and working to meet or exceed them. Evidence of the degree to which health care organizations are attempting to become quality-focused can be seen in the multitude of patient satisfaction instruments currently being used in health care. Patient satisfaction instruments have been developed for use in acute settings (Carey & Seibert, 1993; Cleary, Edgman-Levitan,

* Address correspondence to: Liane R. Soberman, Department of Health Administration, 2nd floor McMurrich Bldg., University of Toronto, 12 Queen's Park Cres. W., Toronto, Ontario, M5S 1A8. E-mail: liane.soberman@utoronto.ca

Walker, Geteis & Delbano, 1993; Meterko, Nelson, & Rubin, 1990; Ware, Davies-Avery & Stewart, 1978), home health care settings (Laferriere, 1993), primary care settings (Pascoe, 1983), with terminal patients (McCusker, 1984), and with long-term care and nursing home residents (Kleinsorge & Koenig, 1991; Norton, von Maris, Soberman, & Murray, 1996; Pablo, 1975).

This chapter examines domains of satisfaction among residents in long-term care and uses a case study from a full-service teaching hospital to demonstrate the method for identifying different domains of satisfaction. Our main goal is to examine what domains should be and are included in satisfaction surveys. There is very little literature on the development of patient satisfaction tools for use in long-term care. This chapter should provide researchers and practitioners with an understanding of how to approach domain construction in patient satisfaction.

One of the primary motivations for conducting a patient, client, or resident satisfaction survey is the identification of improvement opportunities, that is, finding areas or processes of care that need to be better in the eyes of the customer. Although there are instruments that focus on satisfaction with care in general, most include questions about specific aspects of care based on the customer's experience. These different areas have been referred to as domains. Satisfaction questionnaires in many different content areas target different domains, e.g., job satisfaction measures traditionally target five different domains including satisfaction with work, peers, promotion, supervisor, and pay. Identification of domains important to a particular target group is a prerequisite to development of the questionnaire, and conceptualizing and reporting results.

In acute care settings, typical domains of patient satisfaction include such areas as nursing care, medical care, food, pre-hospital and discharge instructions, and so on. There are important reasons why these same domains cannot be used with residents in long-term care settings. The patient experience during an acute stay is quite different from that of a resident living in a long-term care institution. The acute care patient is admitted to hospital for a limited period of time for explicit treatment or surgery, and their medical concern is of the utmost importance during their stay. Long-term care residents, on the other hand, reside in and, in most cases, will die in the institution. While their medical care remains important, there are other important issues that stem from the experience of living in the institution. These are important distinctions, since for a patient satisfaction instrument to have face validity, it needs to reflect questions that are important to the patients completing the questionnaire. While those questions and domains that reflect what is important to long-term and acute patients may overlap, they are clearly not identical. Some of the most important determinants of satisfaction in acute care are physicians' skills, ability to communicate, and attitude toward providing care (Hart , Malinarski, & Djaldetti, 1996), while in long-term care, additional issues, such as caring and dignity, are of paramount importance (Grant, Reimer, & Bannatyne, 1996; Grau , Chandler, & Saundus, 1995; Mitchell, 1993; Pearson, Hocking, Mott, & Riggs, 1993).

In addition to differences in the patient experience which make it necessary to have a unique instrument that specifically reflects what is important to residents in long-term care, there are differences in the population of patients in long-term care and acute care that preclude their using the same instrument. The prevalence of cognitive impairment among many long-term care residents presents a unique challenge to researchers and administrators designing satisfaction instruments. Because some degree of cognitive impairment is found in many long-term care populations, and in some cases it may be as high as 80% (Davis, Sebastian, & Tschetter, 1997), there will always be a proportion of residents who cannot complete a questionnaire. However, philosophically, it is important that a long-term care satisfaction instrument be designed so as to enable as many residents as possible to provide opinions about the care they receive. In order to properly represent the population, it is also important to minimize the non-response bias. Therefore, it is not only the patient experience that necessitates the use of a unique instrument in long-term care. The language and scale complexity that is appropriate for use with acute care patients is not appropriate for many elderly long-term care residents.

LITERATURE REVIEW

While there is a myriad of patient satisfaction instruments that have been developed for use in acute care and other settings (Hall & Dornan, 1988), there are relatively few reported in the literature that have been developed specifically for use with long-term care residents (see Appendix 1). McDaniel & Nash (1990) describe a compendium of instruments that measure patient satisfaction with nursing care. They describe 21 instruments used in different settings with different populations, none of those identified focus on a long-term care or nursing home setting. In some early work, Kahn, Hines, Woodson, & Burkham-Armstrong (1977) developed a 38-item questionnaire to assess resident satisfaction; however, the instrument and domains were professionally driven, and no attempt was made to use the instrument with one third of the residents who were unable to communicate.

Kleinsorge & Koenig (1991) developed a six-domain customer satisfaction scale for use with residents and families in nursing homes. The questionnaire was developed based on two focus groups, one with residents and one with families. They identified 32 items in six dimensions of satisfaction from both the focus groups. The six domains identified in their study are as follows: four pertain to staff groups in the home including nurses and aides, administrators, dietary, and housekeeping. The fifth domain is related to empathy or caring issues and the sixth domain pertains to the environment in the facility. Using the information from the resident focus group, they used factor analysis and tests of construct validity to confirm the dimensions and develop six subscales. Results of their analysis indicated that two of the six scales had reliability levels of 0.7 or greater which they argued was acceptable given the small number of items in each scale and the exploratory nature of the research. Their evaluation of convergent validity (which they achieved by comparing directly worded single items with each multiple item scale) revealed that two of the dimensions (nurses and aides),identified as being distinct by the focus groups should be combined, because both groups of staff were viewed similarly by residents. They found evidence of convergent validity associations on each of the administrators, dietary, housekeeping, and empathy scales.

Kleinsorge and Koenig's (1991) work identified an important domain, the staff empathy/caring domain, that was subsequently recognized as an important aspect of residents' life satisfaction. In a later article, Koenig and Kleinsorge (1994) describe using the same instrument developed for residents to benchmark family member satisfaction across nursing homes. In this later study, family members were surveyed instead of residents because many residents lacked the cognitive or physical ability to complete a survey with the help of an interviewer and because using trained interviewers would have been cost-prohibitive. Given recent research indicating that families not only are different customers, but have different perceptions of what it is important in long-term care (Bleismer & Earl, 1993; Knox & Upchurch, 1992; Meister & Boyle, 1996; van Maris, Soberman, Murray, & Norton, 1996), their methodology raises questions about the degree to which the six domains truly represent the domains of satisfaction from the family's point of view.

Bleismer and Earl (1993) and Meister and Boyle (1996) used a set of 17 quality indicators derived from the National Citizen's Coalition for Nursing Home Reform (NCCNHR) study (1985) in which nursing home residents from around the United States convened for open-ended discussions about the meaning of quality of care. Bleismer and Earl (1993) did not group the 17 indicators into domains, while Meister and Boyle (1996) divided the items into three domains according to Donabedian's (1988) construct of quality care: interpersonal aspects of care, technical aspects of care (process), and attributes of the setting (structure). In both studies, respondents were asked to rank the importance of the items and identify how frequently their facility was meeting these indicators. By validating the NCCNHR quality indicators as being important to long-term care residents, the work of Bleismer and Earl (1993) and Meister and Boyle (1996) has contributed to our understanding of the important areas or domains of satisfaction in long-term care.

The work of the National Citizen's Coalition for Nursing Home Reform (NCCNHR) was carried further by Davis et al. (1997). A factor analysis was conducted to identify the domains of satisfaction based on 52 items derived from the NCCNHR's study. Analyses of the data revealed four factors or dimensions of care: (1) staff responsiveness, (2) dependability and trust, (3) personal control, and (4) food-related services and resources. Four subscales were developed based on these factors. Their study is promising as it recognizes the importance of resident participation in defining how their care is measured. Moreover, by revealing that residents mental status and survey scores were unrelated, their study touches on the important area of patients' mental acuity and patients' ability to provide data using a quantitative satisfaction instrument. However, the fact that residents with a Mini-Mental Status examination score lower than 22 were excluded from the survey suggests that researchers still have a long way to go towards understanding and valuing the perceptions of all long-term care residents, not just those deemed acceptable by staff, families or a mental status examination.

Other studies have used quantitative tools to compare and contrast what is important to residents, staff, and families in long-term care. Knox and Upchurch (1992) surveyed 134 residents, 59 administrators, and 208 staff. Administrators, employees, and residents were each asked to rank, in order of importance to residents, 10 values identified in the literature on quality of life. Rankings from the administrators and employees were compared to nursing home residents' own reports of what they themselves value. The findings revealed a discrepancy between the perceptions of important values assigned by staff and those assigned by residents. This gap has been supported by other research (Bleismer & Earl, 1993; Meister & Boyle, 1996; van Maris et al., 1996).

Other findings from the same study (Knox and Upchurch, 1992) revealed that residents expressed a significantly higher priority for the value choices of family visits and other visitors, clean and comfortable surroundings, and good food than for other value choices such as having caring staff, feeling useful, receiving affection, and participating in religious and social activities. These findings are in conflict with others' findings regarding which items are most important to long-term care residents. For instance, Grant et al. (1996), Davis et al., (1997) and Bleismer and Earl (1993) found caring staff to be more important to residents than visits from family and other visitors. Moreover, good food is absent from the 14 indicators of quality care identified by residents in Grant et al,'s (1996) study and in Bleismer and Earl's (1993) study. These conflicting findings suggest that these areas merit further research using larger, more generalizable samples, so that some of the contradictory findings in the literature can be addressed or hopefully resolved.

Hurwitz (1992) corroborated the relevance of the ten values identified by Knox and Upchurch (1992) by examining the complaints received in her nursing facility by the Resident's Council, family group meetings, and others. Based on this review, her residents most valued the following: personal property/lost clothing, food, family and visitation, and comfortable surroundings. Her method of examining the values in this manner was limited, because only complaints by residents and families were examined in retrospect and no prospective data were collected on evaluating resident and family ratings of these values. The domains in current instruments are summarized in Appendix I.

An area of general concern in the satisfaction literature is the issue of social desirability bias. Often, the concerns voiced by residents are not necessarily the issues that are of utmost concern to them; rather, they represent issues that are important and/or bothersome that they feel comfortable voicing. It is far easier to complain about the food or lost clothing than it is to complain about staff being uncaring or disrespectful. Therefore, to rely on commonly heard complaints as a way of understanding what is most important to residents introduces a social desirability bias—residents complain only about what is socially acceptable and safe to complain about, and not necessarily about those things that are the most important to them. One method of understanding the issues of paramount concern to residents is the use of qualitative data that is collected in a nonthreatening manner by research staff, interviewers, or ombudsman/volunteers not directly employed by the facility in which the resident resides. By using qualitative data from residents about what is important to them, like data from the NCCNHR study, we can begin to understand which areas are critical for resident satisfaction. However, identifying the truly important areas to be included in a satisfaction instrument still does not guarantee that candid responses will be provided by residents. The social desirability bias is reflected not only in the complaints that are voiced by residents, but it persists in sensitive areas, such as those related to the manner in which care is provided by staff.

The literature review (see also Appendix I) highlights the fact that the area of resident satisfaction has limited empirical data that is generalizable across different populations and settings. This is especially true with regard to the empirical data on developing the domains of satisfaction based on the residents' perspective. However, there has been some preliminary and significant qualitative work which helps us to identify issues that are important to nursing home and long-term care residents (Bleismer & Earl, 1993; Grant et al. 1996; Grau et al., 1995; Knox & Upchurch, 1992; NCCNHR, 1985; Pablo, 1975). Some or all of these studies identified the importance of a few domains: that of caring staff, a noninstitutional environment, as well as a variety of good food and activities as being important to long-term care residents. This type of qualitative research and the limited quantitative data in the area is very valuable in trying to understand the domains of satisfaction and ensuring that they are designed to reflect things that are important to residents (Speeding , Morrison, Rehr, & Rosenberg 1983). The investigators of the study described in this chapter drew from this literature to conduct a large, systematic study on resident satisfaction, with particular reference to identifying appropriate domains of satisfaction as represented from the perspective of the long-term care resident.

THE DOMAINS OF SATISFACTION: THE LONG-TERM CARE RESIDENT EVALUATION SURVEY

The Long-Term Care Resident Survey© was developed as part of a collaborative venture between the research team from Sunnybrook Health Science Centre (SHSC), a full-service teaching hospital affiliated with the University of Toronto (UofT), a member of the Department of Health Administration at UofT, and members from eight long-term care facilities in the province of Ontario, Canada. The research team decided to develop the domains of satisfaction and related questions based on a variety of sources, including information from existing qualitative data and data from focus groups. It was also important that these data came from independent research settings. Qualitative data from various research and focus groups would be grouped together and validated with residents and health care professionals, and then pilot-tested with a sample of residents.

An additional objective of the project was the development of a satisfaction survey for family members. The perception that many residents are unable to provide reliable satisfaction data due to cognitive impairment, as well as the added resources required to collect satisfaction data from a long-term or chronic care population, has meant that family members have traditionally been used as surrogates for collecting resident data. Our research sought to understand whether families could, in fact be used as reliable surrogates for collecting resident data. It was therefore decided that the eight organizations pilot-testing the resident instrument would send the same survey to family members asking them to report on the resident experience. As anticipated, the findings indicated that family members are unable to provide accurate surrogate data. These data have been reported elsewhere (van Maris et al., 1996) and mirror other similar findings reported in the literature (Lavizzo-Mourey, Zinn, & Taylor, 1992). Although the accuracy and reliability of family members' reports of what residents desire is suspect, families remain important customers of long-term care facilities with needs and expectations of their own. Because family members are distinct customers of the health care system, it was decided that the resident instrument was not appropriate for use with families and a separate instrument, designed to reflect those issues that are important to families, has been developed. This instrument was designed based on data from multiple focus groups at three different institutions. However, the focus of this chapter is on the domains of resident satisfaction, and so the family instrument is not described here.

The first step in the process of developing the resident instrument involved identifying independent qualitative data sets that could be content analyzed by the research team. The three criteria for identifying data sets were that they (a) were independent of one another, (b) were collected for the express purpose of identifying what is important to residents and what the indicators of quality care are from their perspective, and (c) had raw data that could be made available to the research team. Because it is the philosophy of the research team that cognitively impaired residents can provide information about their experiences, no stipulation was made regarding the cognitive abilities of the residents who contributed to the original qualitative studies. Three data sets were identified that met these criteria: (1) the 1985 study by the NCCNHR in which nursing home residents from 15 cities across the United States convened for open-ended discussions about what quality care means; (2) a 1991 study by two Alberta researchers, Grant and Reimer, completed with residents, significant others, and nurses in 5 Calgary long-term care centers asking them to identify the kind of care they liked best and least; and (3) 1993 in-depth interview data that was collected from residents by G. Mitchell, asking about the quality of life experiences of persons living in a chronic care facility. While Mitchell's data were collected from only one site, much effort was made to include residents suffering from cognitive impairment in the data collection. For this reason, her data were considered to be particularly valuable to the research team, since it was believed that congruence between her data and data in the other studies, if found, would bolster the argument to include all residents in satisfaction studies, not simply those deemed able by family members, caregivers, or mental status examinations.

Despite their origin in separate jurisdictions, these qualitative data showed remarkable congruence, and were mirrored by qualitative focus group data collected in four of the organizations. From these studies, approximately 100 items were identified as important to residents. These items were placed into logical groupings by the researchers, long-term care staff, and representatives from the eight participating organizations. The resulting initial questionnaire was pilot tested with 20 residents living in the long-term and chronic care wings at SHSC. Following these maneuvers, the study team removed redundant items resulting in a total of 60 items in the following seven domains:

- Living environment
- Laundry
- Food
- Activities
- Staff
- Dignity
- Autonomy

After the first eight facilities implemented the first round of the survey, a final set of revisions to the questionnaire were made. As part of the revisions, items considered by the research team to be redundant were verified by residents, and removed, the Activity domain was redrafted in order to measure resident satisfaction more accurately in this area, and the Laundry domain was removed. These revisions will be discussed in more detail in the following discussion of each domain and the reasons for the domain's inclusion as an important indicator of resident satisfaction.

As noted, a qualitative study out of Alberta, Canada was used by the research team to help construct the Long-Term Care Resident Survey described here (Grant & Reimer, 1991). In the Alberta Study, 14 major indicators of quality of care were identified by residents, families, and staff from several long-term care facilities. The researchers used the critical incident technique, in which respondents are asked to identify those aspects of care they like the best and the least. Results of the Alberta study (Grant & Reimer, 1991) have been published since the development of this questionnaire (Grant , Reimer & Bannatyre, 1996). A closer look at these indicators is helpful in illustrating why the research team selected this final set of domains (see Table 3.1).

Table 3.1 Fourteen indicators of quality care from the Alberta Study

The nature of the facility

The nature of relationships

The acknowledgment of the personhood of the resident

The nature of communication with residents

The disposition of decision making

Judgments about assistance required

The degree and nature of surveillance

The presence of planning and judgments about care

The nature of communication with the health care team

Do or assist with activities of living which residents cannot do for themselves

Do or assist with therapeutic activities which residents cannot do for themselves

The manner in which activities of living and therapeutic activities are carried out

The nature of interaction with significant others

The provision, use, and attributes of resources

Living Environment

The importance of the environment to long-term care residents is reflected in the home-versus-institutional view of the long-term care facility (Fogel, 1992; Willcocks, Peace, & Kellaher, 1987). By living environment, we are referring to residents' physical surroundings, including their rooms, nursing units, and the facility as a whole. Items related to the aesthetics of the environment, such as whether the residence is dull, as well as issues related to odor, noise, and cleanliness are included. Additionally, the perceived safety of the environment is addressed in this domain, as is the issue of a homelike environment often cited by residents. Sample items from this domain are: "Is this place homelike?" and "Does the noise around here bother you?".

Laundry

The second domain included in the Long-Term Care Resident Survey at the first eight organizations was the Laundry domain. The fact that the

Laundry domain was included in the initial instrument is reflective of the challenge administrators and researchers face as they try to move away from using professionally driven instruments and try to develop customer-defined satisfaction tools. Laundry was included in the initial instrument to appease professionals and administrators working in the long-term care area who remained certain that, despite its absence from residents' reports of what is important to them in the qualitative data, Laundry was highly important to residents. In fact, in the qualitative data sets, the only persistent reference to Laundry services concerned loss of personal belongings. As previously noted, because it is far easier for residents to complain about things like food and Laundry, understandably, these are issues that professionals assume are important. The inclusion and subsequent removal of the Laundry domain is a good example of why we need to be cautious of instruments and domains that are professionally conceived, with little or no input from the residents themselves.

In addition to its absence in the qualitative data, there were other factors that contributed to the decision by the research team to remove the Laundry domain. For instance, data analysis conducted after the first eight organizations completed the survey indicated that the Laundry questions had lower correlations to global satisfaction than questions in the other six domains, Those findings, coupled with Laundry's absence from the qualitative data and the need to keep the instrument to a reasonable length, contributed to the decision to remove the Laundry domain from the questionnaire. The argument is not that Laundry is unimportant to long-term care residents. As noted, the idea that the loss of personal belongings is a concern to residents is supported in the qualitative data . However, when one considers what is most important to long-term care residents, our analysis of qualitative data as well as quantitative data collected from several hundred residents across Canada in our first eight facilities reveals that issues related to staff, dignity, autonomy, the environment, food, and activities are more important to residents than Laundry.

Food

The next domain in the survey relates to food and food services. This domain includes not only important aspects residents identified specifically about food, such as taste, temperature, and variety, but it also addresses the issue of whether residents who need help eating receive the help they require from staff. The importance of food to long-term care residents and its inclusion in the questionnaire is supported by the NCC-NHR data and focus group data from the initial eight participating institutions. For long-term care residents living in an institution, food becomes an integral part of the resident experience (O'Hara et al., 1997) and is therefore included as a domain of satisfaction. Sample items from this domain are: "Is the temperature of the food OK?" and "Do you get help eating when you need it?".

Activities

Initially, the Activity domain in the Long-Term Care Resident Survey included very general questions about whether the activities offered were interesting, whether residents received help to get to and take part in the activities, whether there were activities outside the facility, etc. When inter-item correlations were calculated for each domain after the eight pilot facilities tested the questionnaire, the activity domain had the lowest internal consistency, with an alpha of .39. The low alpha, coupled with responses from residents indicating that activities constituted a variety of different things, and feedback from professionals telling us that the data provided by this domain would be difficult to use because the questions were vague, suggested that while the domain is important, the questions within it needed to be redefined. There was little question that "activities" and "out-ings" were an important area for residents. What was less certain was what, precisely, constitutes an "activity".

The research team re-reviewed the qualitative data in an effort to develop more specific questions that would accurately represent the resident's conception of activities. Two additional focus groups were also conducted in the long-term care wings at Sunnybrook that focused specifically on the question of identifying what the important issues were with respect to activities and outings. The domain was then redrafted, and it presently contains nine very specific questions about different types of activities (i.e., trips, activities that use the mind) as well as time and location of activities, whether the necessary help is provided, etc. With the new questions, the internal consistency for the domain has an alpha of .87. Sample items from this domain are: "Are there enough activities that use your mind?" and "Are activities offered at the right time for you?".

Staff and Dignity

In the Long-Term Care Resident Survey, the two domains with the questions that correlated most highly with global satisfaction are the "Staff" and "Dignity" domains. Fourteen out of fifteen questions in the survey most highly correlated with global satisfaction are from the Staff or Dignity domains. Evidence of the importance of Staff and Dignity issues to residents is also seen in the Alberta study (Grant & Reimer, 1991, see Table 3.1), Mitchell's work (1993), the NCCNHR study (1985) and the focus groups (conducted in 1995) at the participating organizations. It is important to note that the questions in the Staff and Dignity domains are highly correlated, and the separation into two different domains was done to make the data more meaningful for the end users, the staff. For residents, having truly caring staff that treat them with respect, try to understand their feelings, and do things like helping them to look nice are perhaps the most critical factors of resident satisfaction. It makes intuitive sense that residents viewed the Staff and Dignity domains as being closely related, since these questions referred to resident-staff interaction and interrelationships. Sample items from the staff domain are: "Do the staff show you that they care about you?" and "Do the staff answer promptly when you call?" Sample items from the dignity domain are: "When staff come to your room, do they tell you what they have come for?" and "Do the staff call you by your name?"

Autonomy

The importance of independence for residents is captured in the Autonomy domain. Autonomy was included as an important area for a number of reasons. In the last decade, when researchers and administrators began to recognize the importance of having customer input into the definition of the domains of satisfaction, they discovered the importance of dignity and autonomy in the minds of long-term care residents. Most previous instruments (Bleismer & Earle, 1993; Kleinsorge & Koenig, 1991; Meister & Boyle, 1996; Pearson et al., 1993) dealt with items about food, the environment, and some nurse- and physician-related variables. The questions within this domain therefore, relate to the autonomy of the resident—something akin to the personal control dimension found by Davis et al. (1997). For instance, the residents are asked if they are the ones to decide what they do each day, whether they are free to come and go as they please, whether they are provided with equipment that enables them to be independent, and whether they are ever forced to do things that they don't want to do. These are behaviors that might be defined as autonomous; however, the word "autonomy" while meaningful for staff and administrators, might not be understood by all residents. The word "autonomy" is therefore never used during the administration of the questionnaire with the resident. In this case, the title "autonomy" meets the need of having an instrument that not only reflects issues that are of importance to residents, but that is meaningful for those who will need to understand and act on the results, i.e., staff and administrators. Sample items from this domain are: "Is equipment available that enables you to be independent?" and "Are you ever forced to do things that you do not want to?" In summary, while we have suggested that there are six domains of satisfaction, it is important to recognize that not all domains in any satisfaction survey are equally important to residents (La Monica, Oberst, Madea, & Olf, 1986). As noted, when each question is correlated with global satisfaction, Staff and Dignity issues appear to be critical determinants of satisfaction. However, it is worth noting that certain questions in all of the other domains also correlate highly with overall satisfaction. These findings are in line with the original data from the Alberta Study (Gtant & Reimer, 1991) and Mitchell's study (1993) and, to a less extent, the NCC-NHR study (1985).

PROCEDURES

Sample

After the Long-Term Care Resident Survey was tested in the first eight organizations and revisions were made to the questionnaire as described above, the instrument was implemented a total of 12 additional times at the time this chapter was written (in six of the original eight organizations as a follow-up 18 months after the initial survey, as well as in six new organizations). The 12 organizations, therefore, formed the core group that provided the data to test and refine the instrument. A wide range of organizations were selected and included a 72-bed chronic-care unit in a community health center and a 670-bed hospital and nursing home exclusively for geriatric care drawn from two Canadian provinces, Ontario and British Columbia. Culturally, the populations in the 12 organizations were quite diverse. There were some facilities with homogeneous Jewish, Catholic, or Anglo veteran populations, as well as several multiethnic centers that reflect the diversity of the populations in Toronto and Vancouver.

In some organizations, attempts were made to survey all residents; in others, a random sample was selected. In organizations with fewer than 300 beds, an attempt was made to interview all residents. In larger facilities, a stratified random sample was drawn from certain units. Prior to implementing the survey, organizations were asked to logically group several nursing units together and the sampling was drawn from those groupings. In some organizations, these groupings were based on residents' degree of physical limitation, in others, they were based on cognitive limitation. The most important thing was that the groupings made sense to the organization, as they would ultimately be provided with satisfaction data for each patient group they identified. Data for individual nursing units (where there are typically fewer than 20 respondents) have never been provided because providing data at the unit level could potentially compromise the confidentiality of residents. Unit groupings of cognitively impaired residents were typically oversampled to ensure that enough interviews could be completed from within this group.

The average completion rate across the 12 organizations was approximately 50%, and ranged from 29% to 62%. Interviewers attempted to interview every resident on their list at three different times. If after three attempts they were unable to complete an interview, they recorded the reason and did not make additional attempts. The main reason that an interview could not be completed was resident unresponsiveness or cognitive limitation that precluded the interviewer from carrying on a short conversation with the resident. Organizations with a higher proportion of cognitively impaired residents therefore tended to have lower response rates. Recall that none of the facilities that implemented the LTC Resident Survey prescreened residents based on their cognitive or physical ability. An exercise the authors conducted at SHSC, after the survey was first implemented there in 1994, indicated that staff and family members could not do an accurate job of predicting which residents could be successfully interviewed. Had SHSC relied on nursing staff to prescreen residents, 30% of those who completed an interview would have been eliminated from the survey and 15% of residents whom the interviewers could not successfully interview would have been considered eligible to participate. Other reasons that interviews could not be completed include the resident being too ill, refusals, inability to locate the resident, and discharges or deaths that occurred after the interviewer lists were created. In our experience, helpful staff and dedicated interviewers seem to help to improve the survey completion rate.

Reliability Analysis

Although the items in the questionnaire could be examined individually, investigators conducted reliability analyses to ensure that the items in each domain were not only conceptually related, but internally consistent from a statistical viewpoint. Cronbach's Alpha coefficients were calculated to assess internal consistency for each of the six domains. Table 3.2 shows the alpha coefficients and the average inter-item correlations for each domain.

Alphas ranged from 0.63 to 0.87. Two of the domains (Staff and Activities) had a high internal consistency (.85) while the rest, with the exception of the Autonomy domain which had the lowest alpha of .63, had acceptable alphas (Nunnally, 1978). For each domain, removal of any item resulted in a lower alpha.

Table 3.2 Cronbach's alpha and mean inter-item correlation

Domain	Number of items 36	Alpha	Mean inter-item correlation
Living environment	9	.688	.207
Food	7	.681	.248
Activities	9	.869	.424
Staff	9	.865	.434
Dignity	11	.788	.267
Autonomy	9	.630	.163

$n = 1518$

Discriminant Validity

Discriminant validity was calculated to determine whether each domain was measuring something different and to ensure that each item was placed in the correct domain. Discriminant validity examines the correlation of each item to the other domains, and is supported if the item is more highly correlated with the domain it is in versus any of the other domains. Additionally, correlations between each domain are also calculated.

Of the 54 questions in six domains, all but eight questions were more highly correlated with the domain they are in than with any of the other five domains. All of the eight questions that were more highly correlated with a domain other than the one in which they were conceptually placed related to staffing issues. Two questions currently placed in the Dignity domain, one from the Food domain, and five from the Autonomy domain correlated more highly with the questions in the Staff domain. These findings are not surprising given the fact that both the Dignity and Autonomy domains have elements in common in relation to Staffing issues. The item related to food that correlated more highly with the staff domain asks residents if they get help eating if they need it. Because it is the individual item in each domain that is of interest to the end users of the data, the eight questions remain in the domain in which they are conceptually relevant.

Table 3.3 shows the mean correlations between the six domains. To some extent, the domains do seem to be tapping different dimensions. As noted, the Staff and Dignity domains are the most highly correlated (.68). Autonomy is more highly correlated with Staff and Dignity than any of the other inter -domain correlations. All others are between .37 and .48, indicating moderate discrimination.

Table 3.3 Mean inter-domain correlation

	Living Environment	Food	Activities	Staff	Dignity	Autonomy
Living environment						
Food	.46					
Activities	.368	.441				
Staff	.457	.481	.423			
Dignity	.481	.462	.429	.682		
Autonomy	.396	.38	.416	.535	.585	

$n = 1518$

Table 3.4 shows the correlations between each domain and the global satisfaction question that asks residents, overall, how they would rate the quality of care and services at the facility. The Staff and Dignity domains are most highly correlated with this global satisfaction question.

FUTURE RESEARCH

In this chapter we have outlined the present state of knowledge concerning domains of satisfaction for satisfaction surveys in long-term care. Our review of the literature indicates that this is an area that deserves further investigation. We have also outlined our own experience in this area as we, with our partners, developed The Long-term Care Resident Evaluation Survey©.

Investigators of the study recognize certain limitations of the data presented in this chapter. It seems to us that several questions need to be addressed in this area. First, what is the effect of defining domains on the larger phenomenon of resident satisfaction? What we choose to measure will help define the underlying construct of resident satisfaction. If we choose the wrong domains, or an incomplete set, we may not adequately represent the totality of resident satisfaction. For example, if we only had a questionnaire with Food and Activities domains, we would not be measuring all aspects of resident satisfaction. As researchers work with residents to come up with more rigorous definitions of what the domains of long-term care satisfaction are, the construct validity of "resident satisfaction" will be enhanced. Second, we must continue to use domains that are defined on the basis of qualitative data from residents themselves since,

Table 3.4 Pearson correlations of mean domain scores and global satisfaction

	r
Living environment	.35
Food	.31
Activities	.29
Staff	.44
Dignity	.43
Autonomy	.36

$n = 1518$

we argue, these domains will help keep our instruments patient-focused, rather than focused on the needs and beliefs of caregivers. Having patient-focused instruments is the first step toward ensuring that patient-focused data are available to guide improvement efforts. Whether certain domains or certain ways of characterizing the domains are more amenable to intervention, and the question of how we can better link the domains with the information staff need to improve care, are related and important questions. Third, does the development of domains enhance the utility of the data? In particular, does it help or improve prospects for utilizing the data for quality improvement?

This third question is important in the broader context of patient satisfaction in health care. As organizations become increasingly proficient at collecting patient satisfaction data, there is a pressing need to direct our attention towards understanding how patient satisfaction data are ultimately used by staff to make improvements in the delivery of care and services (Meterko, 1996). Rosenthal and Shannon (1997) identify issues that are emerging in the area of patient satisfaction and, like Meterko, discuss the need to investigate how satisfaction data are used in organizations. They also discuss the value of using standardized measurement tools across organizations and the need to design special instruments for use with populations traditionally surveyed through surrogates (e.g., children and nursing home residents)—two areas that, while only tangentially related to this paper, have been central to our experience over the last 3 years of developing and testing the instrument described here.

Additional questions of interest surround the question of how valid these domains of satisfaction will continue to be, given the increasing acuity and frailty of nursing home residents.

Finally, perhaps one of the most contentious issues surrounding the use of patient satisfaction instruments in long-term and chronic care settings relates to the use of these instruments with cognitively impaired individuals. Patient satisfaction data provide caregivers with information about the patient's perceived experience. Ignoring data from cognitively impaired patients says that their perceptions and experiences are of little or no value. However, if organizations truly want to measure and improve patient satisfaction levels, then they need to use the patient's experience as the baseline, regardless of whether they understand it or believe it. Moreover, evidence of the difference between caregivers' and patients' perceptions of care should remind us that we cannot use caregivers to ascertain either the worth or believability of patients' responses.

Empirically, our data indicates that cognitively impaired residents can both understand and respond to a relatively simple set of closed-ended questions. When data provided by patients from several cognitive support units are compared with data provided by physical support patients, the similarity of responses is very high. For patients in both cognitive and physical support areas, the rank order of results for questions in each domain is nearly identical, supporting both the instrument's reliability and, more importantly, the reliability of responses from cognitively impaired residents in general. Nonetheless, evidence of the inclusion of cognitively impaired residents in satisfaction surveys and survey development remains elusive, and this is therefore an issue requiring further attention.

Finally, it is necessary to briefly discuss one of the limitations of this study. The issue of social desirability bias is a potential limitation of the instrument, and it particularly relates to the domains of satisfaction. If one considers the domains of satisfaction that we have outlined here (Living environment, Food, Activities, Staff, Dignity, and Autonomy), as well as the fact that residents are very concerned with the confidentiality of their answers and require assurances that their caregivers will not see their individual answers, it might be anticipated that certain questions are not always answered honestly.

For instance, residents are quite likely to feel comfortable answering questions about the environment, food, and perhaps activities. Questions in these domains are not overly sensitive or threatening to respondents, and any negative responses are usually attributed to the environment or the system, as opposed to individuals. If patients are unhappy with any of these areas, there is every reason to assume that this dissatisfaction would be expressed in the survey. However, if one considers the Staff, Dignity and Autonomy domains, the situation is quite different. Questions in these domains are often very sensitive (i.e., "Do the day-to-day things you do make you feel worthwhile?") and negative responses are attributed directly to staff for many of these questions (e.g. "Do the staff always treat you like a human being?" or "Are you ever forced to do things that you do not want to?"). Therefore, out of a fear of reprisal or even not wanting to admit to being treated in an undignified manner, residents might be cautious of expressing their dissatisfaction with staff. It is therefore possible that responses to questions in the Staff, Dignity, and Autonomy domains might contain some element of social desirability.

Resident concerns regarding confidentiality became evident prior to the pilot study, when the study team was defining the instrument (based on the qualitative data, a question in the Autonomy domain asked: "Will staff get back at you if you say or do something they do not like?") and again during the pilot test at SHSC, when this concern was openly expressed by residents. Because the study team was aware of these confidentiality concerns from the start, efforts to address respondents concerns and minimize the social desirability bias were built into the interview methodology and study design. Interviewers were trained to be discreet when interviewing, and when a random sample was drawn (i.e., in those facilities with more than 300 residents) interviewers were provided with resident room numbers in an attempt to maintain the anonymity of the subjects selected to participate in the study . Ultimately, however, social desirability remains a possible limitation of the study, and indeed any study that includes an instrument with questions that are of a sensitive nature.

CONCLUSIONS

Over the last decade, health care organizations have gradually come to recognize the importance of customer feedback. In long-term care settings, this transformation has been slower, evidence of which can be seen by the few studies that have empirically examined the domains of satisfaction based on residents' own perceptions. In many ways, it can be argued that understanding the satisfaction of long-term care residents is more important than other patient groups because of the fact that the organization is their home and that most residents will live out their lives there. Researchers and administrators have been reluctant to embrace the notion that chronic care patients can tell us how they feel about the care they receive. This reluctance is based on the perception that many elderly patients with chronic illnesses, often involving some degree of cognitive impairment, are unable to provide reliable information about their experiences. Our philosophy and our experience suggest just the opposite.

There have been many valuable qualitative studies that help to validate which areas are central to residents' satisfaction (Grant, Reimer &

Bannatyre, 1996; Grau, Chandler & Saunders, 1995; Peason, Hockings, Mott & Riggs, 1993). These qualitative studies also help validate the importance of the questions included in the Long-Term Care Resident Survey described here. The fact that the domains described here draw on data from several important and independent sources (i.e., the NCCNHR study (1985), the work of Grant, Reimer & Bannatyre, (1996) the work of Mitchell (1993), and multiple focus groups) that are based on residents' perceptions of what is important, suggests that living environment, food, activities, staff, dignity, and autonomy are all important dimensions of resident satisfaction.

REFERENCES

Bleismer, M., & Earl, P. (1993). Research considerations: Nursing home quality perceptions. *Journal of Gerontological Nursing, 19*(6), 27–34.

Carey, R. G., & Seibert, J. H. (1993). A patient survey system to measure quality improvement: Questionnaire reliability and validity. *Medical Care, 31* (9), 834–845.

Cleary, P. D., Edgman-Levitan, S., Walker, J. D., Gerteis, M., & Delbano, T. L. (1993). Using patient reports to improve medical care: A preliminary report from 10 hospitals. *Quality Management in Health Care, 2*(1), 31–38.

Davis, M. A., Sebastian, J. G., & Tschetter, J. (1997). Measuring quality of nursing home service: Residents' perspective. *Psychological Reports, 81,* 531–542.

Deming, W. E. (1986). *Out of the crisis.* Cambridge, Mass: MIT Center for Advanced Engineering Studies.

Donabedian, A. (1988). The quality of care: How can it be assessed? *Journal of the American Medical Association, 260,* 1743–1748.

Fogel, B. S. (1992). Psychological aspects of staying at home. *Generations, 16,* 15–19.

Grant, N. K., & Reimer, M. (1991). *Indicators of quality of care as perceived by residents, significant others and nursing staff in long-term care agencies.* Working paper, Faculty of nursing, University of Calgary, Alberta, Canada.

Grant, N. K., Reimer, M., & Bannatyne, J. (1996). Indicators of quality in long-term care facilities. *International Journal of Nursing Studies, 33*(5), 469–478.

Grau, L., Chandler, B., & Saunders, C. (1995). Nursing home residents' perceptions of the quality of their care. Journal of Psychosocial Nursing & Mental Health Services, 33(5), 34–41.

Hall, J. A., & Dornan, M. C. (1988). Meta-analysis of satisfaction with medical care: Description of research domain and analysis of overall satisfaction levels. *Social Science & Medicine, 27*(6), 637–644.

Hart, J., Malinarski, Y., & Djaldetti, M. (1996). Survey of patient satisfaction in a community hospital. *Israel Journal of Medical Science, 32*(7), 551–554.

Hurwitz, R. A. (1992). What residents value most. *Journal of Long-term Care Administration, 20*(3), 12.

Juran, J. M. (1988). *Juran on planning for quality*. New York: Free Press.

Kahn, K. A., Hines, W., Woodson, A. S., & Burkham-Armstrong, G. (1977). A multi-disciplinary approach to assessing the quality of care in long-term care facilities. *The Gerontologist, 17*(1), 61–65.

Kleinsorge, I. K., & Koe, H. F. (1991). The silent customers: Measuring customer satisfaction in nursing homes. *Journal of Health Care Marketing, 11*(4), 2–13.

Knox, B., & Upchurch, M. (1992). Values and nursing home life: How residents and care givers compare. *Journal of Long-term Care Administration, 20*(3), 8–10.

Koenig, H. F., & Kleinsorge, I. K. (1994). Perceptual measures of quality: A tool to improve nursing home systems. *Hospital & Health Services Administration, 39*(4), 487–503.

Laferriere, R. (1993). Client satisfaction with home health care nursing. *Journal of Community Health Nursing, 10*(2), 67–76.

La Monica, E., Oberst, M. T., Madea, A. R., & Olf, R. M. (1986). Development of a patient satisfaction scale. *Research in Nursing and Health, 9*, 43–50.

Lavizzo-Mourey, R. J., Zinn, J., & Taylor, L. (1992). Ability of surrogates to represent satisfaction of nursing home residents with quality of care. *Journal of the American Geriatrics Society, 40*(1), 39–47.

McCusker, J. (1984). Development of scales to measure satisfaction and preferences regarding long-term and terminal care. *Medical Care, 22*(5), 298–307.

McDaniel, C., & Nash, J. G. (1990). Compendium of instruments measuring patient satisfaction with nursing care. *Quality Review Bulletin. 16*(5), 182–188.

Meister, C., & Boyle, C. (1996). Perceptions of quality in long-term care: A satisfaction survey. *Journal of Nursing Care Quality, 10*(4), 40–47.

Meterko, M. (1996). The evolution of customer feedback in health care. *The Joint Commission on Quality Improvement, 22*(5), 307–310.

Meterko, M., Nelson, E. C., & Rubin, H. R. (1990). Patient judgments of hospital quality: Report of a pilot study. *Medical Care, 28*, 10–14 (Supplement).

Mitchell, G. (1993). *Quality of life: The patient's perspective*. Working paper, Sunnybrook Health Science Centre, Toronto, Canada.

National Citizens' Coalition for Nursing Home Reform. (1985) *A consumer perspective on quality care: The residents' point of view*. Washington, DC: Author.

Norton, P. G., van Maris, B., Soberman, L., & Murray, M. (1996). Satisfaction of residents and families in long-term care: I. Construction and application of a tool. *Quality Management in Health Care, 4*(3), 38–46.

Nunnally, J. C. (1978). *Psychometric theory* (2nd ed.) New York: McGraw-Hill.

O'Hara, P. A., Harper, D. W., Kangas, M., Dubeau, J., Borsutzky, C., & Lemire, N. (1997). Taste, temperature, and presentation predict satisfaction with food services in a Canadian continuing-care hospital. *Journal of American Dietetic Association, 4*, 401–405.

Pablo, R. Y. (1975). Assessing patient satisfaction in long-term care institutions. *Hospital Administration in Canada, 17*, 22–32.

Pascoe, G. C. (1983). Patient satisfaction in primary health care: A literature review and analysis. *Evaluation and Program Planning, 6*, 185–210.

Pearson, A., Hocking, S., Mott, S., & Riggs, A. (1993). Quality of care in nursing homes: from the resident's perspective. *Journal of Advanced Nursing, 18*(1), 20–24.

Rosenthal, G. E., & Shannon, S. E. (1997). The use of patient perceptions in the evaluation of health-care delivery systems. *Medical Care, 35*(11), Supplement, 58–68.

Speeding, E. J., Morrison, B., Rehr, H., & Rosenberg, G. (1983). Patient satisfaction surveys: Closing the gap between provider and consumer. *Quality Review Bulletin, 9*(8), 224–228.

van Maris, B., Soberman, L., Murray, M., & Norton, P. G. (1996). Satisfaction of residents and families in long-term care: II. lessons learned. *Quality Management in Health Care, 4*(3), 47–53.

Ware, J. E., Davies-Avery, A., & Stewart, A. L. (1978). The measurement and meaning of patient satisfaction. *Health and Medical Care Services Review, 1*, 1–15.

Willcocks, D. M., Peace, S. M., & Kellaher, L.A. (1987). *Private lives in public places: A research-based critique of residential life in local authority old people's homes.* London Tavistock.

Chapter **4**

NURSING STAFF SATISFACTION IN LONG-TERM CARE: AN OVERVIEW

Jiska Cohen-Mansfield and Linda Noelker

The focus of this chapter is on the satisfaction of nursing staff in long-term care facilities because they comprise the majority of employees and have the greatest impact on residents' and family members' satisfaction with care. Virtually all research on job satisfaction among workers in long-term care is directed to nursing staff, and these studies will be reviewed in this chapter. Another reason for the focus on nursing staff is that projections indicate there will be a shortage of nursing assistants that will reach crisis proportions in coming years (Atchley, 1996). Therefore, strategies to enhance nursing assistant job satisfaction, commitment, and retention should be a top priority for administrators, nursing supervisors, researchers, trainers, and educators. More specifically, Silvestri (1993) projects a 45% increase from 1992 to 2005 in the number of nursing assistants needed for institutional care across the nation, which translates to an additional 475,000 nursing assistants. The primary reason for this need is the growing number of the oldest-old (those 85 and over) who make the greatest use of nursing home care.

Anyone who has worked in a nursing home may find obvious the observation that nursing staff experience high levels of stress. The sense of being squeezed between regulations, administration, and residents whose health conditions, despite all efforts, are generally worsening, is difficult. The need to take care of residents in the most comprehensive and basic ways, even when residents frequently respond negatively or strangely, and when care is needed continuously regardless of holidays, nights, snow or other major weather events, is extremely challenging and can cause great strain. The magnitude of the strain is evidenced by the fact that, when RNs, LPNs, and Nurses Aids (NAs) in an acute care setting were compared with their colleagues in a long-term geriatric care unit, the geriatric care providers expressed a greater interest in changing jobs than did the acute care providers (Astrom, Waxman, Nilsson, Norberg, & Winblad, 1991).

Because of the job-related stress nursing entails in long-term care, there is a need to acknowledge the many ways in which nursing staff also feel gratified by this work, especially by their importance in helping people who are in need, and the strong interpersonal relationships that can develop in the long-term care setting. Given these considerations, the questions at the heart of this chapter are: How can institutions understand the issues surrounding staff satisfaction with their job and the work environment and its demands? What are the areas of greatest strain for nursing staff? What areas are rewarding? How can we improve the job satisfaction of these critical health care personnel so that turnover, sick days, and occupational injuries are minimized? What role can satisfaction surveys play in monitoring and improving job satisfaction, and how much of a role do such surveys play at the present time?

This chapter presents a theoretical model for understanding sources of satisfaction and stress among nursing staff in long-term care, a literature review organized around this model, interventions to improve staff satisfaction, and a brief discussion of the availability and characteristics of staff satisfaction surveys. Whereas we acknowledge that occupational satisfaction, burnout, and stress are different constructs, several considerations prompted us to include all three in this chapter: (a) job satisfaction, burnout, and stress have been consistently shown to be related (e.g., Shaefer & Moos, 1996); (b) all are related to the outcomes of interest: turnover, quality of care, and absenteeism; (c) the difference between the constructs in terms of predictors and outcomes has not yet been clarified, and (d) it has yet to be determined whether satisfaction or stress is a better construct for which to survey employees, and which yields information that is more amenable to improvement efforts.

MODEL OF JOB SATISFACTION AND STRESS
AMONG NURSING STAFF IN LONG-TERM CARE:
SOURCES AND OUTCOMES

On the basis of previous work (Cohen-Mansfield, 1989; 1995), we have developed a model for understanding the sources and outcomes of job satisfaction and stress among nursing staff in long-term care (Fig. 4.1). Job satisfaction and stress are affected by four primary sources: (1) organizational features of institutions, (2) unit level organization, (3) the specific work involved, including resident care and relationships with residents and their family members, and (4) the personal life of the staff member. The first of these sources, the institution itself, must be responsive to outside forces such as regulators and funders, the corporate owner or board of directors, and the financial and legal complexities of evolving health care systems. Each of these four primary sources of staff stress will be described in more detail below, along with a summary of research findings supporting their role as sources of stress.

The staff stress which results from this compilation of forces has important repercussions for the quality of care given to residents and for the physical and emotional well-being, job satisfaction, turnover, and absenteeism among nursing staff. Specifically, staff dissatisfaction and stress result in high costs through their effect on turnover and absenteeism. Kiyak, Namazi, and Kahana (1997) showed that the best predictor of turnover was intent to leave, which in turn was best predicted by job dissatisfaction. Staff attitudes and the organizational climate also affect the quality of care provided (Sheridan, White, & Fairchild, 1992). Greater turnover and absenteeism among nursing staff and reductions in care quality directly affect the residents and their families who depend on the institution for good care. In response to perceived deficiencies in care, residents and families are likely to make greater demands on the facility and its nursing staff. Thus, a cyclical process occurs, whereby the factors that increase stress are in turn heightened by the stress they engender, thus further escalating the level of stress and reducing quality of care.

An example can elucidate the cyclical or recursive nature of the problem of staff stress in long-term care. When a nursing assistant experiences high levels of personal and/or job-related stress, she may display negative attitudes toward work, perform more poorly, and be tardy or absent from work more frequently. Other nursing assistants will then be required to manage her work, possibly through overtime assignments, heightening the demands on the remaining staff and continuing the cycle of increasing job stress, diminished teamwork, greater job dissatisfaction, lower commitment, and higher turnover. In order to appreciate the difficulties and

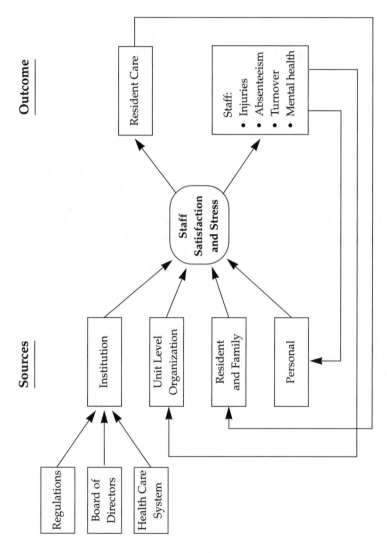

Figure 4.1 The Recursive Cycle of Occupational Satisfaction and Stress in Long-Term Care

importance of reducing staff stress in long-term care, it is essential that the cyclical or recursive nature of the problem be appreciated and addressed. To that end, the four primary sources of stress are described in more detail in the following section.

SOURCES OF OCCUPATIONAL SATISFACTION AND STRESS

External and Internal Institutional Factors

The external institutional factors affecting staff satisfaction and stress, such as federal and state regulations for long-term care services, and demands posed by funders, accrediting organizations, and linkages with other providers in a health care system, may appear tangential to the daily work life of nursing staff. However, they affect nursing staff, through attracting their impact on facility policies, reimbursement, census, competitive edge for residents and staff, and expectations for services. In contrast, the internal institutional sources of stress are focal in our model and include factors which are characteristic of the facility as they impact an individual's job, for example, ownership or auspice, rate of pay and benefits, to name a few.

PAY AND BENEFITS

In an effort to delineate institutional differences between nursing homes and other health care settings, Cotler & Kane (1988) mailed survey questionnaires to all registered nurses in Los Angeles County. The purpose of the survey was to contrast the job perceptions of nurses in Skilled Nursing Facilities (SNF) with those of nurses working in other settings. They found that the SNF nurses ($n = 72$) earned approximately $4000 per year less than nurses in other settings ($n = 1610$), and that SNF nurses had lower pensions and less vacation and sick leave.

Furthermore, SNF nurses did not perceive their opportunity for promotion to be as high as that for hospital nurses ($n = 1202$), and the SNF nurses were more frustrated than the other nurses with excess paperwork, overall work load, and conflict between nursing and management goals. Most nurses who responded to the survey indicated they would prefer to work in a hospital, whereas only 2% of the respondents expressed a preference for a nursing home setting. Finally, nurses in all types of work settings indicated that, in comparison to other types of institutions, SNF jobs were lower in prestige, less interesting, had less pleasant work environments, and offered lower rates of pay. The finding of lower salaries among nursing home staff has been replicated by Dunn, Rout, Carson, and Ritter (1994), Brannon, Cohn, and Smyer (1990), and Caudill & Patrick (1989) who have also reported that nursing homes offer poorer job security than other types of health care facilities.

CONTROL ISSUES, STAFF APPRECIATION, SUPPLIES AND RESOURCES

Institutionally based sources of stress which have been uncovered include administrative policies involving "rigid control" over staff, insufficient appreciation by management staff, and limited availability of supplies (Cohen-Mansfield, 1989; Dunn , Rout, Carson, & Ritter, 1994).

JOB DESCRIPTION/RESPONSIBILITIES

Another institutional-level stressor is the content and scope of the nursing staff's job descriptions. In many facilities, the nursing assistant's job is restricted to direct care. Most of what nursing assistants do has been referred to as the "bed and body work" of changing linens and bathing, toileting, turning, transferring, dressing, and feeding the residents (Gubrium, 1975). While this work is essential to the residents' quality of care and life, and can provide intrinsic rewards for nursing assistants as the residents' primary caregivers, it is repetitious and physically demanding, and its importance often goes unacknowledged. Research suggests that this restriction of nursing assistant responsibilities to direct care contributes to burnout and turnover (Banaszak-Holl & Hines, 1996; Institute of Medicine, 1986; Smyer, Brannon, & Cohn, 1992). Examples of other responsibilities which could be included in the nursing assistants' job are participation in resident care plan development, orientation of new residents to the facility, and the training and orientation of new nursing assistants (Noelker, Schur, Looman, Ejaz, and Whitlatch, in review).

Regarding licensed nurses in SNFs, their job responsibilities may preclude them from participating in resident care and the potential rewards it offers. These include extensive charting and other paper work demands (Cotler & Kane, 1988).

Unit-level factors

In addition to sources of satisfaction and stress generated at the institutional level, unit-level factors also provide distinct sources of satisfaction

and stress for nursing staff. Some examples include work load, staff relationships, unit supervision, and management style. Obviously, the distinction between unit characteristics and institutional characteristics is
somewhat arbitrary, because the two entities are not independent. For that
reason, most research that has undertaken an assessment of institutional
factors affecting staff stress has also included an assessment of unit characteristics, and vice versa.

Relationships with co-workers have been identified as an important
source of stress and satisfaction among staff in long-term care (Brannon,
et al., 1990; Cohen-Mansfield, 1989). Unit level factors that can increase job
dissatisfaction include understaffing, lazy or incompetent coworkers, and
problems with supervisors (Cohen-Mansfield, 1989). In another study
examining these issues, Carr and Kazanowski (1994) compared job satisfaction between nurses working in long-term care (LTC) and nurses in
other settings. Of the 1000 questionnaires sent out, responses were received
from 347 nurses. The primary reasons for nurses in LTC to be dissatisfied
were issues specific to their work units, including a "tremendous workload" (29%), "poor staff cohesiveness" (25%), and "poor staffing" (23%).
In contrast, the most commonly cited reasons for job dissatisfaction among
nurses in other settings were "inadequate salary" (16%), lack of recognition (14%), and "tremendous workload" (13%). Other complaints more
common among the LTC nurses compared to other nurses were inadequate salary (17%) and lack of recognition (18%).

A similar study was undertaken by Dunn et al. (1994) who found that
the most important factors causing stress among LTC nursing staff
included having little opportunity for input into decisions that affect them,
being criticized but not praised, and lack of support from other staff.
Findings from Hare, Pratt, and Andrews' (1988) study are consistent, indicating that supportive relationships reduced feelings of staff stress. It is
possible that these results occurred due to a process in which the staff's
feelings of being appreciated or accepted "buffered" or moderated sources
of job-related stress. However, this explanation did not receive support in
Chappell and Novak's study (1992) which tested for a buffing effect.

WORK LOAD

Findings from Chappell and Novak's study (1992) showed that work load
was the most significant factor affecting stress among 245 nursing assistants employed in nursing homes. Similarly, staffing and scheduling stressors were shown to have the largest impact on staff satisfaction in a study
of 405 nursing staff in 14 nursing care facilities (Schaefer & Moos, 1996).
Also, a smaller study of a nursing home unit for patients with Alzheimer's

disease indicated major sources of stress were "too little time for the amount of work required" and communication problems (McCarthy, 1992).

STAFF RELATIONSHIPS

In a study involving both long-term care and acute settings, Hare et al. (1988) found the Work Relationship Index to be the most powerful predictor of burnout. The Work Relationship Index, based on earlier work by Moos (1981), assesses peer cohesion, supervisor support, and work involvement. The investigators concluded that the causal relationships were circular, in that poor work relationships contributed to burnout which, in turn, decreased peer cohesion and work involvement. Similar findings were reported by Schaefer and Moos (1996) who found that job satisfaction was related to relationships with supervisors and physicians, coworker cohesion (how friendly and supportive employees are to each other), and clarity about work expectations, rules, and policies.

The conceptualization of unit-level support factors reflects two widely recognized dimensions of social support that have differing effects on the outcomes of stress: instrumental and emotional support (House, 1981; Lin, 1986). Examples of instrumental support are hands-on assistance from co-workers and the availability of good supplies and equipment. Emotional support has been shown to have two dimensions, positive and negative support (Antonucci, 1985). Positive support results from social interaction that produces pleasant feelings such as reassurance, understanding, respect, and encouragement. The concept of negative support reflects the fact that social interaction can be decidedly unhelpful to an individual by evoking unpleasant feelings such as anger, frustration, guilt, grief, loneliness, and disrespect.

Negative support has been shown to have a more powerful effect than positive support on satisfaction with support (Krause, 1995). One hypothesis for explaining this phenomenon is that individuals come to expect and generally experience positive interactions with others in their social network. When negative interaction occurs, it stands out clearly because it is unanticipated and generally departs from normative standards in a group. Thus, hurtful interactions tend to have greater potential to produce adverse effects than helpful interactions do to deter them.

UNIT SUPERVISION/MANAGERIAL STYLE

In one study, the extent and nature of feedback at work was the most important predictor of burnout among 60 nursing staff in geriatric and psychogeriatric care (Astrom, Nillson, Norberg, Sandman, & Winblad, 1991). Different aspects of managerial style were highlighted in Noelker's studies (Noelker, 1993; Noelker & Schur; Schur, Noelker, Looman, Whitlatch, & Ejaz, 1998) which found that in some facilities, staff occupational stress was exacerbated by poor management and supervisory procedures and staffing policies. For example, in some skilled nursing facilities, overtime was mandatory when staffing was short, leaving the nursing assistant no choice but to comply in order to avoid disciplinary action. Such unexpected schedule changes create a feeling of powerlessness and may disrupt important family and personal obligations such as child care and transportation arrangements.

Other findings from these studies showed that more than half the nursing assistants expressed dissatisfaction with the way management and nursing staff worked together. The majority were also dissatisfied with the amount of feedback they received, the lack of recognition for good job performance and encouragement to use their nursing skills fully, and teamwork between supervisors and nursing assistants, all of which point to the need for better supervision in skilled nursing facilities. Anecdotal data from these studies lends further support to this conclusion. For example, nursing assistants commented that supervisors "talk down to us," "act like they're better than us," and "ignore what we have to say." This latter comment is supported by findings that more than half of nursing assistants (from a total of 114 nursing assistants from five nursing homes) never or only minimally participate in resident care planning conferences, and three out of four never or only minimally participate in attending residents' preadmission conferences (Schur et al., 1998). These findings support the assertion that nursing assistants, although involved in direct care, are generally excluded from the decision-making processes related to that care.

From the perspective of professional nurses, one barrier to functioning as an effective supervisor are nursing attitudes that foster caring for and nurturing others rather than managing them. Others are a lack of training in supervisory skills and uncertainty about what the supervisory role encompasses (Berger, 1987; Ford, 1996).

JOB-RELATED INJURIES

Job-related injuries can be conceptualized as both sources and consequences of job dissatisfaction. The choice to include them among the sources of dissatisfaction was based on several reasons: (1) job-related injuries have a major impact, and (2) though stress contributes to injuries, other aspects of the job, such as the specific job requirement of lifting and moving people, the ergonomic design of the environment, and training in job-related procedures play an even larger role in contributing to injuries. Nursing staff in long-term care had a period prevalence of back injuries nearly 1.5 times higher than all employees of long-term care facilities and six times higher than all occupations combined industry-wide (Cohen-Mansfield, Culpepper, & Carter, 1996). A survey by the Bureau of Labor Statistics on the rate of non-fatal job-related injuries found that nursing homes were the second most hazardous place to work after automobile manufacturing plants (Buss, 1995). In 1994, nursing home workers experienced more than 221,000 injuries or about 16.9 injuries per 100 workers. Furthermore, the number of lost workdays due to injuries among nursing home employees doubled from 1983 to 1993. The most common injuries are sprains and strains to the back and shoulders that result from lifting or transferring residents. The workers' compensation costs for back injuries are substantial, averaging more than $8,400 per injury.

Recent research has linked job dissatisfaction to work-related injuries, specifically to lower back injuries (Nier, 1996). Nier notes that job dissatisfaction is manifested in certain behaviors, including inattentiveness, depression, tardiness, anxiety, and absenteeism, that can lead to incidents or injury. These behaviors reflect "unhealthy stress" in the workplace and are a function of poor supervision, tense work relationships, poor communication, and inadequate recognition.

Work level: Resident and family factors

As might be intuitively obvious, one of the greatest sources of strain as well as satisfaction among nursing staff in LTC is the resident population itself. In the studies by Brannon, Cohn, and Smyer (1990) and by Cohen-Mansfield (1989), the significance of the work and the sense of being helpful to elderly residents were the main sources of satisfaction. In the latter study, resident disability and agitation were both found to constitute sources of staff stress. The experience of resident decline in cognitive and physical function, as well as the need to handle the most basic daily living activities, such as toileting and feeding, are among the greatest resident-related stressors.

Both residents and their family members can be major sources of satisfaction. Qualitative data obtained from residents, family members, and nursing assistants from Noelker's studies revealed that a sizable portion of assistants remained on the job, despite the low pay and other problems, because of the job's intrinsic rewards, that is, the happiness they derived from giving good care to residents and the closeness of their relationships with them and the residents' families (Looman, Noelker, Schur, Whitlatch, & Ejaz, 1997; Noelker & Schur in review). Similarly, interpersonal relations and communication with residents were reported to be among the more frequent sources of satisfaction for nursing staff in long-term care (Cohen-Mansfield, 1989).

DEMENTIA / BEHAVIOR PROBLEMS

Establishing and maintaining positive relationships with residents suffering from dementia, especially when they exhibit disruptive behaviors, present special challenges for nursing staff. In a study of 132 nurses on wards specializing in the care of demented persons, Hallberg and Norberg (1993) found that agitation, not being responsive, and unruly behavior were the most common problems, while emptiness and agony were the most difficult problems to handle. When staff felt that patients were leading empty lives, they had more difficulty in the provision of care (Hallberg & Norberg, 1995). Another study found that the following symptoms were reported by nursing staff caring for residents with Alzheimer's disease: reluctance to go to work, irritability with family and friends, irritability with patients, headaches, spending less than 15 minutes eating lunch, personal needs not being met, drinking, and smoking (McCarthy, 1992)

Astrom, Nilsson, Norberg, and Winblad (1990) found that nursing staff caring for cognitively impaired residents in nursing homes experienced more burnout than nursing staff in long-term care institutions for physically disabled, nondemented residents. They attributed the difference to the "growing physical and psychological workload connected with the number of demented patients in these institutions" (p. 1243). This finding may be clarified by Clinton , Moyle, Weir and Edwards' (1995) study, which found that the most common stressors mentioned by nurses caring for residents suffering from dementia involved resident behaviors which were characterized as difficult, disruptive, noisy, or attention-seeking. Although small in size (n = 28), Dougherty, Bolger, Preston, Jones, and Payne (1992) shed further light on these findings by showing very high correlations between resident aggressive behavior and staff job dissatisfaction in a long-term care facility. Similar findings were reported by Everitt, Fields, Soumerai, and Avorn (1991) who examined behavior problems among 346 residents of intermediate care facilities who were receiving psychoactive medication. Resident behaviors that caused severe staff distress included physically abusive behaviors, bizarre behaviors, noisy behaviors and verbally abusive behaviors. Similarly, Lusk (1992) describes verbal and physical violence which residents inflict on staff members, and the ensuing injuries, including those to staff eyes, arms, shoulders, knees, jaw, and thumb.

INCONTINENCE

Incontinence is such a basic and common problem among nursing homes residents that its impact on the staff is easily overlooked. However, research indicates that dealing with resident incontinence causes great dissatisfaction among direct care staff. For example, incontinence results in odors that were at least sometimes disliked by 80% of nursing staff in nursing homes, and 45% reported that at least some of the time they disliked changing wet clothes and beddings. About 40% felt depressed about their work and about the extra work associated with urinary incontinence, and 20% felt like resigning from their job because of the patients' urinary incontinence (Yu & Kaltreider, 1987; Yu et al., 1991).

RESIDENT DEATH

Approximately 42% of the nursing staff in a continuing care and rehabilitation hospital reported being negatively affected by patients' deaths. The impact contributed to low morale and, for some, to a reported loss of efficiency at work (O'Hara, Harper, Chartrand, & Johnston, 1996).

SOCIAL RELATIONSHIPS AND MUTUAL RESPECT BETWEEN NURSING ASSISTANTS AND RESIDENTS

The most satisfying factor for the more than 1,200 long-term care nurses who returned a questionnaire in Fisher-Robertson and Cummings' (1991) study was recognition from patients. Findings from Noelker's (1993) first study of relationships between nursing assistants and cognitively intact residents demonstrated that attachment and mutual respect in the nursing assistant-resident relationship were central to both nursing assistant job satisfaction and resident satisfaction with the nursing home and its care. When nursing assistants and residents felt they had a greater appreciation of one another's individuality, were affectionate, and had a broader understanding of their personal histories and lives outside the facility, levels of satisfaction were significantly higher. In contrast, when nursing assistants and residents perceived negative affect in their interaction, evidenced by anger or irritation, they were more dissatisfied. These findings are consistent with other studies indicating that nursing homes are not emotionally neutral environments, but that expressions of negative emotion can come to dominate the social milieu (Noelker & Poulshock, 1982; Pillemer & Moore, 1989).

SOCIAL RELATIONSHIPS AND MUTUAL RESPECT BETWEEN NURSING ASSISTANTS AND RESIDENTS' FAMILY MEMBERS

In Noelker's subsequent study (Noelker, Schur, Looman, Ejaz, & Whitlatch, in review) on the nature of relationships between nursing assistants and the family members of residents with dementia, important relationships were found between job satisfaction and perceived respect by residents' families. Furthermore, findings indicated that perceived respect from residents' families had an influence on multiple dimensions of nursing assistant job satisfaction, including satisfaction with management and supervision.

Qualitative data from this research showed how distressed nursing assistants felt when family members accused them of mistreatment when they noticed a bruise on a resident, or theft when something was missing from the resident's belongings. In turn, nursing assistants expressed resentment about the ways some of "their" residents were treated by relatives, such as sporadic visiting and decisions to withhold antibiotics, hydration, and/or nutrition. Some family members were viewed as having little understanding of the nursing assistant's important role in resident care, and a lack of appreciation of their skills at caregiving, while others were seen by nursing assistants as empathetic supporters who were grateful for the quality of care they gave to their relatives (Looman et al., 1997).

When family members are overly stressed, most commonly because they are upset about the quality of care, it can manifest itself in physical and verbal aggression towards nursing home personnel (Vinton & Mazza, 1994). In their study of administrators at 70 Florida nursing homes, 1,193 acts of verbal aggression and 13 acts of physical aggression were reported to be directed at staff by residents' families over a six-month period.

Personal factors

LIMITED FINANCIAL RESOURCES COMBINED WITH FAMILY RESPONSIBILITIES

Prior ethnographic studies have poignantly documented the personal burdens borne by nursing assistants who are typically racial and ethnic minorities, women, unmarried with dependents, and living on the edge of poverty as the lowest-paid workers in the health care labor force (Foner, 1994; Tellis-Nyak & Tellis-Nyak, 1989). Most nursing assistants live in poor neighborhoods, and many are immigrants. Those factors are, by themselves, known risk factors for stress because of economic pressures, high crime levels in their neighborhoods, and poorer support mechanisms. Two personal sources of stress that proved to be significant predictors of job dissatisfaction were worries about family while at work and financial worries (Noelker, 1993).

Discussions of these findings with the directors of local nursing assistant training programs reinforced the extent to which transportation, housing, and child care problems contribute to job stress and job loss, particularly among young unmarried mothers who are moving off welfare. One director noted that a key predictor of a nursing assistant making it through the probationary period at a nursing home is whether the facility is on a bus line, because most are dependent on public transportation. Although subsidized child care is sometimes available to these workers, there are constraints on its use. Nursing assistants working the night-shift are dependent on family or friends to take care of their children, because child care programs do not operate at this time. After the night shift, these employees must choose between sleeping or watching their children, because night-shift workers are ineligible for reimbursement for daytime child care.

Nursing assistants moving off welfare and those in subsidized housing face additional threats to keeping their jobs because of mandatory meetings during the work day with their case manager and housing official to verify their continued eligibility for benefits. During the 90-day probationary period in many facilities, nursing assistants are automatically terminated after three absences from work. Nursing assistants sometimes forget to notify the housing authority that a meeting must be rescheduled because of their work requirements. Many opt to attend the meeting and miss work, especially with housing officials, because they cannot risk becoming homeless or losing their supplemental income and food stamps, even if it means losing their job.

INTERVENING FACTORS: SELF-ESTEEM, DEPRESSION, AND COPING SKILLS

Intervening factors are not stressors in themselves, but factors that can moderate the impact of stressors on outcomes. These are resources or liabilities that the individual brings to the job that affect job performance, social relationships, and job outcomes (Cohen-Mansfield, 1995). In fact, previous research has shown these personal factors are related to occupational stress; for example, lower self-esteem among workers was associated with poorer outcomes (Cronin-Stubbs & Velsor-Friedrich, 1981).

In a sample of 289 nursing assistants from 14 northeast Ohio skilled nursing facilities, depression was relatively prevalent, with almost one-third (31%) scoring 16 or higher on the CES-Depression measure which indicates possible clinical levels of depression (Noelker & Schur, 1999). In the general population, the incidence of depression is approximately half the percentage found in these samples. It is possible that the higher rate is partially due to the fact that most nursing assistants were women, who generally tend to report higher levels of depression than men. Also, their low-income status, having financial dependents, and other stressful life events could heighten their vulnerability to this psychiatric disorder. It is acknowledged that depression can be an intervening variable or an outcome of stress.

Coping mechanisms have been demonstrated to have significant effects on the outcomes of stress (Williamson & Schulz, 1993). Coping mechanisms used in the workplace may be adaptive, such as careful problem-solving, positive reappraisal, and prayer, or they may be maladaptive, such as confrontation, withdrawal, or substance use (Hare et al., 1988).

INTERVENTIONS TO REDUCE STRESS AND ENHANCE JOB SATISFACTION AMONG NURSING STAFF IN LONG-TERM CARE

The weight of evidence that the nursing profession in long-term care involves a high degree of stress and a corresponding high rate of staff turnover (see Cohen-Mansfield, 1997) suggests that there should be substantial research on interventions for reducing stress in nursing home settings. In fact, there are few studies that have addressed this issue. Some aspects of this issue which have been addressed include the use of additional clinical supervision, the implementation of informal support groups focused on professional issues (Balint groups), and specialized training often tied to career ladders.

Clinical Supervision Combined with Individualized Care

Clinical supervision combined with individualized care was reported to result in a reduction in burnout among staff on a dementia unit (Berg, Hansson, & Hallberg, 1994; Hallberg & Norberg, 1993). For these studies, RNs, LPNs, LMNs, and NAs on the unit underwent a year of systematic clinical supervision combined with the implementation of individualized care routines for residents with dementia. In addition to reduced burnout, staff members reported improved feelings of devotion and beneficence to the residents, and viewed the residents as more responsive and easier to handle. A control unit manifested no decrease in burnout.

Balint Groups

In another intervention study, Rabinowitz, Kushnir, and Ribak (1996) assessed the effectiveness of "Balint Groups" on preventing burnout in primary care nurses. Balint Groups are designed to provide health professionals with an accepting atmosphere in which they can focus on issues related to the client-professional relationship and discuss any related issues which might be sources of stress or discomfort for them. The groups are not intended to serve as "therapy" for the professionals, in that they do not focus on emotional issues; rather they are problem-solving groups designed to help maximize the professionals' performance. Rabinowitz et al. (1996) reported that, over time, the Balint Groups reduced emotional exhaustion and cognitive weariness, but emphasized that decreases in burnout occur gradually.

Advanced Training and Career Ladders

Skilled nursing facilities increasingly recognize the value of providing advanced training and career advancement as a tool to improve recruitment, retention, and recognition for nursing staff, particularly nursing assistants (as examples, see Harris & Chermak, 1987; McDonald, 1991–1992; Ripka & Fouser, 1992). The training can be linked to specialty care on dementia, hospice, or rehabilitation units and involves advanced training in the area with corresponding title change and promotion. Alternatively, it can involve additional training in gerontology and adult learning with promotion and title change linked to nursing assistant status (e.g., Resident Care Specialist I, II and III; Nursing Assistant Specialist, Senior Nursing Assistant; and Senior Aide Coordinator). Adding career ladders and associated pay increases is costly, yet it can be cost-effective when the prohibitive costs of turnover are taken into account. Although the benefits for employee satisfaction and retention are commonly reported, most of this literature is based on the experiences of one facility, or chain of facilities, rather than on more rigorous research evaluations.

POSSIBLE AREAS FOR FUTURE INTERVENTIONS

Interpersonal Relationships Among Staff Residents and Families

Noelker's results suggest that several steps can be taken to foster stronger bonds between residents and nursing assistants. One fruitful tactic might be to institute the practice of permanent assignment, in which nursing assistants care for the same residents daily. This strategy has the potential to maximize opportunities for staff to become acquainted with residents and families, thereby developing closer bonds. Second, nursing assistants could be given biographies of residents upon admission to help them appreciate the resident's personal history, lifestyle, and accomplishments, and thus encourage more individualized care. Third, supervisory and social service staff could be encouraged to be more attentive to the nature and quality of the interactions among nursing assistants and residents in order to ensure that negativity and impatience do not dominate over positive affect. Methods by which mutual respect could be enhanced among nursing assistants, residents, and residents' families are described by Heiselman and Noelker (1991) and can be used to educate staff and family members. Family/staff conferences represent another mechanism for enhancing relationships between staff members and informal caregivers. Better staff training in promotion of positive interpersonal relationships with cognitively impaired residents may be useful. Finally, mental health interventions should be initiated with residents showing signs of depression, paranoia, or other conditions that contribute to negativity in interaction.

Staff Support and Training

Clinton et al. (1995) reported that over half of 10 nurses on a dementia unit relied heavily on maladaptive coping behaviors, such as withdrawal, smoking, or getting nervous. In response, the authors developed an intervention that included counseling to nurses who relied on maladaptive coping strategies, and a workshop on stress management. However, the results of the intervention were not reported.

Staff support and training is continuously advocated in the staff stress literature, but its effects have not been consistently tested via intervention studies. Training in handling behavior problems or in avoiding injuries would seem to be an obvious need, based on known high rates of injury. It should be emphasized, however, that staff training must go beyond educational lectures in order to impact behavior or satisfaction; effective staff training is a complex process (Burgio & Burgio, 1990; L. D. Burgio & Scilley, 1994; Cohn, Horgas, & Marsiske, 1990; Maas, Buckwalter, Swanson, & Mobily, 1994).

Job redesign and training have been used by Smyer, Brannon, and Cohn (1992). Although job satisfaction was not measured, job performance was not significantly affected. Career ladders and recognition awards have been suggested as job redesign features to enhance staff motivation.

A stress management program involving music therapy, deep breathing exercises, yoga positions, and imagery is described by McCarthy (1992). The program was met with low levels of attendance because staff had difficulty attending during their workday, and were not willing to devote non-work time to the program. Much of the literature on informal caregivers of persons with dementia stresses the need for support with this difficult task. It therefore stands to reason that caring for the caregivers is an important component for enhancing satisfaction among formal caregivers as well.

Resources and Outside Obstacles to Satisfaction

One important area for intervention relates to public policy and to forces outside the institution. Issues of staff shortages, staff pay, and regulations concerning staff-to-resident ratios may need to change if a comprehensive change in staff morale is to take place in long-term care.

Using Satisfaction Surveys within a Quality Improvement Framework

Using satisfaction surveys within a quality improvement framework is a methodology for enhancing staff satisfaction that is glaringly absent from the literature. No interventions studies of this method were found, though an article by Zemans (1995) describes such a program, as does his chapter in this book (see Chapter 10).

LIMITATIONS OF THE FINDINGS

Most striking in a topic of such magnitude as staff satisfaction and stress in long-term care is the dearth of information. The literature is limited both in amount and in scope. Interestingly, some of the important research has been performed outside the US (e.g., Sweden—Astrom, Waxman et al.,

1991; Berg et al., 1994; Hallberg & Norberg, 1993; Canada—Chappell & Novak, 1992; UK—Dunn et al., 1994; Australia—Clinton et al., 1995) and most studies address only portions of the model, limiting the ability to understand the relative importance of the various sources of satisfaction.

A limitation of most studies cited above is the use of a cross-sectional design that does not allow for the determination of the causal order of relationships between the "source" and staff job satisfaction. For example, in examining the sense of respect from others in the facility, nursing assistants who disliked the job may have felt less respected by others in the facility, or disrespect from others could have resulted in less satisfaction with the job. Similarly, the causal order of relationships between other important study variables such as nursing assistant stressors (e.g., family and financial worries, depression) and dimensions of social support on nursing assistant job outcomes can only be determined using a longitudinal design.

A third limitation relates to the insufficient differentiation between nursing assistants, registered nurses, and other nursing staff members. Many studies combine these categories, whereas it stands to reason that the issues which relate to their satisfaction are quite different, given that their actual job responsibilities and their place in the career ladder of the organization.

ASSESSMENT OF STAFF SATISFACTION

Assessment instruments which have been used to investigate staff satisfaction in long-term care are summarized in Appendix I, Table I.2. As can be seen, most have used existing scales for job satisfaction, such as Pine's burnout scale, or the Minnesota Satisfaction Scale. However, several (e.g., Helmer, Olson, & Heim, 1993; Dunn et al., 1994) attempted to develop instruments specifically for this population. Although the domains covered generally involve the areas described above as sources of satisfaction and stress, they vary greatly among instruments. The fact that domains were defined independently for each assessment using different methods and different terminologies defies adequate comparisons of domains across the instruments. Assessment instruments range in length from 15 to 44 items, with scales ranging from 1–4 to 1–7. Information on reliability is generally scarce, and most instruments have only been used in one or two studies. As mentioned above, instruments used specifically for staff surveys and quality improvement processes are conspicuous by their absence.

It is clear from this review that the assessment of staff satisfaction in the nursing home is still in its infancy. Basic questions still need to be clarified: What critical elements should be included in a staff satisfaction survey? What are the differences between stress and satisfaction, and which is more meaningful for the organization, for the employee, and for the quality of care? Are different surveys needed for employees who are involved in direct care to residents versus those who provide ancillary care or supportive services? Additionally, the literature is lacking norms or benchmarking from a large number of facilities to which data for specific job titles could be compared. This review could serve as a basis for determining initial domains to be included in staff satisfaction or stress surveys and in quality improvement programs. However, only additional research could determine the relative utility of specific sources of stress or satisfaction in such surveys and in improvement programs to be implemented.

SUMMARY

Although the literature on employee satisfaction in long-term care is limited, some conclusions can be drawn. Staff dissatisfaction and stress pose a significant problem to long-term care institutions, with concomitant high turnover, frequent burnout, and low morale among staff. These in turn commonly lead to low productivity, low quality of care, and increased personnel costs related to recruitment and training of new staff. Some aspects of dissatisfaction are unique to the long-term industry. For example, some of the stress is related to the growing proportion of nursing home residents who suffer from Alzheimer's disease or other types of illness which lead to memory impairments and behavioral problems. Dealing with such populations is particularly stressful when the initial training or continuing education received by direct-care staff is deficient in information on how to handle problematic resident behaviors. Low pay, inadequate managerial style, and stressors in their personal lives are also among the most commonly cited stresses amongst long-term care staff. The use of staff satisfaction surveys in long-term care may be more common than would be surmised, given the availability of research literature on the topic. However, if this is the case, the use of such data for increasing staff satisfaction, either through systematic interventions or through quality improvement processes, needs to be documented and disseminated.

REFERENCES

Antonucci, T. C. (1985). Personal characteristics, social support, and social behavior. In R. H. Binstock & E. Shanas (Eds.), *Handbook of aging and the social sciences* (pp. 94–120). New York: Van Nostrand Reinhold.

Astrom, S., Nilsson, M., Norberg, A., Sandman, P-O., & Winblad, B. (1991). Staff burnout in dementia care: Relations to empathy and attitudes. *International Journal of Nursing Studies, 28*(1), 65–75.

Astrom, S., Nilsson, M., Norberg, A., & Winblad, B. (1990). Empathy, experience of burnout and attitudes towards demented patients among nursing staff in geriatric care. *Journal of Advanced Nursing, 15,* 1236–1244.

Astrom, S., Waxman, H. M., Nilsson, M., Norberg, A., & Winblad, B. (1991). Wish to transfer to other jobs among long-term care workers. *Aging, 3*(3), 247–256.

Atchley, R. C. (1996). Frontline workers in long-term care: Recruitment, retention, and turnover issues in an era of rapid growth. Monograph, The Scripps Gerontology Center, Miami University, Oxford, Ohio.

Banaszak-Holl, J., & Hines, M.A. (1996). Factors associated with nursing home staff turnover. *The Gerontologist, 36*(4), 512–517.

Berg, A., Hansson, U. W., & Hallberg, I. R. (1994). Nurse's creativity, tedium and burnout during 1 year of clinical supervision and implementation of individually planned nursing care: Comparisons between a ward for severely demented patients and a similar control ward. *Journal of Advanced Nursing, 20,* 742–749.

Berger, S. G. (1987, April). How nurses relate to nursing assistants. *Provider,* 14–17.

Brannon, D., Cohn, M. D., & Smyer, M. A. (1990). Care giving as work: How nurse's aides rate it. *The Journal of Long-Term Care Administration, 18*(1), 10–14.

Burgio, L. D., & Burgio, K. L. (1990). Institutional staff training and management: A review of the literature and a model for geriatric, long-term care facilities. *International Journal of Aging and Human Development, 34*(4), 287–302.

Burgio, L. D., & Scilley, K. (1994). Caregiver performance in the nursing home: The use of staff training and management procedures. *Seminars in Speech and Language, 15*(4), 331–322.

Buss, D. (1995). Nursing homes rank high in workplace injuries. *Contemporary Long-Term Care,* April: 11.

Carr, K. K., & Kazanowski, M. K. (1994). Factors affecting job satisfaction of nurses who work in long-term care. *Journal of Advanced Nursing, 19,* 878–883.

Caudill, M., & Patrick, M. (1989). Nursing assistant turnover in nursing homes and need satisfaction. *Journal of Gerontological Nursing, 15*(6), 24–30.

Chappell, N. L., & Novak, M. (1992). The role of support in alleviating stress among nursing assistants. *The Gerontologist, 32*(3), 351–359.

Clinton, M., Moyle, W., Weir, D., & Edwards, H. (1995). Perceptions of stressors and reported coping strategies in nurses caring for residents with Alzheimer's disease in a dementia unit. *Australian and New Zealand Journal of Mental Health Nursing, 4*(1), 5–13.

Cohen-Mansfield, J. (1989). Sources of satisfaction and stress in nursing home caregivers: Preliminary results. *Journal of Advanced Nursing, 14,* 383–388.

Cohen-Mansfield, J. (1995). Stress in nursing home staff: A review and a theoretical model. *The Journal of Applied Gerontology, 14*(4), 444–466.

Cohen-Mansfield, J. (1997). Turnover in nursing home caregivers: a review. *Nursing Management, 28*(5), 59–64.

Cohen-Mansfield, J., Culpepper, J., & Carter, P. (1996). Back injuries to nursing staff in long-term care facilities. *AAOHN, 44*(1), 9–17.

Cohn, M. D., Horgas, A. L., & Marsiske, M. (1990). Behavior management training for nurse aides: Is it effective? *Journal of Gerontological Nursing, 16*(11), 21–25.

Cotler, M. P., & Kane, R. (1988). Registered nurses and nursing home shortages: Job conditions and attitudes among RNs. *Journal of Long-Term Care Administration, 16*(4), 13–18.

Cronin-Stubbs, D., & Velsor-Friedrich, B. (1981). Professional and personal stress: A survey. *Nursing Leadership, 4*(1), 21–26.

Dougherty, L. M., Bolger, J. P., Preston, D. G., Jones, S. S., & Payne, H. C. (1992). Effects of exposure to aggressive behavior on job satisfaction of health care staff. *The Journal of Applied Gerontology, 11*(2), 160–172.

Dunn, L. A., Rout, U., Carson, & J., Ritter, S. A. (1994). Occupational stress amongst care staff working in nursing homes: An empirical investigation. *Journal of Clinical Nursing, 3*, 177–183.

Everitt, D. E., Fields, D. R., Soumerai, S. S., & Avorn, J. (1991). Resident behavior and staff distress in the nursing home. *Journal of the American Geriatric Society, 39*(8), 792–798.

Fisher-Robertson, J., & Cummings, C. C. (1991). What makes long-term care nursing attractive? *American Journal of Nursing, 91*(11), 41–46.

Foner, N. (1994). Nursing home aides: Saints or monsters? *The Gerontologist, 34*(2), 245–250.

Ford, W. (1996, May). Shoring up nurse supervisors. *Nursing Homes, 45*(5), 14–16.

Gubrium, J. F. (1975). *Living and dying at Murray Manor.* New York: St. Martin's Press.

Hallberg, I. R., & Norberg, A. (1993). Strain among nurses and their emotional reactions during one year of systematic clinical supervision combined with the implementation of individualized care in dementia nursing. *Journal of Advanced Nursing, 18*, 1860–1875.

Hallberg, I. R., & Norberg, A. (1995). Nurses' experiences of strain and their reactions in the care of severely demented patients. *International Journal of Geriatric Psychiatry, 10*, 757–766.

Hare, J., Pratt, C. C., & Andrews, D. (1988). Predictors of burnout in professional and paraprofessional nurses working in hospitals and nursing homes. *International Journal of Nursing Studies, 25*(2), 105–115.

Harris, A., & Chermak, J. B. (1987, April). "PCAs": Hillhaven's career ladder option. *Provider,* 32–33.

Heiselman, T., & Noelker, L. S. (1991). Enhancing mutual respect among nursing assistants, residents, and residents' families. *The Gerontologist, 31*(4), 552–555.

Helmer, F. T., Olson, S. F., & Heim, R. I. (1993). Strategies for nurse aide job satisfaction. *The Journal of Long-Term Care Administration, 21*(2), 10–14.

House, J. S. (1981). *Work stress and social support.* Reading, MA: Addison-Wesley.

Institute of Medicine. (1986). *Improving the quality of care in nursing homes.* Washington, DC: National Academy Press.

Kiyak, H. A., Namazi, K. H., & Kahana, E. F. (1997). Job commitment and turnover among women working in facilities serving older persons. *Research on Aging, 19*(2), 223–246.

Krause, N. (1995). Negative interaction and satisfaction with social support among older adults. *Journal of Gerontology: Psychological Sciences, 50B*(2), P59–P73.

Lin, N. (1986).Conceptualizing social support. In N. Lin, A. Dean, & W. Ensel (Eds.), *Social support, life events and depression* (pp. 17–30). Orlando, FL: Academic.

Looman, W. J., Noelker, L. S., Schur, D., Whitlatch, C. J., & Ejaz, F. K. (1997). Nursing assistants caring for dementia residents in nursing homes: The family's perspective on the high quality of care. *American Journal of Alzheimer's Disease, 12*(5), 221–226.

Lusk, S. L. (1992). Violence experienced by nurse's aides in nursing homes: An exploratory study. *AAOHN, 40*(5), 237–241.

Maas, M., Buckwalter, K. C., Swanson, E., & Mobily, P. R. (1994). Training key to job satisfaction. *The Journal of Long-Term Care Administration, 22*(1), 23–26.

McCarthy, K. M. (1992). Stress management in the health care field: A pilot program for staff in a nursing home unit for patients with Alzheimer's disease. *Music Therapy Perspectives, 10*, 110–113.

McDonald, C. A. (1991–1992, Winter). Career ladder: Tool for recruitment, retention, and recognition. *The Journal of Long-Term Care Administration, 19*(4), 6–7.

Moos, R. (1981). *Work Environment Scale Manual*, Palo Alto, CA: Consulting Psychologists Press.

Nier, L. (1996, June). On-the-job injury tied to job satisfaction. *Provider*, 47–48.

Noelker, L. S., & Schur, D. (1999, March). *Depression among nursing assistants: Explanatory factors and interventions.* Paper session presented at the 45th Annual Meeting of the American Society on Aging, Orlando, FL.

Noelker, L. S. (1993). *Improving the quality of nurse assistant-resident relations in nursing homes. (Final report to The Cleveland Foundation).* Cleveland: The Benjamin Rose Institute.

Noelker, L. S., & Poulshock, S. W. (1982). *The effects on families of caring for impaired elderly in residence.* (Final report to the Administration on Aging). Cleveland: The Benjamin Rose Institute.

Noelker, L. S., Schur, D., Looman, W., Ejaz, F. K., & Whitlatch, C. J. (in Review). Sources and consequences of stress for nursing assistants caring for residents with dementia. Manuscript submitted for publications. *Research in Aging.*

O'Hara, P. A., Harper, D. W., Chartrand, L. D., & Johnston, S. F. (1996). Patient death in a long-term care hospital: A study of the effect on nursing staff. *Journal of Gerontological Nursing, 22*(8), 27–35.

Pillemer, K., & Moore, D. (1989). Abuse of patients in nursing homes: Findings from a survey of staff. *The Gerontologist, 29*, 314–320.

Rabinowitz, S., Kushnir, T., & Ribak, J. (1996). Preventing burnout: Increasing professional self primary care nurses in a Balint Group. *AAOHN, 44*(1), 28–32.

Ripka, G., & Fouser, C. (1992, September). Implementing a clinical ladder program. *Caring Magazine*, 54–57.

Schur, D., Noelker, L. S., Looman, W., Whitlatch, C. J., & Ejaz, F. K. (1998). 4 steps to more committed nursing assistants. *Balance, 2*(1), 29–32.

Shcaefer, J. A., & Moos, R. H. (1996). Effects of work stressors and work climate on long-term care staff's job morale and functioning. *Research in Nursing and Health, 19*(1), 63–73.

Sheridan, J. E., White, J., & Fairchild, T. J. (1992). Ineffective staff, ineffective supervision or ineffective administration? Why some nursing homes fail to provide adequate care. *The Gerontologist, 32*(3), 334–341.

Silvestri, G. T. (1993). The American Work Force, 1992-2005. *Monthly Labor Review*, November, pp. 58–86.

Smyer, M., Brannon, D., & Cohn, M. (1992). Improving nursing home care through training and job redesign. *The Gerontologist, 32*, 327–333.

Tellis-Nyak, V. & Tellis-Nyak, M. (1989). Quality of care and the burden of two cultures: When the world of the nurse's aide enters the nursing home. *The Gerontologist, 29*, 307–313.

Vinton, L., & Mazza, N. (1994). Aggressive behavior directed at nursing home personnel by residents' family members. *The Gerontologist, 34*(4), 528–533.

Williamson, G. M., & Schulz, R. (1993). Coping with specific stressors in Alzheimer's disease caregiving. *The Gerontologist, 33* (6), 747–755.

Yu, L. C., Johnson, K., Kaltreider, D. L., Hu, T. W., Brannon, D., & Ory, M. (1991). Urinary incontinence: Nursing home staff reaction toward residents. *Journal of Gerontological Nursing, 17*(11), 34–41.

Yu, L. C., & Kaltreider, D. L. (1987). Stressed nurses dealing with incontinent patients. *Journal of Gerontological Nursing, 13*(1), 27–30.

Zemans, J. R. (1995). How opinion surveys improve employee morale and resident satisfaction. *Journal of Long-Term Care Administration. 23*(2), 10–11.

Chapter 5

CORRELATES OF NURSING HOME SATISFACTION

Jean M. Kruzich

OVERVIEW OF QUALITY OF NURSING HOME LITERATURE

A recent Institute of Medicine report identified older persons' satisfaction with care deserving of special attention by researchers and policy makers (Feasley, 1996). Binstock and Spector (1997), when charged to set forth the five most important research areas for long-term care, identified the development and refinement of quality of care measures as the most important, with satisfaction with care seen as an increasingly important outcome measure. Patient satisfaction has clearly emerged as a central focus of health care delivery and quality assurance efforts across health care settings, and nursing homes are no exception (Aharony & Strasser, 1993). In long-term care, satisfaction is a relative newcomer compared to other measures that have dominated efforts to assess nursing home quality.

While the primary emphasis in this chapter is on correlates of residents' and family members' satisfaction with the nursing home, studies of staff satisfaction will also be discussed. The goals of this chapter are twofold:

first, to summarize what is known about organizational and individual correlates of nursing home satisfaction, and secondly, to identify individual and organizational variables that merit attention in future studies of nursing home satisfaction.

To understand the context for the increasing interest in nursing home satisfaction as an outcome measure of nursing home quality, it is useful to have a historical picture of how quality of care has been conceptualized in the past few decades. The dominant paradigm for assessing quality includes three categories of indicators of quality: structure, process, and outcome (Donabedian, 1988). Figure 5.1 illustrates the conceptual linkages among the three categories which assume that good structure increases the likelihood of good process, which increases the likelihood of good outcomes.

Nursing home studies can be grouped into three lines of inquiry that reflect a shift in interest over the past 20 years. The majority of studies of quality of care in nursing homes are included in the first line of inquiry, with its focus on the interrelationship of organizational structure and process characteristics, with no link to outcome measures of care. "Structure" refers to the attributes of the setting in which care occurs, and the facility's capacity to provide high quality care. Frequently used measures of structure include nursing hours per patient, expenditures per resident, ratings of a facility's physical environment, and occupancy rates (Sainfort, Ramsay, & Manato, 1995). As Davis' extensive review of the literature (1991) documents, most nursing home studies have examined the relationship of these variables and other structural factors such as ownership and facility size. Structural components of care are more objective, reliable, and easily measurable than process or outcome components, and

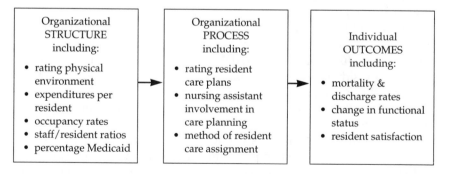

Figure 5.1 Conceptual relationships among categories of quality of care measures.

have been the most commonly used in nursing home studies (Kurowski & Shaughnessy, 1985).

However, an exclusive focus on structural factors has major limitations. Oftentimes, studies have treated an input measure such as expenditures per resident as an indicator of quality of care, and all other organizational variables are examined for their relationship to this proxy for quality (Kane & Kane, 1987). Input measures of quality of care make sense in relation to the needs of the residents being served—information that is lacking when only organizational characteristics are considered (Hammerman, Friedsam, & Shore, 1975). One problem with this approach is that there is frequently little empirical support for a relationship between structural variables, such as RN/resident ratio, and resident outcomes (R. L. Kane, 1998). An assumption cannot be made that higher expenditures leads to higher quality of care. While numerous studies have found lower staff/resident ratios in for-profit homes (W. D. Spector & Takada, 1991), it may be true that expenditures are used more efficiently in for-profit facilities (Koetting, 1980), leading to the same quality of care at lower costs. In spite of all the studies focusing on the interrelationships among structural components, the findings have been inconclusive and inconsistent (Davis, 1991).

Because of the "predictive impotence of structural measures" (Brannon, 1992, p. 293), efforts have begun to incorporate measures of processes in studies of nursing home quality of care. Process components of care refer to the manner in which care is delivered (Donabedian, 1988; Kurowski & Shaughnessy, 1985). Considerably more difficult and time-consuming to measure than structural factors, these components include such factors as ratings of care plans and meals (Nyman, 1988), the rigidity of resident management practices (Kruzich, Clinton, & Kelber, 1992), nursing assistant participation in shift reports where daily updates are shared with incoming staff, and nursing assistants' influence in resident care decisions (Kruzich, 1995).

The aim of the second set of studies is to link organizational structure and process components to resident outcomes. Examples of outcome measures include functional status (ADLs, IADLs), mortality and discharge rates, and resident satisfaction. Because the effects of care are strongly related to health-related resident characteristics, researchers wanting to identify the influence of organizational factors on resident outcomes have to account for the variation in resident characteristics that influence the outcome. Both facility case-mix variables, which attempt to measure the average severity of resident impairment, and inclusion of a variety of individual resident health-related characteristics as control variables in the model are aimed at sorting out the unique influence of organizational and resident influences on outcomes (Donabedian, 1988).

In addition to studying the linkage between organizational factors and resident outcomes, a second shared characteristic of this set of studies is that resident outcomes are assessed by someone other than the resident, a knowledgeable staff person or outside expert who usually focuses on measures of physical functioning. An example of this type of study is the work of Linn, Gurel, and Linn (1977), who found with a sample of 1000 men transferred to 40 community nursing homes that, at 6 months follow-up testing, patients in homes with more RN hours per patient were more likely to be alive, improved, and discharged from the home. Higher professional staff-patient ratio, better medical records, and more services were related to being discharged from the nursing home.

In an assessment of a national sample of 658 nursing homes and 2,663 residents, Cohen and Spector (1996) found that the intensity of RN staffing, as measured by number of full-time equivalents per 100 residents (adjusted for case-mix), influenced mortality rates, while the intensity of LPN staffing affected functional outcomes. In a third study, residents' functional ability was positively associated with fewer levels of supervision within the facility and nurse work assignments allowing greater discretion (Rohrer, Momany, & Chang, 1993). These studies typify the second line of inquiry, where outcome ratings were made about the resident by an expert, with primary interest in the outcome measures related to resident's physical functioning. In a few instances such studies included a measure called "resident satisfaction" (Greenwald & Linn, 1971; Nyman, 1988), which was based on an observer's perception and rating of the resident.

Only recently has nursing home satisfaction, as perceived by the resident, family member, or staff person, gained credence as an outcome measure of significant interest to those interested in improving the quality of nursing home care. The National Citizens' Coalition for Nursing Home Reform designed the first major study to identify nursing home residents' views on quality of care (Spalding, 1985). Using a large sample of residents from over 100 nursing homes, the Coalition found that residents attached the highest importance to the receipt of dignified, courteous, and responsive care by competent staff. Residents' ability to maintain control over their daily life activities was also a key factor in how they assessed their quality of care in the nursing home. A subsequent study found that the quality of interpersonal relationships with staff was the basis for the majority of both residents' best and worst experiences (Grau, Chandler, & Saunders, 1995), providing further support for the importance of the staff-resident relationship in the nursing home. Before reviewing what we know about organizational and individual correlates of nursing home satisfaction, it is important to conceptually clarify the relationship between satisfaction and quality of care.

THE CONCEPTUALIZATION OF SATISFACTION AND NURSING HOME CARE

Making sense of the nursing home satisfaction literature is difficult for a number of reasons. One difficulty lies in differences in how satisfaction is conceptualized. Some researchers use "customer satisfaction" and "quality" synonymously (Kleinsorge & Koenig, 1991; Steffen & Nystrom, 1997) while other researchers consider quality to be a more far reaching construct (Cleary & McNeil, 1988). Another difference is how satisfaction is operationalized. For example, one study (Nyman, 1988) identified one of their outcomes as "resident satisfaction," but it was an outside observer's rating of residents' satisfaction; while in another study (Zinn, Lavizzo-Mourey, & Taylor, 1993) "resident satisfaction" actually referred to residents' own perception of their satisfaction.

What is included in the phrase "nursing home care" also varies. Some researchers operationally define nursing home care as the level of RN staffing, while other studies encompass a much broader view that includes the physical and social environment as well as multiple measures of staffing. Unlike outpatient settings, nursing home care is both a treatment and a living situation, which means that care includes the physical, psychosocial, and environmental circumstances of care (Institute of Medicine, 1986). Other issues which lack any consensus are the value and relative importance of resident satisfaction as an outcome criteria for quality of care, as well as the extent to which residents are able to assess various dimensions of quality of care (Davies & Ware, 1988).

Satisfaction has been conceptualized in a number of different ways, with some authors focusing on the affective part of the concept while others stress the cognitive or judging component (Pascoe, 1983). A model that incorporates both dimensions and is applicable to resident, family, and staff nursing home satisfaction is the work of Strasser and Davis (1991), who define patient satisfaction as an individual's value judgments and subsequent reactions to the stimuli they perceive. For example, strong odors (stimuli) in a resident's room may lead to a thought "This nursing home is unacceptable" (value judgment), which can lead to a number of different reactions—feelings of anger (affective), or an expression of anger to the charge nurse (behavior) on the part of the resident or family member. Similarly, a nursing assistant who observes other staff reporting for shift report (stimuli) when she is not asked to participate may decide that her knowledge of residents is not valued (judgment), which may lead to a variety of reactions—feeling sad or angry (affective) or deciding to be less attentive to answering call lights quickly (behavior), thereby influencing resident or family satisfaction with the care provided to residents. Strasser and Davis' model (1991) recognizes that individual differences, including personality characteristics, life and health care experiences, expectations, and values moderate the value judgments and reactions individuals have to various stimuli in the nursing home. Measures of nursing home satisfaction need to include those stimuli that are crucial to the group of individuals whose satisfaction with the facility is being measured. Residents, family members, and staff have different experiences and relationships with the nursing home. For residents, it is a home; for family members or frequent visitors, it is a place where they visit a loved one; and for staff, it is their place of employment. We might expect that there would be some differences in the stimuli that were important to the three groups, and therefore in the correlates influencing their satisfaction.

RESIDENT AND FAMILY CHARACTERISTICS RELATED TO NURSING HOME SATISFACTION

The third set of studies of nursing home quality has as its focus an understanding of how facility and individual factors are related to individuals' self-perceived satisfaction with the nursing home. Table 5.1 provides a summary of these studies, their design and selected findings. As mentioned earlier, individuals' value judgments and therefore ratings of nursing home satisfaction are influenced by the expectations, personal experiences, and standards they use when evaluating various stimuli in the nursing home. The fact that residents' or family members' ratings are likely to be influenced by individual characteristics does not undermine the validity of their assessment. It does mean we need to know how individual characteristics are systematically related to satisfaction, so that we can take it into account when reviewing their ratings (Davies & Wares, 1988) and in sorting out the effect of organizational and individual factors.

We know little about how individuals' perceptions of nursing homes are influenced by their sociodemographic characteristics. In part, this is due to the fact that so few studies having used satisfaction as an outcome of importance. In some cases, the interest in identifying relevant organizational variables meant that little attention was given to the inter-relationships of resident characteristics with resident satisfaction, and therefore this data was not included in publications (Harel, 1981). In other cases, only aggregate measures of residents were gathered and, therefore, analyses did not allow identifying organizational variables that were relevant at the individual level (Lemke & Moos, 1989). Broadening the scope of the literature reviewed to include studies of individual correlates of satisfaction with care in other health care settings increases our understanding of factors that may be relevant to nursing home residents.

Table 5.1 Selected studies of resident and family satisfaction with nursing home.

Source	Study purpose	Study design	Respondent sample size	Facility sample size	Selected findings
Davis, Sebastian, & Tschetter (1997)	Study 1: Development of Nursing Home Service Quality Inventory.	148 items based on resident comments from Spalding (1985) study were rated by long-term care experts, resulting in 52 items included on an interview questionnaire administered by volunteers to residents.	103 residents	23	Reliability analysis and correlations between resident scores on the Nursing Home Service Quality Inventory and overall rating of facility quality support measures validity.
	Study 2: Refinement and evaluation of measure.		194 residents	1	All subscale scores and total scores was unrelated to residents' cognitive functioning, functional status, and length of stay.
Kruzich et al, (1992)	To determine how organizational factors influence residents' satisfaction with the nursing home and if there are differential impacts based on varying levels of functional ability.	Residents interviewed by research staff were randomly selected from a list of residents who met study criteria. Fifty one nursing homes in Wisconsin comprised the sample. Data was also collected from nursing, social service and activity staff. Medical record reviews and observational ratings of units supplemented interview data.	289 residents	51	For residents who needed major assistance with tub baths, dressing and toileting, longevity of nursing assistants and personalization of residents' rooms were significant predictors. Predictors of satisfaction for residents able to complete ADLs with little assistance included RN turnover, higher benefit levels for NAs, and residents on units where NAs perceived the charge nurse as competent.

Source	Purpose	Method	Sample		Findings
Kleinsorge & Koenig (1991)	To develop a tool to monitor and assess ongoing satisfaction of nursing home residents and family members.	Results of two focus groups, one comprised of residents and the other of family members, used participants' statements to develop a 32-item survey instrument administered to sample of residents and family members. Sampling method and response rate not provided.	50 residents and family members	1	Length of stay in facility was negatively related to satisfaction with nurses and aides, as well as food. Greater length of time spent in a facility was related to lower ratings of nurse and nurse aides.
Bitzan & Kruzich (1990)	To identify patterns of interpersonal relationships among nursing home residents.	All residents in randomly selected units in 54 nursing homes were included in the sampling frame if they met study criteria (i.e., over 60 years old, not comatose, not aphasic, not diagnosed with Alzheimer's disease).	332 residents	54	Residents who stated they felt close to others in the facility had significantly higher satisfaction scores. A significantly higher proportion of residents who identified a staff person as "close" were on units with permanent resident care assignments.

Table 5.1 (continued)

Source	Study purpose	Study design	Respondent sample size	Facility sample size	Selected findings
Norton, van Maris, Soberman, & Murray (1996); van Maris, Soberman, Murray, & Norton (1996)	Construction and pilot testing of instruments to measure patient satisfaction.	Based on a review of the literature and focus group information, a 60-item measure was created and administered by volunteers to residents. 54% of residents selected completed the interview. The family questionnaire achieved a 69% response rate.	127 residents 145 family members	1	On overall measure, family members rated care more highly than did residents, but on individual items, family members were more critical. Variability in responses to items suggests that individuals with moderate cognitive impairment could discriminate between various aspects of care.
Steffen & Nystrom (1997)	To determine relationship of family members' perception of service quality to organizational factors.	25 residents were randomly selected from each nursing home, and a questionnaire was mailed to the person listed as the closest family member or health care representative, resulting in a 41% response rate	416 family members	41	Nonprofit facilities and smaller facilities received higher ratings on three of the five service dimensions. Rate of RN fulltime equivalent (FTE) to residents was unrelated to any dimension of the measure.
Zinn et al. (1993)	To develop and evaluate a survey instrument to measure residents' satisfaction with nursing home care.	Item selection was based on review of literature with initial form piloted in 2 Philadelphia homes. Results led to a 10-item measure, completed by 85% of residents who met eligibility criteria.	168 residents	4	No significant correlations were found between level of satisfaction and age, cognitive functioning, gender, or facility of residence.

Sociodemographic Characteristics

Extensive reviews of patient satisfaction, including both hospital and outpatient settings, have identified a few characteristics that tend to be related to older persons' satisfaction. Several studies of adults have found age and gender consistently related to service satisfaction, with older persons reporting higher levels of satisfaction than younger patients, and with women more satisfied than men (Aharony & Strasser, 1993; Cleary & McNeil, 1988). A large-scale national study of 6,455 adults recently discharged from 62 hospitals used a survey designed to focus on specific actions taken by hospital staff. For example, instead of asking patients to evaluate general aspects of care such as "helpfulness of your doctors," patients were asked, "Were you told about the purpose of medications in a way you could understand?" Survey questions were developed with input from patients, their families and friends, and health care providers, and resulted in 52 items. The response options were dichotomous, and a summary score was created by averaging its scores in each of these areas. The survey focused on areas where patients were seen as the best judges including: communication with provider, provider respect for patient professions and needs, provision of emotional and physical comfort, and family involvement. They found that patients 65 years and older reported fewer problems with their care than other age groups. Low-income patients were significantly more likely to have higher problem scores, even after controlling for potentially confounding factors such as patients' perceived health status (Cleary et al., 1991). While these findings cannot be generalized to nursing homes, the results do suggest factors that need to be considered in future studies of individual correlates of nursing home satisfaction.

While age has been found to be consistently correlated with satisfaction in samples of adults 18 years and older, when considering the truncated age range that exists among nursing home residents, the relationship between age and resident satisfaction with nursing home care is not supported. In the three nursing home studies that considered the relationship between age and satisfaction (Kruzich, Clinton, & Kelber, 1992; Reinardy, 1995; Zinn et al., 1993) none found a significant correlation. Findings regarding gender were mixed: Reinardy and Kruzich et al. (1992) found females more satisfied than males while Zinn et al. (1993) found no significant differences between men and women.

Self-perception of health was the strongest predictor of having problems with care in a national survey of discharged hospital patients (Cleary et al., 1991). Persons who perceived their health as poor on average had problem scores twice as high as patients who reported excellent health. Greeley & Schoenherr (1982) also found a positive relationship between perceived health status and satisfaction in a large sample of individuals receiving outpatient services. Self-reported health status was also found to be positively related to nursing home resident satisfaction in the Kruzich et al. study (1992).

A review of nursing home satisfaction studies reveals considerable differences among researchers regarding the inclusion of residents with mild or moderate cognitive impairments in satisfaction studies, and the issues involved are discussed in considerable detail in Chapter 8. Because of different sampling approaches and criteria for subject inclusion in the studies discussed in this section, there is a good deal of variation in the proportion of cognitively impaired residents included in the samples. What is interesting is that in all four studies of nursing home residents (Davis, Sebastian, & Tschetter, 1997; Kruzich et al., 1992; Norton et al., 1996; Zinn et al., 1993), cognitive functioning was not related to satisfaction.

Functional level as measured by activities of daily living is not a variable considered in the broader patient satisfaction literature, and so we have to rely solely on nursing home studies for understanding its influence on satisfaction. The findings of two nursing home studies are inconclusive: level of assistance required to complete activities of daily living was found to be negatively related to resident nursing home satisfaction in one study (Kruzich et al., 1992), while a second found no relationship between functional status and resident perception of nursing home quality (Davis et al., 1997).

Kruzich et al. (1992) study included a number of additional individual predictors that have not been included in other studies attempting to model resident and organizational influences on individuals' nursing home satisfaction. This study found significantly higher levels of nursing home satisfaction for residents who identified someone in the home they felt close to, as well as for residents who felt close to their roommate.

Family Characteristics

A few researchers have conducted studies to find out about family members' satisfaction with nursing home care. For the most part, these efforts have been focused on measurement development (Kleinsorge & Koenig, 1991), the relationship of family members' perceptions to organizational characteristics (Steffen & Nystrom, 1997), or comparisons between family members' and residents' perceptions (van Maris et al., 1996). None reported any data on the relationship between family members' perceptions of nursing home quality and their attitudes, expectations, and sociodemographic characteristics.

One study that has identified a few individual correlates of satisfaction included families of residents in 7 nursing homes (Prawitz et al., 1991). A survey sent with billing statements produced 411 responses (a 40% return rate). Results indicated that family members who investigated all nursing homes in the area prior to selection were more satisfied than were others who had not taken this action before they chose the facility. Also, where there was a unanimous decision among family members to choose a particular home, and where they did not feel that they had been forced to make a quick decision prior to the selection of the nursing home, family members were more satisfied with the facility.

While we know little about how family members' income, gender, age, and other individual factors may impact their perceptions of nursing homes, studies that have surveyed family members' and residents' perceptions of satisfaction with care do show similarities and difference between the two groups. The most detailed data is provided by van Maris et al., (1996). On an overall measure of quality, family members were more likely to rate the overall quality as excellent (36%) than residents (27%). There was also a good deal of variation between the two groups on specific items. Residents were far more likely to rate the choice of roommate, dining partners, and times for bathing and sleep as important. A greater proportion of family members (70%) saw the facility as dreary as compared to residents (55%). Residents also gave more positive ratings for the smell and cleanliness of the facility than did family members. A second study (Kleinsorge & Koenig, 1991) surveyed both groups but only published the results of the residents sample.

FACILITY CORRELATES OF RESIDENT SATISFACTION

While numerous studies have examined the relationship between facility characteristics and resident outcomes as measured by mortality or functional status changes, much less attention has been paid to how the facility's structure and process characteristics may relate to family members' or residents' self-perceived satisfaction. The literature is replete with articles by individuals sharing their perspectives on which environmental factors impact on residents' satisfaction with nursing homes or their quality of life in long-term care settings. Yet, only two published studies could be located that included a sufficient number of organizational units of analysis and residents or family members to empirically assess the relationship of environmental factors to self-reported nursing home satisfaction (Kruzich et al., 1992; Steffen & Nystrom, 1997).

It is not surprising that individual correlates of nursing home satisfaction have been a focus of more study than have organizational correlates. The latter requires the facility or operational units of a facility (wing, floor) to be the unit of analysis, which increases the number of facilities that need to be included in order to describe the organizational influences on satisfaction. As a result, only one published study has attempted to model both resident and organizational characteristics as predictors of residents' self-reported nursing home satisfaction.

Using a sample of 289 residents from 51 nursing homes, Kruzich et al., (1992) examined the influence of a wide range of organizational structure and process variables on residents' perceived nursing home satisfaction. To assess the possible differential influence of the environment on residents with high and low functional abilities, six items on an activity of daily living (ADLs)—adapted from the Physical Self-Maintenance Scale, a subscale of the Philadelphia Geriatric Center Multilevel Assessment Instrument (Lawton & Brody, 1969)—was completed by the staff person on duty identified as most familiar with the individual resident. The sample was divided into two groups: a high ADL group of residents (n = 145) who were able to function on most activities independently or with minor assistance, and a low ADL group of residents (n = 144) who needed moderate or major assistance.

Bivariate results indicated that organizational correlates of nursing home satisfaction were different for the two groups. The only correlates shared by both groups were lower satisfaction levels for residents in for-profit facilities and for individuals residing on units with higher levels of depersonalized residents' rooms.

Regression analyses conducted separately for residents with high and low ADLs found distinct organizational attributes predicting nursing home satisfaction. For those individuals who needed greater assistance, longevity of the nursing assistants' tenure on the unit and personalization of the residents' rooms were the most relevant attributes. For individuals able to complete ADLs with little or no assistance, higher levels of RN turnover was related to lower resident satisfaction. Residents in facilities that provided higher health insurance benefits for nursing assistants and residing on units where the nursing assistants perceived the charge nurse as competent were more likely to be satisfied. Organizational predictors of nursing home satisfaction explained more of the variance for high ADL residents than for those with low ADL scores (24% versus 11%). Findings that organizational predictors were different for the two supports the proposition that residents' functional abilities influence their experience of the facility environment. Figure 5.2 includes resident and organizational correlates that have been empirically supported. In many instances, the correlate was only included in one study and so more extensive research of these factors are needed to have greater confidence in their relationship to nursing home satisfaction.

FACILITY CORRELATES OF FAMILY MEMBER SATISFACTION

Steffen et al., (1997) aim was to identify the organizational determinants of family members' perception of service quality in nursing homes. They used an adapted version of Parasuraman, Zeithaml, and Berry's (1988) measure of customer satisfaction, which included five dimensions: responsiveness, reliability, assurance, empathy, and tangibles or physical facilities. Items used to assess the four interpersonal dimensions asked family members to assess nursing staff's demonstration of these qualities. For each of the 41 nursing homes included in their sample, 25 residents were selected from a facility section (floor), and a questionnaire was mailed to the closest family member or health care representative. Results found that for-profit status was related to lower family member satisfaction with responsiveness, empathy, and tangibles dimensions of service quality. The higher percentage of Medicaid residents in a nursing home, the more likely family members were less satisfied with all dimensions of quality, with the strongest relationship between the tangibles dimension and percent Medicaid (-.56). Smaller homes received higher ratings by family members on all dimensions of service quality except tangibles such as the physical appearance of facility. Regression analysis was performed with the five dimensions of quality treated as dependent variables in separate regression analyses . Results indicated that for-profit ownership and larger facility size were significant predictors of two dimensions of quality, i.e., lower ratings on responsiveness and empathy of staff (Steffen & Nystrom, 1997).

Studies of client satisfaction in other human service settings can augment the limited research in nursing homes by suggesting organizational factors that need to be considered in future nursing home studies. Greeley and Schoenherr (1981) surveyed 417 staff members and 411 patients and clients in 11 health and human service organizations to identify organizational effects on one dimension of client satisfaction—humaneness of service. An additive index was constructed based on five items concerning staff courtesy, warmth, respect, consideration, and concern for the patient. After controlling for the influence of patient characteristics, attitudes, problems, and experiences, they found client satisfaction was positively related both to agencies' autonomy from their parent organization and greater

RESIDENT CORRELATES

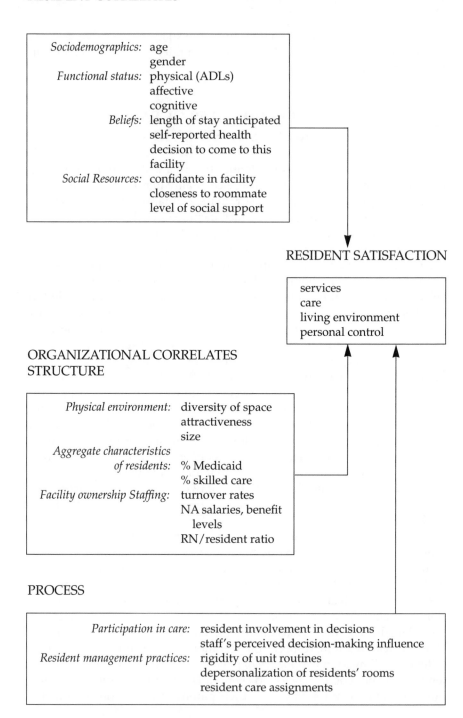

Sociodemographics: age
gender
Functional status: physical (ADLs)
affective
cognitive
Beliefs: length of stay anticipated
self-reported health
decision to come to this
facility
Social Resources: confidante in facility
closeness to roommate
level of social support

RESIDENT SATISFACTION

services
care
living environment
personal control

ORGANIZATIONAL CORRELATES
STRUCTURE

Physical environment: diversity of space
attractiveness
size
Aggregate characteristics
of residents: % Medicaid
% skilled care
Facility ownership Staffing: turnover rates
NA salaries, benefit
levels
RN/resident ratio

PROCESS

Participation in care: resident involvement in decisions
staff's perceived decision-making influence
Resident management practices: rigidity of unit routines
depersonalization of residents' rooms
resident care assignments

Figure 5.2 Organizational and resident correlates of residents' nursing home satisfaction

interagency communication. The extent to which staff had role discretion or flexibility in handling job tasks was the only internal organizational attribute related to client satisfaction with humaneness of service. Organizations where employees reported more professional consideration, more pro-client attitudes, and less commitment to organizational rules had more satisfied clients and patients. Although client/patient characteristics accounted for the majority of variation in satisfaction with humaneness of service, organizational factors alone accounted for 20% of the variance.

The relationship between job satisfaction of nursing staff and client satisfaction was examined by Weisman and Nathanson (1985) in one type of setting—family planning clinics. Based on data obtained from 344 nurses working in 77 clinics and 2,900 clients (80% response rate) who received services from them, Weisman and Nathanson found job satisfaction of staff to be a significant predictor of client satisfaction, which in turn was related to client compliance with medical regimens.

These studies help us recognize that the organizational and administrative context in which care is delivered is crucial to creating caring relationships among staff and clients in a variety of health care settings (Scott, Aiken, Mechanic, & Moravesik, 1995). These illustrated how characteristics of the organization's structure and processes influence staff attitudes and feelings, factors residents identified as most important in determining their judgments of quality of care in nursing homes (Spalding, 1985).

CORRELATES OF STAFF SATISFACTION WITH THE NURSING HOME

Nursing home staff satisfaction has not been a topic that has generated a great deal of interest. Nursing home turnover which engenders discontinuity of care and increases personnel costs, has been the major focus of researchers interested in staffing issues in long-term care (Cohen-Mansfield, 1997). While we might expect staff dissatisfaction to lead to high turnover, the findings are inconclusive. Particularly in the case of nursing home assistants whose employment opportunities may be significantly limited, there is not a clean and consistent relationship between turnover and staff dissatisfaction across studies (Caudill & Patrick, 1989; Waxman, Carner, & Berkenstock, 1984). Regardless of its relationship to turnover, staff satisfaction remains an important factor because of its likely influence on the quality of care that is provided to residents.

Staff satisfaction with the nursing home is comprised of dimensions that are crucial to residents as well. The source of the measure, however—job satisfaction scales emerging from the work of sociologists and psychologists—is different than for resident and family member measures. Personal contexts and autonomy, and quality of the physical and social environment are important to both staff and residents. In some cases, a dimension is shared by the two groups, but the focus is different. For residents, the responsiveness and empathy of the staff is key to their satisfaction; for staff, these same qualities are looked for in their supervisor. Salary and benefit levels are an important dimension of staff satisfaction, but have no parallel in measures of resident and family satisfaction.

To relate organizational factors to individual correlates of staff satisfaction with the nursing home requires a research design that includes multiple facilities so that variations in organizations can be identified. Such studies are aimed at better understanding how the organizational features and individual employee characteristics relate to job satisfaction in the nursing home. Only studies where the measure of satisfaction was included in the study or publicly available in print were included in this chapter's review.

Table 5.2 describes the purpose, design, and measures used in 4 studies whose results provide an empirical basis for what we know about nursing home staff satisfaction. Grau, Chandler, Burton, and Kolditz' (1991) study of nursing assistants was notable for its use of measures that had been validated and used in prior studies. They found that none of the six dimensions of job satisfaction were related to job tenure. Long-stay workers did not vary from short stayers, indicating that job dissatisfaction does not predict nursing assistants' decision to quit. Grau et al. (1991) also found no relationship between ethnicity, nursing home site, or unit organization with measures of job satisfaction. Their careful articulation and measurement of multiple dimensions of satisfaction, as well as their use of researchers not affiliated with the facility to administer the questionnaire, supports the validity and reliability of their findings. The fact that the study was conducted in two reputable, high-quality facilities means care must be taken in generalizing their findings to a broader, more representative sample of nursing homes.

A second study by Helmer, Olson, and Heim (1993) surveyed a convenience sample of nursing assistants in 36 facilities. Unfortunately, analyses did not tie job satisfaction ratings to other organizational factors. Their measure of job satisfaction included some components shared by the Grau et al. study (1991), but the reliability and validity of the measures they constructed was not reported. Respondents were particularly dissatisfied with their salary (71%) and the lack of respect administrators and charge nurses showed for nurse aides (71%). The authors reported that turnover was not related to remuneration.

Mullins et al., (1988) focused on identifying whether organizational structure and managerial influence were related to nursing assistants' job satisfaction. They considered six aspects of organizational structure: standardization of work, formalization of policies, staff coordination, participation in decision making, centralization of decision making, and motivation, measured by employees' perception that organizational rewards were tied to performance.

Regression analyses were performed for the total sample as well as separately for supervisory and nonsupervisory staff. Findings indicated that participation in decision making was a predictor of job satisfaction for supervisory personnel and for the combined staff sample. The authors suggested that the lack of relationship between participation in decisionmaking and satisfaction for nonsupervisory personnel may reflect a perception that involvement was an additional responsibility to existing work demands. A perception that organizational rewards were tied to performance was a significant correlate of job satisfaction for all groups. Both supervisory and nonsupervisory staff who perceived their immediate superiors as using rewards and positive support to influence work behavior instead of coercive or punitive methods were significantly more satisfied with their jobs.

Waxman et al. (1984) sought to examine the association between nurse aides' perceptions of their work environment, job turnover, and job satisfaction. Using a satisfaction measure with well demonstrated psychometric support (Price & Mueller, 1986), they found, paradoxically, that job satisfaction was greatest in facilities with high turnover. In addition, an assessment of the overall quality of the facilities in the sample was completed by two independent experts and a review of code violations were completed. Results indicated that higher quality homes had higher turnover rates. The authors suggest that union status may explain the paradoxical findings, since the 3 homes with the lowest turnover rates included unionized staff, whereas the 4 with the highest turnover rates were nonunionized. Their remarks highlight the importance of considering a broad range of organizational factors and the need for facility samples large enough to tease out potential confounding factors.

DIRECTIONS FOR FUTURE NURSING HOME SATISFACTION RESEARCH

We are at the beginning of the journey of understanding correlates of nursing home satisfaction. Additional theoretical, empirical, and methodological efforts are needed. Three areas , if addressed by future studies, would improve our capacity to increase resident, family member and staff satisfaction: (1) fuller descriptions of individual characteristics, (2) examina-

Table 5.2 Selected studies of staff satisfaction with nursing home

Source	Study purpose	Study design	Respondent sample size	Facility sample size	Selected findings
Grau et al. (1991)	An examination of the relationship of job tenure to dimensions of job satisfaction.	In groups, nursing assistants from day, evening, and night shifts who reported for work during a 24-hour period completed a questionnaire administered by outside researchers (85% response rate). Large, unionized not-for-profit homes in New York were the study sites.	29	2	Job tenure and job benefits were unrelated to job satisfaction.
Helmer et al. (1993)	To analyze factors correlated with high turnover.	Facility administrators in nursing homes were mailed 600 surveys. They distributed and returned completed surveys from nursing assistants (response rate of 41%).	246	40	Nurse aides were most dissatisfied with their pay. Lack of respect from supervisors was second area of least satisfaction.

Source	Study purpose	Study design	Respondent sample size	Facility sample size	Selected findings
Mullins, Nelson, Busciglia, & Weiner (1988)	A study of the influence of organizational structure and management influence on job satisfaction.	56 for-profit facilities in West Central Florida (88%) participated. Number of staff responding ranged from 3 to 16 per facility with a 73% completion rate. DON distributed forms to staff RN, LPN, and aides—at their discretion.	397	46	Job satisfaction was significantly related to the immediate supervisor using rewards instead of coercion to influence behavior.
Waxman et al. (1984)	A study of the relationship of turnover rate to job satisfaction and perceptions of environmental climate.	In groups, day and evening shift nursing assistants in proprietary nursing homes (3 urban, 4 suburban) in the Philadelphia area completed a questionnaire that was distributed and orally administered by researchers. All aides approached completed the survey.	234	7	Homes with the highest turnover had staff with the highest level of job satisfaction.

tion of relationships between satisfaction and other outcome measures and (3) more comprehensive assessment of organizational factors, with greater attention to process measures.

First, increasing the breadth of information gathered on individual respondents is crucial for a number of reasons. If we are going to meaningfully compare results across studies of nursing home satisfaction, we need to know in what ways study samples are similar or different. The more knowledge we have about the population we survey, the more precise and accurate our satisfaction survey conclusions will be (Strasser & Davis, 1991). Greater attention to gathering multiple measures of individuals' functioning, attitudes and demographic information is also needed, so that variables that may have a direct or indirect influence on satisfaction can be included in the research design and statistical analyses of future investigations (Aharony & Strasser, 1993). Variables deserving additional attention include cultural and ethnic factors, which are recognized as important influences on attitudes and behaviors (Cleary & Edgman-Levitan, 1997; Ellmer & Olbrisch, 1983), but have yet to be incorporated into any study of nursing home satisfaction. The major source of financial support for resident care and resident level of discomfort and pain at the time they evaluate a facility have been found to be important to satisfaction in other settings. While researchers recognize that an individual's expectations are likely to influence his/her evaluations of nursing homes, with few exceptions, studies have not included attitudinal measures.

Second, including multiple outcome measures in studies of nursing home satisfaction would be an efficient method of expanding our knowledge base. Findings in other settings suggest that certain organizational features may simlutaneously increase staff satisfaction and result in better client outcomes (Weisman & Nathanson, 1985). Examining the interrelationship of resident and family members' satisfaction, or resident and staff satisfaction, would be helpful. Currently we do not know if satisfied residents experience better clinical outcomes, therefore, examining the relationship between resident satisfaction and physiological and functional outcomes would be instructive.

Third, future studies need to gather sufficient data to allow generalizations concerning the impact of specific organizational attributes on nursing home satisfaction. Satisfaction studies conducted in other health care settings have identified a number of organizational correlates, including organizational autonomy, staff discretion, and interorganizational communication, none of which have been included in any published study of nursing home satisfaction. The increase in multiunit organizations brings more complex internal relationships between corporate management and facility administration which may impact on resident, staff, and family member satisfaction. Including affiliation, number of facilities owned by a parent corporation, or proximity to organizational headquarters would be valuable.

Yet, as Sheridan, White, and Fairchild note (1992), after 20 years of research, the empirical evidence suggests structural variables explain little of the variation in resident nursing home care. The greater need is for investigators to include, and when necessary, develop measures of organizational processes that are the bridge between structural variables and outcome measures, including satisfaction. Studies of nursing home satisfaction have seldom included any measures of facilities' human resource policies, resident care practices, methods of patient care assignment, and nursing leadership. In the rare instances where they have, the results have been fruitful.

REFERENCES

Aharony, L., & Strasser, S. (1993). Patient satisfaction: What we know about and what we still need to explore. *Medicare Care Review, 50*(1), 352–382.

Binstock, R. H., & Spector, W. D. (1997). Five priority areas for research on long-term care. *Health Services Research, 32*, 715–730.

Bitzan, J. E., & Kruzich, J. M. (1990). Interpersonal relationships of nursing home residents. *The Gerontologist, 30*, 385–390.

Bleismer, M., & Earl, P. (1993). Research considerations: Nursing home quality perceptions. *Journal of Gerontological Nursing, 19*(6), 27–34.

Brannon, D. (1992). Toward second-generation nursing home research. *Gerontologist, 32*, 293–294.

Caudill, M.., & Patric, K. M. (1989). Nursing assistant turnover in nursing homes and need satisfaction. *Journal of Gerontological Nursing, 15*(6), 24–30.

Cleary, P. D., & Edgman-Levitan, S. (1997). Health care quality: Incorporating consumer perspectives. *Journal of the American Medical Association, 278*(19), 1608–1612.

Cleary, P. D., & Edgman-Levitan, S., Roberts, M., Moloney, T., McMullen, W., Walker, J., & Delbanco, T. L. (1991). Patients evaluate their hospital care: A national survey. *Health Affairs, 278*(19), 254–267.

Cleary, P. D., & McNeil, B. J. (1988). Patient satisfaction as an indicator of quality care. *Inquiry, 25*, 25–36.

Cohen, J. W., & Spector, W. D. (1996). The effect of Medicaid reimbursement on quality of care in nursing homes. *Journal of Health Economics, 15*, 23–48.

Cohen-Mansfield, J. (1997). Turnover among nursing home staff. *Nursing Management, 15*, 23–48.

Davis, M. A. (1991). On nursing home quality: A review and analysis. *Medical Care Review, 7*(1), 33–48.

Davies, A. R., & Ware, J. E. (1988). Involving consumers in quality of care assessment. *Human Affairs, 81*, 531–542.

Davis, M. A., Sebastian, J. G., & Tschetter, J. (1997). Measuring quality of nursing home service: The residents' perspective. *Psychological Reports, 81,* 531–542.

Donabedian, A. (1988). The quality of care: How can it be assessed? *Journal of the American Medical Association, 260*(12), 1743–1748.

Ellmer, R., & Olbrisch, M. (1983). The contribution of a cultural perspective in understanding and evaluating client satisfaction. *Evaluation and Program Planning, 6,* 275–281.

Eustis, N., & Patten, S. (1984). The effectivenes of long-term care. In D. Mangen & W. Peterson (Eds.) *Health, program evaluation and demography* (Vol. 3, pp. 217–316). Minneapolis, MN: University of Minnesota Press.

Feasley, J. C. (1996). *Health outcomes for older people: Questions for the coming decade.* Division of Health Care Services, Institute of Medicine. Washington, DC: National Academy Press.

Grau, L., Chandler, B., Burton, B., & Kolditz. D. (1991). Institutional loyalty and job satisfaction among nurse aides in nursing homes. *Journal of Aging, 3*(1), 47–65.

Grau, L., Chandler, B., & Saunders, D. (1995). Nursing home residents' perceptions of the quality of their care. *Journal of Psychosocial Nursing, 33*(5), 34–41.

Greeley, J. R., & Schoenherr, R. A. (1981). Organization effects on client satisfaction with humaneness of service. *Journal of Health and Human Behavior, 22,* 2–18.

Greenwald, S. R., & Linn, M. W. (1971). Intercorrelation of data on nursing homes. *Gerontologist, 11,* 337–340.

Gustafson, D., Sainfort, F., Konigsveld, R., & Zimmerman. (1990). The quality assessment index (QAI) for measuring nursing home quality. *Health Services Research,* (25)1, 97–127.

Hammerman, J., Friedsam, H., & Shore, H. (1975). Management perspectives in long-term care facilities. In S. Sherwood (Ed.), *Long-term care* (pp. 179–212). New York: Spectrum.

Harel, Z. (1981). Quality of care, congruence and well-being among institutionalized aged. *The Gerontologist, 21,* 523–531.

Helmer, T., Olson, S., & Heim, R. (1993). Strategies for nurse aide satisfaction. *Journal of Long-Term Case Administration, 21*(2), 10–14.

Institute of Medicine. (1986). *Improving the quality of care in nursing homes.* Washington, DC: National Academy Press.

Kane, R. A., & Kane, R. L. (1987). *Long-Term care: Principles, programs, and policies.* New York: Springer Publishing Company.

Kane, R. L. (1995). Improving the quality of long-term care. *JAMA, 273*(17), 1376–1380.

Kane, R. L. (1998). Assuring quality in nursing home care. *Journal of the American Geriatric Society, 46,* 232–237.

Kane, R. L., Bell, R., Riegler, S., Wilson, A., & Kam, R. (1983). Assessing the outcomes of nursing home patients. *Journal of Gerontology, 38,* 385–393.

Kleinsorge, I. K., & Koenig, H. F. (1991). The silent customers: Measuring customer satisfaction in nursing homes. *Journal of Health Care Marketing, 11*(4), 2–13.

Koetting, M. (1980). *Nursing home organization and efficiency.* Lexington, MA: Lexington Books.

Kruzich, J. M. (1995). Empowering organizational contexts: Patterns and predictors of perceived decision-making influence among staff in nursing homes. *The Gerontologist, 35,* 207–216.

Kruzich, J. M., Clinton, J. F., & Kelber, S. T. (1992). Personal and environmental influences on nursing home satisfaction. *The Gerontologist, 32,* 342–350.

Kurowski, B. O., & Shaughnessy, P. W. (1985). The measurement and assurance of quality. In R. Vogel & H. Palmer (Eds.), *Long-term care: Perspectives from research and demonstrations.* Rockville, MD: Aspen.

Lawton, M. P., & Brody, E. M. (1969). Assessment of older people: Self-maintaining and instrumental activities of daily living. *The Gerontologist, 9,* 179–186.

Lemke, S., & Moos, R. (1989). Ownership and quality of care in residential facilities for the elderly. *The Gerontologist, 29,* 209–215.

Linn, M., Gurel, L., & Linn, B. (1977). Patient outcomes as a measure of quality of nursing home care. *American Journal of Public Health, 67,* 337–344.

Mullins, L. C., Nelson, C. E., Busciglia, H., & Weiner, H. (1988). Job satisfaction among nursing home personnel: The impact of organizational structure and supervisory power. *Journal of Long-Term Care Administration, 6*(1), 12–19.

Norton, P., van Maris, B., Soberman, L., & Murray, H. (1996). Satisfaction of residents and families in long-term care: I. Construction and application of an instrument. *Quality Management in Health Care,* (4)3, 38–40.

Nyman, J. A. (1988). Improving the quality of nursing home outcomes: Are adequacy or incentive-oriented policies more effective? *Medical Care, 26,* 1158–1171.

Parasuramon, A., Zeithmal, V., & Berry, L. (1998). SERVQUAL: A multi-item scale for measuring consumer perceptions of service quality. *Journal of Retailing, 64,* 12–40.

Pascoe, G. C. (1983). Patient satisfaction in primary health care: A literature review and analysis. *Evaluation and Program Planning, 6,* 185–210.

Pearson, A., Hocking, S., Mott, S., & Riggs, A. (1993). Quality of care in nursing homes: From the resident's perspective. *Journal of Advanced Nursing, 18*(1), 20–24.

Prawitz, A., Lawrence, F., Draughn, P., & Wozniak, P. (1991). Relationships between steps taken in selecting a nursing home and consumers' satisfaction. *Psychological Reports, 69,* 404–406.

Price, J. L., & Mueller, C. W. (1986). *Handbook of organizational measurement.* Cambridge, MA: Ballinger.

Reinardy, J. R. (1995). Relocation to a new environment: Decisional control and the move to a nursing home. *Health & Social Work, 20*(1), 31–38.

Rohrer, J., Momany, E., & Chang, W.. (1993). Organizational predictors of outcomes of long-stay nursing home residents. *Social Science and Medicine, 37,* 549–554.

Sainfort, F., Ramsay, J. D., & Manato, H. (1995). Conceptual and methodological sources of variation in the measurement of nursing facility quality: An evaluation of 24 models and an empirical study. *Medical Care Research and Review, 52,* 60–87.

Scott, R. A., Aiken, L. H., Mechanic, D., & Moravesik, J. (1995). Organizational aspects of caring. *Milbank Quarterly, 73*(1), 77–95.

Sheridan, J. E., White, J., & Fairchild, T. (1992). Ineffective staff, ineffective supervision, or ineffective administration? Why some nursing homes fail to provide adequate care. *The Gerontologist, 32,* 334–341.

Spalding, J. (1985). *A consumer perspective on quality care: The residents' point of view.* Washington, DC: National Citizen's Coalition for Nursing Home Reform.

Spector, P. E. (1985). Measurement of human service staff satisfaction: Development of job satisfaction survey. *American Journal of Community Psychology, 13,* 693–713.

Spector, W. D., & Takada, H. A. (1991). Characteristics of nursing homes that affect residential outcomes. *Journal of Aging and Health, 3,* 427–454.

Steffen, T. M., & Nystrom, P. C. (1997). Organizational determinants of service quality in nursing homes. *Hospital & Health Services Administration, 42*(2), 179–191.

Steffen, T. M., Nystrom, P. C., & O'Connor, S. J. (1996). Satisfaction with nursing homes. *Journal of Health Care Marketing, 16*(3), 34–38.

Strasser, S., & Davis, R. M. (1991). *Measuring patient satisfaction for improved patient services.* Ann Arbor, MI: American College of Health Care Executives.

van Maris, B., Soberman, L., Murray, M., & Norton, P. (1996). Satisfaction of residents and families in long term care: II Lessons learned. *Quality Management in Health Care, 4*(3), 47–53.

Waxman, H. M., Carner, E. A., & Berkenstock, G. (1984). Job turnover and job satisfaction among nursing home aides. *Gerontologist, 24,* 503–509.

Weisman, C. S., & Nathanson, C. A. (1985). Professional satisfaction and client outcomes. *Medical Care, 23,* 1179–1192.

Zinn, J. S., Lavizzo-Mourey, R., & Taylor, L.. (1993). Measuring satisfaction with care in the nursing home setting: The Nursing Home Resident Satisfaction Scale. *The Journal of Applied Gerontology, 12,* 452–465.

Chapter 6

TRENDS IN THE USE OF SATISFACTION SURVEYS IN LONG-TERM CARE AND IN-HOUSE VERSUS CONSULTING-FIRM QUESTIONNAIRE ADMINISTRATION

J. Mac Crawford

INTRODUCTION

This chapter presents trends in the use of satisfaction surveys. Information is provided on the evolution of satisfaction surveys, changes in the health care industry which have spurred increased utilization of and reliance on satisfaction research in decision making, the various entities conducting satisfaction research, costs involved, and the advantages and disadvantages of hiring outside consultants to do this kind of work.

THE EVOLUTION OF SATISFACTION SURVEYS

With the publication of Ralph Nader's *Unsafe At Any Speed* in 1965, American society entered into a period of intensified concern for the safety and well-being of consumers. The proliferation of products and services has served to make consumers increasingly aware of quality and value. This focus has a parallel in the health care industry, motivated both by the increasing use of health services by an aging population and by increases in costs in excess of recent inflation rates. The failed attempt to reform the health care industry has had the paradoxical effect of galvanizing quality initiatives nationwide.

One consequence of the failure of President Clinton's health care reform initiative has been the proliferation of managed care. Managed care is seen both as a way to control costs and as a natural mechanism for promoting preventive care and services. Federal government expenditures for health services have increased from $14.7 billion in 1970 to $303.6 billion in 1995, and expenditures for nursing home care have risen from $4.2 billion to $77.9 billion over the same period (American College of Healthcare Executives, 1997). These two components of health care expenditures have seen a roughly proportionate increase in the past 25 years; federal outlays have increased over 20-fold, while expenditures for nursing home care have increased over 18-fold. Obviously, growth in health care expenditures has greatly surpassed what might be attributed to inflation. In this climate, it is easy to see why there is a renewed call for accountability and quality; not only in inpatient, outpatient, emergency, and primary care physician settings, but also in long-term care.

The aging Baby Boom generation poses a challenge to health care systems in general, but it poses the particularly difficult challenge of skyrocketing demand for long-term care services. In addition to the large numbers of retirees who will eventually seek long-term care, persons with developmental disabilities, younger persons disabled as a result of injury or illness, and persons with debilitating chronic diseases (such as AIDS) will all need, at the very least, extended-care rehabilitation services. The Congressional Budget Office (1991) estimates that the nursing home population will increase 50% between 1990 and 2010, will double by 2030, and will triple by 2050.

While congressional budgetmakers are concerned with holding down Medicaid and Medicare expenditures, there may be important consequences, resulting from austerity measures, for quality of care. These converging trends—increasing rates of long-term care utilization and political/economic pressure to reduce federal health outlays—point to the critical need for vigilant and improving methods of monitoring quality of care. Kleinsorge and Koenig (1991) make the point that the emphasis on quality and satisfaction needs to be a priority for all industries, including manufacturing and service industries.

HISTORY AND EMERGENCE OF SATISFACTION SURVEYS

Techniques for measurement of patient satisfaction have been evolving for many years. Abdellah and Levine (1957) reported on the development of a measure of patient satisfaction with nursing care and Rice, et al. (1963) developed a "ward evaluation scale." The 1970s saw the proliferation of publications in the area of patient satisfaction: Houston and Pasanen (1972) wrote on patient's perceptions of hospital care, and Ware (1978) addressed methodological issues such as the effects of acquiescent response set (the tendency of some respondents to answer positively, regardless of their true opinion) on patient satisfaction ratings. Aharony and Strasser (1993), in their review, cite Donabedian (1981), Pascoe (1983), and Cleary and McNeil (1988) respectively for establishing patient satisfaction as an outcome of care; reviewing definitions, models, and empirical studies; and reviewing the theoretical work on patient satisfaction. The '80s and '90s have witnessed the proliferation of entities focused on measuring patient satisfaction, as well as a technological revolution which has made possible the handling of very large databases. In the past, analysis of such massive amounts of data would have required a great deal of programming and processing power, however, it is not uncommon today for researchers to conduct complex analyses on data sets containing hundreds of thousands of records using desktop computers. Besides enhanced data manipulation capabilities, today's researchers are able to enter data more efficiently through the use of scannable forms and Computer Aided Telephone Interviewing (CATI) systems.

EVOLUTION OF METHODOLOGIES

Likert, in 1932, published an article describing his now well-known technique for the measurement of attitudes in *Archives of Psychology*. The evolution of attitude measurement theory allowed for researchers to have greater confidence that their instruments were measuring the underlying attitudes of interest. However, data analysis lagged far behind until the advent of modern data processing after World War II. Kerlinger (1992) traces the development of modern behavioral research through the 1940s, 1950s, and into the present. Kerlinger himself has contributed to the field of psychometrics with his documentation and exposition of the methods of measurement and the assessment of validity and reliability.

Measurement of residents' and family members' opinions may be accomplished by gathering several types of information: reports of facts, ratings and/or evaluations, and reports of future intentions. Facts can range from simple demographic information (such as age, gender, and race) to relatively complex information about the specifics of the care process and living environment.

Ratings and evaluations may be elicited on various aspects of long-term care, such as nursing care, physician care, physical environment, food, activities, and communication. The Likert scale elicits the degree to which respondents agree or disagree with a series of statements about care received. An example might look like the following:

The nurses treated you with respect.	SD	A	N	D	SA
	1	2	3	4	5

The abbreviation SD stands for Strongly Disagree, and the other choices are constructed similarly. Other rating scales ask for degree of satisfaction with some dimension of care, while still others ask for a rating from "poor" to "excellent." For example, a respondent might be asked to indicate his or her level of satisfaction with pain control, or the respondent could be asked to rate pain control efforts from poor to excellent. An example of the later might look like the following:

The measures used to control my pain are:	Poor	Fair	Good	Very Good	Excellent
	1	2	3	4	5

The point is that there are many ways to ask satisfaction questions, but there is very little consensus on which method is best.

Future intentions may be measured by asking respondents for the likelihood of some behavior, such as changing to another care facility, or intention to recommend the facility to friends or family. Response categories such as "Very likely, likely, neutral, unlikely, or very unlikely" might be used. Or, an agreement scale, as previously mentioned, could be used in conjunction with statements about future intentions such as "I would recommend this facility to my family and friends."

Whatever scales are used, it is important to be consistent. Detailed discussion of questionnaire writing is beyond the scope of this chapter, but there are several books available which are excellent guides (e.g., *Improving survey questions* by Fowler, 1995).

ENTITIES CONDUCTING THESE STUDIES

There are many companies, universities, and regulatory bodies either conducting patient satisfaction research or contracting for such research among patients being seen in inpatient, emergency room, outpatient, primary care physician, and long-term care settings. Some of the larger market research firms, such as SRI Gallup (Health Care Group), Market Facts, Maritz Marketing Research, and HCIA, conduct patient satisfaction surveys. These firms also work for clients interested in client reaction to and satisfaction with a broad spectrum of products and services. The number of research entities is somewhat smaller when attention is focused on health care in general or on residents of long-term care facilities. Companies such as The Picker Institute, Press,Ganey Associates, Inc., National Research Corporation, and Parkside Associates, Inc. focus almost exclusively on customer satisfaction in health care settings. In the following sections, lack of a mention of revenues in health care or work done in the long-term care arena for a particular firm implies a lack of specific information. Most firms, however, are happy to entertain enquiries from any potential clients.

Larger Research Firms

The Gallup Organization is a very well-known opinion research firm, with yearly gross revenues close to $170 million per year, roughly $10 million of which are related to health care survey research. Gallup is based in Lincoln, Nebraska, but has offices all over the U.S. and the world. Gallup employs both mail and telephone methodologies and works with managed care and health care providers. Gallup includes long-term care entities among its clients.

Maritz Marketing Research, Inc. is a large research firm based in Fenton, Missouri. Maritz' gross revenues exceed $130 million, with approximately $12 million coming from the health care sector. Maritz employs both mail and telephone methodologies and focuses on the managed care environment.

Market Facts, Inc. and HCIA, Inc. are large firms which are national in scope. Market Facts is located in Arlington Heights, Illinois and has gross revenues in excess of $90 million, $10 million of which come from the health care industry. Market Facts uses both mail and telephone methodologies and focuses on managed care.

HCIA, based in Baltimore, is essentially a financial analysis and management company, with yearly revenues of about $90 million. Near the end of 1995, HCIA acquired a company called Response Technologies, which became a division of HCIA. This division is now known as HCIA Response and currently has gross revenues on the order of $5 million per year. They use both mail and telephone methodologies and focus on health care providers.

Smaller Research Firms Focusing on
the Health Care Industry

National Research Corporation (NRCI) located in Lincoln, Nebraska, has revenues from health care-related satisfaction research on the order of $23 million per year. NRCI's clients include managed care organizations as well as providers of long-term care. NRCI's products cover the spectrum of satisfaction, from nurses and physicians to physical facilities. NRCI employs both mail and telephone methodologies in surveying long-term care residents and family members, and they have conducted face-to-face interviews with nursing home employees.

Parkside Associates, Inc. is a subsidiary of Advocate Health Care, based in Oak Brook, Illinois. Advocate is a large group of hospitals, nursing homes, managed care organizations, and physician practices and is one of the top 10 employers in the Chicago region. Parkside is a full-service patient satisfaction research firm operating nationwide. Parkside conducts long-term care resident satisfaction surveys as well as surveys of patients in various health care settings.

Press, Ganey Associates, Inc. was founded in 1985 in South Bend, Indiana. Press, Ganey processes more than 3 million questionnaires annually and has revenues of around $7.5 million. Press, Ganey does satisfaction work in the long-term care arena and focuses on health care providers in terms of clientele. Press, Ganey primarily conducts mailed surveys.

The Picker Institute (formerly the Picker/Commonwealth Program for Patient-Centered Care) has been assessing patient satisfaction since 1987. Picker has interviewed more than 160,000 patients from all types of health care settings, including long-term care. They subcontract the actual data collection to other firms using Picker's measurement instruments. They have roughly $3 million in annual revenues.

In-House Surveys

Undoubtedly there are many long-term care facility managers who support ongoing, in-house resident, family, and employee satisfaction surveys. Ejaz (1996) described an in-house survey process in which research staff reviewed an exhaustive list of questions they had developed, requested instruments from other long-term care facilities, conducted a literature review, and formed a committee to develop a set of instruments. These instruments were then passed on to the administrative staff, research staff, and the operations committee of the board of trustees. The research staff worked with the billing department to establish the sampling frame, identification numbers were assigned to residents' family members, and cover letters were prepared. The cover letters included information on the purpose of the survey, who was conducting it, issues of confidentiality, and a time frame for completion (3 weeks requested). The letters were signed by the Executive Director and were distributed with questionnaires and stamped, self-addressed envelopes to be returned to the Executive Director. A separate protocol was developed for interviewing residents. Results were presented to the facility administrator, the board of trustees, the facility's management staff, and all other staff. They then developed an action plan for improvement and a process for providing feedback to family members. This example illustrates many of the complex issues that will be encountered when implementing a customer satisfaction program. Davies, in an interview by Kennedy (1996), makes the point that the process must begin with a determination of the needs of the organization. In the long-term care setting, this could include deciding how many instruments will be needed because the "customers" are not only residents, but family, friends, and guardians as well. In Davies' parlance, multiple targets of satisfaction research require a "family of instruments."

VARIOUS SURVEY METHODOLOGIES

Dillman (1978) authored an important reference on mail and telephone surveying. These two methodologies account for the vast majority of surveys conducted today. Additionally, face-to-face interviews may be conducted, but these are seldom seen in traditional health care-related satisfaction research. The recent technological revolution has opened up some other avenues for opinion research. Most notable among these are Internet questionnaires and Interactive Voice Response (IVR). The proliferation of computers has also allowed for the assembly of large panels of potential respondents (over 500,000 households represented in some instances) to surveys covering almost any topic.

Face-to-Face Interviews

Until recently, face-to-face interviewing was considered to be the only acceptable way to conduct survey research. One advantage to this technique is that interviewers who take the time to visit a home are generally accorded at least a chance to persuade the respondent to participate. Mailed questionnaires, on the other hand, frequently end up in the wastebasket. Telephone interviewers also have the opportunity to sway reluctant participants, but phone surveys must now compete with the burgeoning numbers of solicitations to sell products. Many householders, fatigued by the constant assault in their off-work hours, steadfastly refuse to convey any personal information over the telephone. The face-to-face interviewer is better able to provide valid identification and assure the householder that he or she is working for a bona fide research firm. In the 1960s, it was not uncommon for research firms to achieve response rates in the range of 80 to 85%. Another advantage is that illiterate respondents or respondents without telephones can be successfully interviewed, thus reducing the potential bias of exclusively including wealthier and better-educated respondents.

In spite of these apparent advantages, face-to-face interviewing has become less successful at engaging large proportions of samples, and other factors, such as cost, have conspired to make this method less attractive to researchers. A fairly large segment of U.S. households are made up of males and females, each of whom works. The increasing phenomenon of dual incomes has lead to an increased need for return visits when no one is found to be at home. Additionally, with the higher relative price for fuel, difficulty in finding reliable interviewers, and increasing threats to personal safety, costs per completed questionnaire have substantially increased (Dillman, 1978). Recently it has been estimated that face-to-face interviews comprise fewer than 10% of all surveys conducted, and response rates to this type of interview are falling, just as they are for mail and telephone surveys (Dillman, 1991).

There may also be some methodological reasons why personal interviewing is less than optimal. There is a well-documented tendency for respondents to personal interviews (telephone respondents, as well) to answer in socially desirable ways (Bainbridge, 1989; Kane, 1997). This phenomenon manifests itself in generally higher satisfaction scores or rankings as respondents desire to appear in a more positive light. This is particularly likely if respondents have reason to doubt the complete confidentiality of their responses. In the extended-care setting, this tendency is predictable, given the intimate, ongoing interrelationships between residents and their physicians, nurses, and aides. It does not take much imagination to understand why residents might be hesitant to criticize staff, upon whom they are, in many ways, dependent. All of the above points lead to the conclusion that face-to-face interviews, except in certain circumstances, are not practical for conducting patient satisfaction research. Face-to-face interviews may be most cost-effective for long-term care facilities conducting in-house surveys of residents. The trade-off is, of course, the confidentiality issue.

Mail Methodology

Mail surveying has been used for gathering opinions for many years, but has a rather tarnished reputation. One of the major problems with using mail methodology is the typically poor response rates achieved. Dillman (1991) has proposed a Total Design Method (TDM) which may be applied differentially to both mail and telephone methods. The essence of the TDM is to personalize and legitimize the survey effort and to make it as simple as possible for individuals to participate. Dillman has very detailed prescriptions for conducting every aspect of the effort: pre-survey letters announcing the study, cover letters accompanying the questionnaires, postcard reminders, mailing second (and sometimes third) questionnaires to nonresponders, and mailing thank-you cards after the study is complete. Dillman has reported response rates in excess of 70% in mail surveys employing his TDM. Readers intending to conduct their own surveys are strongly encouraged to read Dillman (1978, 1991) carefully and follow the protocols.

Mailed surveys may be conducted in two essential ways: respondents can check answers to satisfaction questions and write in comments when prompted, or respondents can carefully fill in bubbles on a questionnaire which will be scanned directly into the computer. The former method requires data entry and verification, both of which can be costly processes. Open-ended responses must be coded and entered as well. The advantage is ease of completion for the respondent, who is less intimidated by a large number of circles to fill in for large data fields, such as name and address. Less care is required in answering closed-ended questions as well. This ease in answering may translate into higher response rates.

Scannable questionnaires make data entry much easier, but data-checking efforts need to be intensive. Modern scanning machines are able to handle ink, as well as the traditional "Number 2" pencil. However, if respondents are sloppy in filling in the bubbles or change their minds and erase, the scanner can erroneously read certain questions. For this reason, researchers must be very careful to ensure that electronic data files correspond exactly with what the study subjects have indicated on paper. Still, substantial savings may be realized, making this method among the most cost-effective ways to gather patient satisfaction data. In long-term care settings this method is rarely, if ever, used with residents. Questionnaires designed for family and friends of residents, as well as staff, would be good candidates for scannable formats.

Costs for traditional and scannable questionnaires include printing, paper, envelopes, postage, data system setup, and data entry. Costs per completed questionnaire using mail methodology can range from $5 to

$10, depending on the degree of automation, the size of the study, and the number of questions being asked. Prices at the low end of the range would not include analysis and reporting, while prices at the high end would include these services. On the whole, mailed surveys remain the method of choice in many cases.

Telephone Methodology

It has been possible to conduct telephone surveys since the advent of the telephone in the 19th century. In fact, two famous examples, the predicted victories of Landon over Roosevelt and Dewey over Truman, respectively, in the 1936 and 1948 U.S. presidential elections, pointed to a central problem with telephone interviewing: those without telephones are quite likely to differ, in a systematic way, from those who do have phones.

In 1936, only 35% of the population had telephones. To make matters worse, a major poll was conducted using the subscription list to the periodical *Literary Digest*. It does not take much imagination to infer that this particular sample consisted of an elite segment of the population, one that might, on the whole, have supported a Republican candidate. Landon was predicted to win, but Roosevelt won in a landslide victory. In the case of Dewey and Truman, 12 years later, a preponderance of wealthier Republicans who had been polled by phone indicated that they would vote for Dewey. At that time, a substantial proportion of the population (greater than 35%) had not acquired telephones. Newspaper editors who had printed headlines proclaiming Dewey's victory on election night were stunned and embarrassed to find on the following morning that Truman had actually won a close race.

The situation is not so bleak now, as more than 95% of U.S. households have at least one telephone. Indeed, the computer revolution has enabled researchers to take full advantage of the telephone in conducting surveys. Phone and computer systems have been merged so that the distinction is becoming blurry. Computer Aided Telephone Interviewing (CATI) stations allow interviewers to automatically dial sampled phone numbers, follow prompts from the computer monitor, enter the data directly as the interview proceeds, and compile statistics on the disposition of each call (i.e., whether the interview was completed or refused, the phone was disconnected or busy, etc.). Telephone interviewing is probably not an option in long-term care settings because of the wide range of sensory, cognitive, and motor functioning encountered among residents: while those with poor eyesight or motor skills would have an easier time with the interview, those with hearing deficits would have difficulty completing a telephone interview. Telephone interviews would, however, be effective with family, friends, and perhaps staff. As with face-to-face interviews, telephone interviewers are able to provide respondents with additional information as needed. This may assure that responses accurately reflect respondents' understanding of the questions. Of course, this advantage has to be weighed against the possibility of interviewers leading respondents to answer in a certain way. This phenomenon may be subconsciously manifested, but it underscores the necessity for adequate training and monitoring of interviewers. Costs per completed interview might range from $10 to $15, depending on the number of questions and the accuracy of the sampling frame. Prices at the low end of the range would not include analysis and reporting, while prices at the higher end would include these services. An inaccurate sampling frame results in interviewers contacting a greater proportion of ineligibles, driving up costs of interviewer payroll and telephone charges.

Mixed-Mode Methodology

It is possible to use combinations of methodologies when there is a need to improve sample size. One of the drawbacks of mailed surveys is the typically poor response rates. Researchers can, if necessary, follow-up nonresponders to the mailed survey with telephone interviews. Costs for this approach will probably fall between those of pure mail and pure telephone methodologies, although the costs for a mail study diligently following Dillman's TDM will be almost as high as costs for a telephone survey. One point to keep in mind is the need for careful analysis and the awareness that expressed satisfaction levels are likely to be slightly higher (typically less than one-tenth of a point on a 5-point scale) in a telephone study than in a mail survey . Another consideration is the degree to which late responders (those followed up by telephone) and earlier responders might systematically differ. Looking for variations in satisfaction by relative promptness of response may shed light on the degree to which responders represent the target population. For example, as the time between initial survey administration and receipt of the final survey grows longer, those who return questionnaires very late in the process might resemble nonresponders in attitudes, beliefs, and various sociodemographic characteristics. This phenomenon could manifest itself through intensity of follow-up in the following way: Assume that 30% of the sample return a questionnaire after the first mailing; another 20% return one after a reminder postcard, another 10% return one after a second mailing; and finally, 5% complete a questionnaire after a third mailing. Sixty-five percent of the targeted sample have now participated, but the last 15% or so required extraordinary diligence to prod into responding. These "reluctant responders" very likely resemble the 35% of the sample who, actively or passively, refused to participate.

Distribution by Hand

In the long-term care setting, a natural way to collect resident satisfaction data is to distribute questionnaires by hand. This is cost-effective and allows staff to say a few personal words to residents about the purpose and importance of the effort during the distribution process. Respondents can drop completed questionnaires into centrally located receptacles (dining and recreation areas are convenient). The receptacles should be secure (locked to assure confidentiality) and clearly marked. The important point here is to ensure that everyone who is eligible for the study has an opportunity to respond.

The Electronic Frontier

The proliferation of the Internet has spurred interest in collecting data on the World Wide Web. Many online surveys are posted on Web sites. Data are easily collected, compiled, and analyzed. The principal difficulty with these surveys is the lack of probability sampling, thus making broad inferences practically impossible. Some European governments have experimented with assembling panels of respondents who complete longitudinal surveys on a regular basis. Volunteers are provided with computers and modems, and are asked to provide new data periodically. If such methods could be used on samples of persons with known probabilities of selection into the study, the result might be considered a useful alternative to Web-based surveys. At this point, Web-based systems are of limited value, especially for long-term care populations.

Another fairly recent development, Interactive Voice Response (IVR), is a computer/telephone-based system which can be used to collect closed-ended survey data (questions for which there are limited response choices). Respondents may call a telephone number and follow a series of instructions for choosing responses by pressing touch-tone keys. The advantages are the flexibility accorded the subject in choosing when to respond, the ease of data compilation, the ability to incorporate foreign languages into the system, and reduced interviewing costs. These methods are very new, however, and there have been no reports on the reliability and validity of such systems. Again, with sufficient attention to methodological rigor, IVR could, in the future, be a viable method of satisfaction data collection. These methods are perhaps the least expensive, but they are also the least understood in terms of reliability and validity. Because of the issues of variability in sensory, cognitive, and motor functioning, IVR is of limited value to administrators wishing to measure satisfaction in long-term care residents. These methods could, however, eventually be applied in surveying family and staff.

Choosing among the various methods of data collection may be facilitated by firms which have experience conducting these studies. Their consultants can provide cost estimates and assist in making the many decisions necessary to get a Continuous Quality Improvement (CQI)/customer relations program up and running. These decisions could include setting goals for the CQI process; deciding how many patients, family members, and staff to survey; how frequently to conduct the studies; what questions to ask; and how effectively to use the data in improving care and the living environment. The next section focuses on some of the issues to be considered in deciding whether or not to hire an outside vendor.

ADVANTAGES OF UTILIZING OUTSIDE VENDORS

Considering the costs involved in conducting survey research, an administrator might reasonably conclude that considerable savings would accrue by conducting satisfaction research in-house. There are, however, some compelling reasons that administrators of long-term care facilities should consider using outside vendors to conduct their patient and family satisfaction research.

Objectivity

Successful health care organizations have invested a great deal of time and money to build a reputation for high-quality care, among potential residents and families alike. Efforts to utilize results of satisfaction studies in marketing campaigns will be facilitated by reporting objective results obtained by third-party vendors. Just as accrediting bodies look for objectivity in data used to assess consumer satisfaction, potential residents and families are concerned that information they use to make decisions about which facility to choose is objective and unbiased.

Database Management

Medical recordkeeping is a costly, complex, and sometimes daunting undertaking. As most administrators know, keeping and updating residents' records requires space, time, and expertise. Given the enormity of the task, it makes all the more sense to turn over the collection, storage, and manipulation of client, family, and employee satisfaction data to an outside vendor. Independent contractors are in the business of maintaining (and backing up) large, complex database files. Most such firms have a dedicated Management Information Systems (MIS) department with programmers and network administrators on staff. Even long-term administrators who are maintaining their own databases may want to engage the services of an outside vendor to conduct the studies.

Benchmarking

Full-service patient satisfaction firms provide assistance in developing benchmarking systems, have large comparative databases readily available, and are better equipped to interpret data meaningfully so that CQI efforts may be precisely targeted and implemented. While tracking one's performance over time is an excellent way of monitoring and using satisfaction data, it is also a very valuable exercise to compare oneself to other facilities of similar size and residential makeup, in similar markets. These kinds of comparisons are extremely difficult, if not impossible, to come by without the services of a vendor dedicated to gathering satisfaction and other outcome data.

Reporting

Automated reporting is usually one of the "economies of scale" provided by outside vendors. Companies dedicated to this kind of work are able to generate reports, based on very large numbers of respondents, in a relatively short time. In reporting, outside vendors are also able to provide insight into changes in satisfaction within a facility over time, are able to pinpoint drivers of satisfaction, and will make recommendations for improving quality.

Confidentiality

Even the most stringent practices and procedures related to data protection cannot absolutely prevent breaches of confidentiality. This issue permeates all health and social sciences research and, as mentioned previously, respondents are less likely to be forthcoming with their true feelings if they suspect that the staff will be privy to their responses. No matter what assurances are made, it may be difficult to persuade residents that their opinions will be withheld (except in the aggregate) from staff, and it might be even more difficult to persuade employees that their opinions will be withheld from administrators. Using outside vendors ensures at least that data will be collected and stored off-site, minimizing or eliminating the likelihood of compromising confidentiality. This is not a guarantee. However, the separation in space of respondents from their data creates one more barrier to unscrupulous or even unintentional snooping. Research firms are usually very concerned with security, both electronic and physical, and have substantial checks built in to their data and facility security systems.

Questionnaire Development

Besides knowing what kinds of questions to ask and what scales (response sets) to use, the administrator needs to be aware that simply putting together a set of questions does not guarantee that the questionnaire, as a whole, is measuring what is intended. Nor does it guarantee that satisfaction will be measured reliably; that is, that residents will display consistency upon repeated responses to the same instruments. These issues, validity and reliability, are covered in detail elsewhere in this volume, and the reader is referred to Chapter 5. The point is that outside vendors have the benefit of experience in testing the psychometric properties of questionnaires, which requires fairly sophisticated statistical skills and knowledge. In addition to testing new survey instruments, vendors' analysts have the expertise to reevaluate existing instruments to ensure that underlying constructs are still being accurately and reliably measured.

Consulting

Outside vendors are able to provide clients with training in utilizing their satisfaction research to improve quality of care and improve the lives of residents, families, and employees. Analyses can pinpoint aspects of long-term care and the living environment which need improvement. Outside vendors can use their experience to help clients allocate resources maximally, ensuring the most cost-effective use of funds dedicated to CQI. It is possible, through analytic techniques, to target areas for improvement which are both highly correlated with patient satisfaction and which receive low satisfaction scores. For example, if a long-term care facility receives relatively low scores on the empathy shown by staff and empathy is highly correlated with overall satisfaction, then improvements in resident satisfaction may be attained by working with the staff to enhance their ability to see the care they provide from the resident's point of view.

Other technical issues, such as the number of patients to be interviewed, are not simple matters. Research firms can recommend the optimal sample size to assure representativeness and statistical power to detect trends over time and estimate satisfaction levels. Once a sample size has been decided on, the process of actually selecting the sample may be done much more efficiently and accurately by an experienced research firm.

It is quite likely that, given the database management capabilities of research firms, results will be available and actionable in a more timely manner. For example, vendors dedicated to patient satisfaction are able to quickly code verbatim responses and provide immediate feedback to administrators when a "red flag" event occurs (for example, potentially dangerous conditions or expressions of extreme dissatisfaction). Management is then able to act quickly to minimize the effects of the event and perhaps prevent a recurrence.

Flexibility of Approach

Outside vendors have the capability of assembling large banks of telephone interviewers, or subcontracting for this service. Additionally, if mail methodology is to be used, research companies are experienced in using electronic scanning machines, and, importantly, are familiar with the protocols for data checking which ensure the accuracy of conversion of pencil or ink markings on paper to a computer database. Most firms also are capable of conducting focus groups for specialized populations for which survey research is unwarranted or impractical. This flexibility in approach and expertise in implementation may actually result in lower costs for institutions contracting for the work.

ADVANTAGES OF IN-HOUSE ADMINISTRATION OF SATISFACTION SURVEYS

Specialized Research Firms are Expensive

Some of the advantages previously listed may also have their negative sides. Depending on the vendor and the capabilities of the organization wishing to contract for satisfaction research, costs will be higher for the outside vendor. All of the technical and analytic capabilities provided by the research firm usually require highly educated (and compensated) individuals, as well as sophisticated data collection hardware and software. Management may realize considerable cost savings by conducting studies in-house.

Familiarity with the Facility or System

A very important consideration is the insight the administrator has into the specific performance issues and needs of his or her facility. Management has knowledge of staffing, census, and performance indicators, which is critical in designing and administering satisfaction surveys. The administrator is also intimately familiar with the expectations of regulating bodies, and hence is probably the best person to map out strategies for achieving accreditation. This in-depth understanding of a multitude of issues allows the administrator to understand and utilize the results better than someone from outside the facility. Additionally, data which might not have originally been considered for analysis may be incorporated into measurement systems at minimal cost, allowing for new perspectives and analyses of trends.

Privacy and Confidentiality

Administrators may not be comfortable with hiring outside vendors to conduct satisfaction studies. Perceptions of "prying" and intrusion into the lives of both residents and employees are understandable. It can be intrusive to allow people outside the facility to contact residents.

Facility administrators may be concerned about confidentiality of the data. This is a very important consideration, and questioning potential vendors about data security is not unreasonable. Some vendors allow Internet or dial-up access to data which employs systems of passwords and other security measures. Protocols should be in place for regularly changing passwords, monitoring who is accessing the system, and providing safeguards for data not relevant to logged-in, legitimate users.

CONSIDERATIONS IN CHOOSING A VENDOR

McGee, Goldfield, Riley, and Morton et al. (1996) recommend considering many of the following items in choosing an outside vendor. The author has filled in the gaps with his own recommendations.

Experience

Keep in mind when "shopping around" for a vendor that not all research companies have experience in the health care industry. Some companies might be able to assemble the correct questions to ask, but the key is analyzing, interpreting, and using the data effectively. Firms without experience in health care may lack this critical knowledge. The vendor should be willing, even eager, to involve stakeholders and decision makers in the pre-survey process of questionnaire development and planning. For example, focus groups are frequently used to determine the critical elements of the questionnaire specifically and the quality improvement effort in general.

Survey Instruments and Implementation

Look for examples of questionnaire items used by the vendors. Verify that these instruments have "face validity," that is, the questions make sense and seem to be getting at the essential issues of resident, family, and staff satisfaction. Ask questions about how the vendor can demonstrate validity and reliability. Likewise, ask questions about how the survey will be administered; will the interviews be conducted face-to-face for residents and staff, and by mail or telephone for family? Ask how sampling will be done; will all residents be surveyed (census sampling) or will a random sample of residents and family be drawn?

Analysis and Reporting

Ask how the data will be analyzed, and ask about how and when reports will be delivered. Also request information about the content of the reports. Look for the ability to provide comparative norms and/or benchmarks of how other facilities are performing.

Quality Control, Personnel, and Costs

Verify quality control measures and security procedures, and ask about staff that will be assigned to the project. What are the qualifications of the vendors, and how accessible will they be? It is not unusual for vendors to supply detailed resumes listing educational attainment, professional experience, and even references from previous clients.

Compare estimated costs quoted by the various vendors and make sure the comparison is appropriate. Ranges of costs were mentioned previously, but keep in mind that costs may vary widely and that vendors can collaborate with management to provide all or just portions of the components of a customer satisfaction system (see next paragraph). Some very inexpensive surveys may be inflexible, may include only rudimentary reports, may take a long time to complete, and may not answer the essential questions about customer satisfaction. Many of these questions should be incorporated into a "Request for Proposals" (RFP) and can be evaluated on a vendor-specific basis. Once the best candidates have been selected, further questioning may be necessary to make the final selection. Table 6.1 on the next page summarizes the important considerations in choosing an outside vendor to conduct satisfaction studies. These items could be used to develop an RFP which allows for systematic review of all components of customer satisfaction systems proposed by vendors.

Alternatives to Outside Vendors and Internal Data Collection

As an alternative to hiring outside vendors to implement every component of a resident satisfaction/customer service program, institutions may work with research firms' consultants to help recognize operational or structural weaknesses and fill in the gaps. Strasser and Davis (1991) suggest that costs may be reduced by purchasing an existing survey instrument which has been carefully designed and tested, or undertaking the process of developing an instrument in-house. Further savings could be realized by conducting all mailings in-house and receiving only raw data from the vendor, who is responsible for data entry and verification.

Consulting firms could supply the expertise of statisticians in conducting more in-depth analyses if desired. The vendor could help interpret results and mobilize resources needed to act on the findings. This approach has the advantage of being less costly, yet allows administrators the flexibility of getting expert advice and impartial analysis and interpretation. Many research firms are happy to meet with prospective clients, at little or no cost, to discuss needs and the services available to meet those needs.

CONCLUSION

This chapter reviewed the history of customer satisfaction in health care settings, the necessity for conducting these studies, the kinds of firms providing these services, the methodologies available, and the pros and cons of contracting with independent research companies. Self-reflection can be a painful process. We do not always like the person in the mirror, but critical self-examination is crucial in life and in business. The ability to learn from mistakes and improve performance are hallmarks of successful people and enterprises.

Table 6.1 Listing of important considerations in choosing an outside vendor

Scope of Work
  Resident
  Family/friend
  Staff
Sampling
  Census
  Sample
Methodology
  Face-to-face interviews (residents, staff)
  Telephone (family, staff)
    Participation in training interviewers
    Monitoring of telephone calls
  Mail (family, staff)
  Hand delivery (residents, staff)
Data Security and Confidentiality
  Policies
  Procedures
Quality Control Procedures
  Data entry and verification
  Data analysis
  Reporting
Survey Instruments (Ask for Samples)
  Validity
  Reliability
Analytic Methods
  Description
    Means
    Standard deviations
    Frequencies and percentages
  Complex Analysis
    Regression
    Analysis of variance (ANOVA)
Reporting
  Sample layout
Personnel
  Contact person
  Research staff
References from other Clients Costs
  Questionnaire development
  Data collection, analysis, reporting

REFERENCES

Abdellah, F. G., & Levine, E. (1957). Developing a measure of patient and personnel satisfaction with nursing care. *Nursing Research, 5,* 100–108.

Aharony, L., & Strasser, S. (1993). Patient satisfaction: What we know and what we still need to explore. *Medical Care Review, 50,* 49–79.

American College of Healthcare Executives, (1997). Key industry facts. *Healthcare Executive, 12,* 53.

Bainbridge, W. S. (1989). *Survey research: A computer-assisted introduction.* Belmont, CA: Wadsworth.

Cleary, P. D., & McNeil, B. J. (1988). Patient satisfaction as an indicator of quality of care. *Inquiry, 25,* 25–36.

Congressional Budget Office (1991). *Policy choices for long-term care.* Washington, DC: Government Printing Office.

Dillman, D. A. (1978). *Mail and telephone surveys: The total design method.* New York: Wiley.

Dillman, D. A. (1991). The design and administration of mail surveys. *Annual Review of Sociology, 17,* 225–249.

Donabedian, A. (1981). Criteria, norms and standards of quality: What do they mean? *American Journal of Public Health, 71,* 409–412.

Ejaz, F. K. (1996, November). *Experiences in Conducting satisfaction surveys: An in-house perspective.* Paper presented at the Annual Meeting of the Gerontological Society of America, Washington, DC.

Fowler, F. J. Jr., (1995). *Improving survey questions.* Thousand Oaks, CA: Sage

Houston, C. S., & Pasanen, W. E. (1972). Patients' perceptions of hospital care. *Hospitals, 46,* 70–74.

Kane, R. L. (1997). *Understanding health care outcomes research.* Gaithersburg, MD: Aspen.

Kennedy, M. (1996). Designing surveys for maximal satisfaction: An interview with Allyson Ross Davies. *Journal on Quality Improvement, 22,* 369–373.

Kerlinger, F. N. (1992). *Foundations of behavioral research* (3rd ed.). New York: Harcourt Brace College Publishers.

Kleinsorge, I. K., & Koenig, H. F. (1991). The silent customers: Measuring customer satisfaction in Nursing Homes. *Journal of Health Care Marketing, 11,* 2–13.

Likert, R. A. (1932). A technique for the measurement of attitudes. *Archives of Psychology, 140,* 1–55.

McGee, J., Goldfield, N., Riley, K., & Morton, J. (1996). *Collecting information from health care consumers.* Gaithersburg, MD: Aspen.

Pascoe, G. C. (1983). Patient satisfaction in primary health care: A literature review and analysis. *Evaluation and Program Planning, 6,* 185–210.

Rice, C. E., Berger, D. G., Klet, S. L., Sewal, L. G., & Lemkaw, P. V. (1963). The Ward Evaluation Scale. *Journal of Clinical Psychology, 19,* 252–260.

Strasser, S., & Davis, R. M. (1991). *Measuring patient satisfaction for improved patient services.* Ann Arbor, MI: Health Administration Press.

Ware, J. E. (1978). Effects of acquiescent response set on patient satisfaction ratings. *Medical Care, 16,* 327–336.

Chapter 7

PREVALENCE AND PROBLEMS IN THE USE OF SATISFACTION SURVEYS: RESULTS FROM RESEARCH ON OHIO NURSING HOMES

Linda S. Noelker, Farida K. Ejaz, and Dorothy Schur

INTRODUCTION

The purpose of this chapter is to investigate the extent to which consumer satisfaction surveys are being conducted in skilled nursing facilities in the state of Ohio, the nature of the survey process and outcomes, and reported problems with satisfaction surveys. To date, research has not examined these issues, hence there is a lack of empirical information to gauge the prevalence and effectiveness of the consumer satisfaction survey process and outcomes from the perspective of facility staff. This study helps to fill the gap in the research literature by providing information on satisfaction surveys, based on interviews with management staff from a random sample of nursing homes throughout the state that are certified by the Ohio Department of Health as licensed providers.

CONCEPTUAL BASIS FOR THE RESEARCH

A number of assumptions guided the study's conceptualization and design. We assumed that the majority of facilities in the study would conduct satisfaction surveys for several reasons. It is increasingly common for skilled nursing facilities to have managed care contracts, and the contracting organizations typically require that facilities survey their enrollees about satisfaction with the care received and report back the results. Second, a growing number of facilities are seeking or have received accreditation from the Joint Commission or other accrediting bodies which mandate that facilities routinely monitor resident satisfaction and use the results in the quality improvement process. Also, the health care environment has become more competitive in recent years with the growth of managed care and merging health care systems. As part of this environment, nursing facilities competing for managed care contracts and private-pay residents must pay careful attention to the quality as well as the cost of care in order to ensure that the customer is indeed satisfied.

To stay abreast of residents' satisfaction with the care and services rendered, we assumed that facilities would conduct a variety of satisfaction surveys. These are necessary to respond to the different types of residents with varying lengths of stay in subacute, short-term rehabilitation, hospice, dementia care, and long-term residential care programs. For short-stay residents in sub- and post-acute or rehabilitative care, satisfaction should ideally be monitored within 48 hours of admission, so that corrections can be made immediately, if, for example, the food service is unsatisfactory or the room accommodations are not up to the resident's standard of cleanliness. Many facilities give the resident a brief checklist, similar to the ones found in hotel rooms and restaurants, within a few days of entry to indicate where improvements can be made to enhance the resident's stay and encourage repeat business.

For residents in hospice and dementia care programs who would not be appropriate respondents for a satisfaction survey, family members typically serve as surrogates. Many facilities, however, routinely survey residents' families as a general policy, even when residents are cognitively alert, because many families remain closely involved in resident care following nursing home placement and participate along with residents in the facility's social and recreational activities (Zarit & Whitlatch, 1992). Long-term care residential facilities thus can be viewed as serving a dual clientele, residents and their families, and must be responsive to the expressed satisfaction of both. Consequently, this study examines the prevalence and process of conducting surveys with residents' family members as well as residents.

We also assumed that some facilities conduct their own in-house satisfaction surveys, while others rely on the growing number of outside organizations and consultants that provide this service. A recent search on the Worldwide Web showed that there are almost 7.9 million matches for "nursing home satisfaction surveys," and it appears that individual consultants and companies are using this communication vehicle to advertise their services. For facilities that are part of a chain, satisfaction surveys are often provided by the corporate office that analyzes the survey data and benchmarks the facility's results against other facilities in the chain.

The use of different methods of data collection for the survey, such as mailed questionnaires and telephone and in-person interviews, is likely to vary in relation to the amount of resources available and the targeted response rate. This research investigates the survey methods used, including who has responsibility for gathering the data, techniques for obtaining information, response rates, and the distribution of results.

Lastly, we assumed that staff satisfaction with the survey outcomes would vary in relation to the process used. Hence, the study focused on management staff's complaints about the process, such as the length of time to complete the survey, as well as their overall satisfaction with the outcomes and recommended changes in the survey process.

OHIO ASSOCIATIONS OFFERING
SATISFACTION SURVEY SERVICES

Because this research study is limited to nursing homes in the state of Ohio, it is important to understand the satisfaction survey services offered by the two statewide associations for nursing homes: the Ohio Health Care Association (OHCA) and the Association of Ohio Philanthropic Homes and Services for the Aged (AOPHA). The state of Ohio is unique in that OHCA offers satisfaction survey services to its membership twice a year at no cost. Currently, between 160 and 200 of the 575 for-profit nursing facilities in OHCA's membership take advantage of this service. According to Mr. Barry Jamieson, Director of Data Services for OHCA (personal communication, September 15, 1998), the service was initiated about 2 years ago to counterbalance the increasing emphasis on "objective" quality indicators, such as frequency of falls and weight loss, that are derived from the Minimum Data Set (MDS+) information. It was felt that equal attention should be given to "subjective" indicators of quality, such as resident satisfaction with the care given, the environment, staff, and services.

The national affiliate of OHCA, the American Health Care Association, developed a 100-item resident satisfaction survey; however, OHCA staff felt that its length and complexity would reduce the response rate. Hence, the long form was adapted to a one-page, 21-item form. The survey forms for residents and family members are shipped to participating facilities twice a year with return envelopes mailed directly to OHCA. The facilities are responsible for the following: screening residents on cognitive status using MDS data to identify those who are cognitively aware and can complete the survey; recruiting and overseeing volunteers who assist residents in completing the survey; and mailing the forms out to residents' families. The OHCA contracts with another firm for scanning services to automate the survey data, and OHCA staff analyze the results and send prepared reports back to the facilities.

Currently, OHCA is preparing to undertake its fourth round of surveys. Information from the first three waves suggests there is a 85–90% participation rate for residents who passed the MDS screening and about a 40% rate for family members. According to Mr. Jamieson, OHCA staff are strongly committed to keeping the form simple and maintaining the confidentiality of the data to ensure a high response rate. As a result, they recommend data collection methods that convey to residents that they can be honest in their reports without fear of retribution. Volunteers, rather than facility staff, are used to assist residents who need assistance to complete the survey, and the volunteers fold and insert the form and seal the envelope in front of the residents after they are finished. When completed, both resident and family survey forms are mailed directly to OHCA.

The not-for-profit counterpart to OHCA, the Association of Ohio Philanthropic Homes and Services for the Aged (AOPHA), currently does not provide satisfaction survey services to its membership. However, according to AOPHA's Executive Director, Mr. Clark Law (personal communication, September 23, 1998), the association plans to offer resident satisfaction surveys as a free service to its membership by year's end. This will be possible through an arrangement with the philanthropic association of homes in the state of Illinois, Life Services Network of Illinois. This statewide association has developed scannable satisfaction survey forms for long-term residents, family members, short-stay residents, and facility employees (Donna Munroe, RN, Ph.D., personal communication, September 23, 1998). It will also automate and analyze the data from participating facilities and provide annual reports with benchmarks.

THE OHIO SURVEY'S DESIGN

Design

The research survey of Ohio homes was designed originally to include 15-minute telephone interviews with the administrators of approximately 90 facilities throughout the state. These facilities were randomly selected from a stratified sample of small (26–99 beds), medium (100–199 beds) and large (over 200 beds) facilities listed as licensed providers by the Ohio Department of Health. Facilities with fewer than 25 beds were eliminated from the sampling pool, leaving 1,119 facilities in the pool. We oversampled from the larger facilities in Ohio to enable us to make meaningful comparisons between facilities of different sizes. Of the 1,119 facilities, 569 (50%) had 26 to 99 beds, 491 (45%) had 100 to 199 beds, and 59 (5%) had 200 or more beds. There were 37 facilities randomly drawn from the group of small facilities, 33 from the middle group, and 21 from the group of large facilities, for a total of 91 facilities. A replacement pool of 78 facilities was also drawn to substitute for those that did not respond or refused to participate.

The survey interview form was developed to elicit information on selected characteristics of a facility, the survey process, and its outcomes. A structured format with forced-choice answers was used for the interview schedule. Several open-ended probing questions were included to identify all the reasons why a facility did not conduct satisfaction surveys, perceived problems with the surveys, and preferred changes in the survey process. A professional interviewer was trained to use the schedule, and she conducted pretests with a small number of facilities that were not in the study sample.

Pretest results indicated that it was extremely difficult to obtain interviews with the administrators of larger facilities, a finding that has been reported by other researchers in Ohio (Robert Atchley, personal communication, November 6, 1998). In most cases, the interviewer was referred to the staff member who had responsibility for the survey, usually someone from Social Services or Admissions. These individuals often requested that the interviewer fax the survey form and they would complete it when they had time available. Consequently, the original telephone interview form was modified into a questionnaire format, and this form was used when faxed versions were requested. A tally showed that 25 of the interviews were received by fax transmission, while 56 were completed by telephone.

The final sample included 46 facilities from the original sample, with the remaining 35 facilities drawn from the replacement pool, resulting in a total of 81 facilities. There were ten facilities that were selected but not included in the final sample, because they did not return the questionnaire by the established deadline for data collection. The sample response rate declined by size of facility, with 65% (24) of the small facilities responding, compared to 42% (14) of the medium size, and 38% (8) of the large facilities. The 51% response rate from the original sample is primarily attributable to facility staff not returning phone calls and faxes in a timely manner.

OHIO SURVEY FINDINGS

The 81 facilities in the sample range in size from 29 to 384 beds, with an average of 131 beds. Most (87%) provide skilled nursing care, 75% offer intermediate care, and 54% provide rehabilitative care. A large majority (82%) are for-profit homes, and 97% accept Medicaid residents. In terms of their location, 22% are in urban areas, 38% are in suburban areas and 40% are in rural areas. Most (72%) report having one or more managed care contracts.

Almost 80% of the sample (64 of the 81 facilities) conduct satisfaction surveys. Of the 17 that do not, most are small facilities, where the respondents noted that they get direct feedback on a regular basis from residents, and that most had lived in their facilities for many years. In those facilities conducting satisfaction surveys, 95% survey both residents and residents' families, generally on an annual basis. A large majority (70%) only solicit information from cognitively alert residents. An additional 20% send satisfaction surveys annually to other persons, such as employees, physicians, and medical staff members, and contract agencies.

In facilities in which annual surveys are done, the respondents reported that it takes 4 weeks, on average, to complete the survey process. However, the times reported ranged from 1 to 12 weeks, with respondents from one out of four facilities noting that it takes 6 weeks to 3 months to complete the survey process.

About one-third (30%) of the facilities conduct ongoing satisfaction surveys with residents. Only one facility reported doing ongoing satisfaction surveys with residents' family members. Several types of ongoing resident surveys are used. One type involves conducting interviews sequentially by unit throughout the year until every resident in the facility is surveyed by year's end. Other facilities randomly select small samples of residents throughout the year for the survey, while others continuously survey residents on certain units, such as short-term rehabilitation and post-acute care.

Almost three-fourths (72%) of the 64 facilities that conduct satisfaction surveys do one or more on an in-house basis, and a majority (62%) also use an outside consultant for one or more surveys. Among those using out-side sources, the most common source is OHCA (52%), followed by private firms (33%), and the facility's corporate office (15%). Among facilities that do in-house surveys, 71% designed their own satisfaction survey form. Among the twelve facilities that use other sources for the survey, five use the corporate office's survey form(s), two adapted the OHCA form, and five have taken or adapted forms from miscellaneous sources. The staff person most commonly responsible for overseeing the satisfaction survey is from Social Services/Admissions (56%), followed by facility administrators (23%). Some others who were mentioned as responsible for the survey include administrative assistants, discharge coordinators, and directors of volunteers.

Three methods for collecting survey data from residents and families were investigated: mailed questionnaires, phone surveys, and in-person interviews. Results show that facilities use a variety of methods and a number use multiple methods to survey residents, and the method(s) used varies in relation to the resident's length of stay. Mailed questionnaires and phone interviews following discharge are generally used for short-stay residents who received post-acute care and/or rehabilitation. Long-term care residents, in contrast, generally receive in-person interviews.

Findings on methods used with residents show that 60% of the facilities use in-person interviews with pre-screened residents, 55% use mailed questionnaires and 5% use phone interviews with residents. In about half (47%) of the facilities in which in-person interviews are conducted with residents, volunteers are enlisted to collect the information. Regarding methods used with the family members of residents, 11% of the facilities conduct in-person interviews, while 95% use mailed questionnaires and 14% do phone interviews. In 20% of the facilities in which mailed questionnaires are used, follow-up phone calls or mailings are used with residents and families that do not respond to the initial mailing in order to increase the response rate. Overall, the estimated response rate to the surveys averages 58%; however, estimates range from a low of 5% to a high of 100%. When responses are broken down by residents and families, it appears that, on average, the response rate for residents is 60%, while it is 45% for families.

According to 98% of the facilities that conduct satisfaction surveys, the primary reason is for quality improvement. Hence, one might expect that the results would be distributed to all facility staff. However, findings show that this varies. In 97% of the facilities, management staff receive the results; in 89% of the cases, governance bodies (e.g., Boards of Trustees or Directors) also receive them; and employees receive the results in 77% of the facilities. Only about one-third of the facilities (36%) share the survey results with residents and with residents' families.

In terms of overall satisfaction with the survey process, most respondents (58%) report that they are "somewhat satisfied," while 39% say they are "very satisfied" and only 3% say they are "somewhat dissatisfied." Possible reasons for the moderate level of satisfaction are shown in Table 7.1 which displays the frequency with which respondents either agreed or disagreed that their facility experienced various problems with the survey process or outcomes. Most of the problems reported relate to a common issue: the information obtained did not provide an adequate knowledge base for guiding the quality improvement process and addressing residents' and family members' sources of dissatisfaction with care. The problem mentioned most frequently by 34% of the respondents is the low response rate, which raises doubts in the minds of facility staff about the reliability of the information. The low response rate seems surprising in view of the fact that the average response rate for the 81 facilities is 58%. Yet, facilities that have 100% participation as their goal may be disappointed by a rate that is any lower, or possibly by the lower rate of response from residents' family members.

The second most common complaint mentioned is the quality of information obtained from the survey, which refers to the information's worth or value compared to its timeliness, usefulness, clarity, and depth that were covered in the other items shown in Table 7.1. These complaints about the survey information may reflect the tension between using a more detailed form that will increase the quality, amount, and clarity of information necessary for guiding the quality improvement process, and avoiding a lengthy interview or questionnaire that would dissuade residents and family members from completing it.

Table 7.1 Reported problems with the satisfaction surveys

Reported problems	%	(N)
Low response rate	34	21
Quality of the information	25	16
Amount of time involved	21	13
Timeliness of the information	18	11
Clarity or usefulness of the information	15	9
Insufficient information	13	8
Lack of application to QI	8	5
Financial cost	5	3

Although we did not pursue additional types of information collection that facilities may be using based on the general survey results, it is possible that follow-up focus groups or phone calls with residents and their families are being used by some to gather more detailed information about a program or service that receives relatively low marks in the general satisfaction survey. These methods can be considered supplemental to the survey and help to determine more precisely what it is about a service, such as food or laundry, that should be targeted for change. Additionally, the use of these methods can by itself result in increased satisfaction because of the closer attention given to the nature of consumer complaints.

Large percentages of respondents also complained about the amount of time taken to complete the survey and, on a similar note, the timeliness of the information. Unless sufficient resources are devoted to the survey process, the time required to complete the work will be extended. As a result, there is a lower chance that complaints can be addressed in a timely manner if months pass from the collection of the data to the time the results are available to take corrective action. For this reason, some facilities opt to conduct the ongoing surveys discussed previously, so that satisfaction information is continually available from samples of residents or residents in different parts of the facility.

The fewest complaints concern: (a) the cost of the survey, possibly because OHCA provides it at no charge and most facilities manage to conduct it with current staff and volunteers; and (b) the failure to use the information in the quality improvement process. The overwhelming majority of facilities (91%) reported that the survey results are used for quality improvement purposes, although the extent to which the use of this information actually led to improved services was not ascertained.

Respondents from 20 out of the 64 facilities (33%) that conduct satisfaction surveys recommend changes in the survey process. The two most widely endorsed recommendations by one-third of these respondents are to improve the quality of the information obtained and provide more timely results. These findings are consistent with the complaints about the survey that were reported earlier. Other recommendations made by respondents are better automation of the data, including more people in the survey, and conducting the survey more frequently.

Lastly, we examined a variety of factors such as size, location, and for- and non-profit status that may be related to the use of satisfaction surveys and complaints about the survey process. The only factor that has a statistically significant relationship to conducting satisfaction surveys is whether or not the facility has managed care contracts. Virtually all facilities that have these contracts use satisfaction surveys, compared to 85% of those without managed care contracts ($p < .03$).

SUMMARY AND DISCUSSION

Findings from the survey of 81 randomly selected nursing homes confirm that satisfaction surveys are being widely used in Ohio facilities and are used primarily for quality improvement purposes. However, the proprietary facilities in the State of Ohio are unique in the support available from their statewide association for conducting satisfaction surveys. Subsequent discussions with staff members at state associations in other Midwestern states, such as Illinois, indicate that plans are underway to replicate the services provided by OHCA to their member facilities.

In most of the Ohio facilities, both residents and their family members are targeted for the survey, and one out of five facilities in the sample also includes other groups such as employees and medical staff. Our data suggest that most facilities use a variety of approaches to obtain satisfaction information, including designing their own in-house survey form, contracting with outside sources such as OHCA for annual surveys of residents and families, and utilizing an ongoing survey process for shorter-stay residents. As expected, these diverse methods are necessary because of the different types of residents served and their varying lengths of stay.

Overall, the respondents from the facilities express moderate levels of satisfaction with the survey process and outcomes. Chief among their complaints are the low response rate and the quality and timeliness of the survey information. Similarly, most recommendations for change in the survey process center on improving the quality of the information and making the findings more immediately available to staff so they can take appropriate action quickly and respond to consumer complaints.

While it may be expected that skilled nursing facilities would initiate satisfaction surveys of their own volition for the variety of reasons discussed in previous chapters, study data suggest that external pressures lead many of them to undertake the survey process. Facilities with managed care contracts, for example, are more likely to use satisfaction surveys than are those without such contracts. Discussions with staff from the state associations also indicate that the momentum to provide satisfaction survey services did not build until more of their members sought accreditation and managed care contracts, or received pressure from their governing boards to monitor consumer satisfaction.

Our experience attempting to conduct phone surveys with the facility administrators or the staff member responsible for the survey underscores the multiple demands and time constraints under which these individuals work. Clearly, the time and resources needed to improve the scope, quality, and timeliness of the consumer satisfaction survey data are in short supply, if available at all. For example, a common complaint is the low response rate; yet only a minority of facilities make follow-up contacts with residents and their families who do not respond in order to increase participation.

Efforts to improve the quality of the survey information require psychometric work on the data, yet few if any of the facilities have the technical proficiency or staff to carry this out. In fact, discussions with staff from the state associations indicate that they too lack the time and skills to establish the validity and reliability of the questions used in their surveys. There are national organizations, such as Healthcare Research Systems, National Research Corporation, and SMR: Century Business Services, that can be engaged to conduct satisfaction surveys, and they have established psychometric properties for their survey items. However, these contracts require more of a financial commitment by facilities, and may not be customized to facility needs. Data from this survey suggest that most facilities are unable or unwilling to expend additional monies for satisfaction survey efforts: existing staff supplemented by volunteers are used, and, at times, the free services of the state association.

To solve the problem of untimely information, two other approaches are used by some facilities in the study sample, most commonly when they contract with an outside consultant for the survey. One approach is to randomly select smaller samples of residents and their family members from throughout the house on a quarterly basis for the survey; the other is to conduct the survey unit by unit throughout the year. Both approaches provide more continuous information on consumer satisfaction for facility staff to use in the quality improvement process. They also can provide more immediate feedback about the impact of quality improvement changes that are made in response to consumer complaints from one quarterly survey to the next.

An important issue that this research did not address, and, that should be examined in future research, is the effectiveness of the survey process and results for improving services. Empirical attention needs to be given to the extent to which the results are actually incorporated into the quality improvement process and how, in turn, services are amended or refined in response to consumer complaints. Additionally, information is lacking about trends in consumer satisfaction rates over time in facilities that conduct satisfaction surveys.

Based on the survey findings, we have two concluding recommendations. First, areas identified as problematic in the general satisfaction survey need to be more thoroughly investigated to obtain the detailed information necessary for quality improvement. General satisfaction surveys cannot provide the level of detail on a specific service, type of staff, or environmental feature that is required to develop an adequate action plan. Several approaches can be taken to obtain more in-depth information: conducting focus groups with residents and their families on the specific area, using follow-up phone calls or mailed questionnaires that probe the nature of the problem, or using resident councils and/or family education or other organized family groups to obtain the information.

The latter approach has particular appeal because it engages both residents and their family members in the development of the quality improvement action plan. This can have decided advantages, such as empowering residents and families, making them partners in the quality improvement process, and underscoring that their complaints have been heard and action will be taken.

This leads to our second recommendation. Survey results should routinely be shared with all residents and families, along with a corresponding action plan. According to the study data, little more than one-third of the facilities currently provide residents and families with a report on the satisfaction survey results. When residents and family members take the time to complete the survey, they deserve to be informed about the results and the effects of their efforts. Furthermore, these reports are likely to reinforce the importance of their contribution and encourage them to continue to complete surveys, thereby increasing the response rate over time.

REFERENCES

Zarit, S. H., & Whitlatch, C. J. (1992). Institutional placement: Phases of transition. *The Gerontologist*, 32(5), 665–672.

P A R T **II**

PRACTICE

AN OVERVIEW OF THE PROCESS OF CONDUCTING CONSUMER SATISFACTION SURVEYS IN NURSING FACILITIES

Farida K. Ejaz

INTRODUCTION

This chapter deals with the process of conducting consumer satisfaction surveys in nursing facilities. It is primarily focused on providing a "do-it-yourself" approach, and deals with issues such as how important staff commitment is before undertaking such an enormous task; whom the consumer is in the nursing home; methods for surveying consumers; tips for developing an instrument in-house; pretesting and piloting instruments; establishing reliability and validity; what tasks are involved in the actual implementation of the survey; how to analyze the data; and how to present the findings. It concludes with a case example of a nursing facility that designed and conducted its own survey. Since the tasks involved in developing an in-house survey are numerous, and require expertise and skill in survey methodology, this chapter is only meant as a overview of the process of conducting consumer satisfaction surveys in long-term care (LTC). Toward that end, the references may be used to obtain more detailed information on the tasks involved.

OBTAINING COMMITMENT FROM UPPER MANAGEMENT

The first step in planning consumer satisfaction surveys is to obtain commitment from staff, especially administrative staff, to "buy" into the utility of conducting these surveys (see Figure 8.1, pp. 150–151). This can be a challenging task, because the nursing home industry as a whole has been slower than the hospital/acute care industry to formally assess the consumer's perspective on quality of care (Zinn, Lavizzo-Mourey, & Taylor, 1993). With the current trend of nursing homes applying for accreditation from the Joint Commission on Accreditation of Healthcare Organization (JCAHO) which requires a facility to have a formal complaint management system, it is likely that the industry at large, including nursing home administrative staff, will become more receptive to utilizing satisfaction surveys. Furthermore, many nursing facilities today are competing for managed care contracts to care for elderly Medicare patients who need a step-down unit once they are discharged from an acute care hospital. One way of proving to managed care companies that nursing facilities provide high-quality services is to demonstrate that they are attentive to the perspective of consumers, that their consumers are satisfied with their services, and that there is a commitment to improve services based on the input of consumers.

Therefore, a well-designed, well-implemented, and well-utilized satisfaction measurement system can help nursing home administrative staff to improve the quality of their clinical and administrative activities. Ultimately these data must be used to improve quality and increase satisfaction levels. At a basic level, nursing facilities can use the information from such surveys for quality assurance purposes (i.e., to identify areas that are excellent and those that require improvement). The areas of excellence can be used to boost employee morale, for publicity and advertising, and for negotiating managed care contracts.

The problematic areas/criticisms could be used positively to develop action plans to address and improve quality of care. Such action plans can be addressed at the facility level or may be broken down at the department level for the sake of manageability. Both excellent and problematic areas can be used to provide feedback to residents and families to ensure that these groups are aware that their opinions are being taken seriously by management (see Chapter 11 by Slavin and Carter on methods of providing feedback).

PREPARING DIFFERENT LEVELS OF STAFF

Consumer satisfaction surveys may be viewed as a threat by staff who provide hands-on care or those who provide ancillary services. Since it is a form of evaluation, some staff might view it as a way to lose their job or becoming demoralized by angry, vengeful, or difficult consumers. Strasser and Davis (1991) have suggested many methods to allay staff anxiety and resistance to such surveys. According to Strasser and Davis, management needs to take a public position that the purpose of consumer satisfaction surveys is not to harm staff, and that they would work with staff to collaboratively resolve and improve problem areas. As a precautionary step, these authors advise never to show one department head the satisfaction scores of another department head; besides breaching confidentiality, this is likely to generate hostility and anger between department heads. Further, it is always important to emphasize that consumer satisfaction data, although extremely important, are only one facet of measuring and evaluating a department's performance.

WHO IS THE CONSUMER IN NURSING HOME SETTINGS?

One of the problems of conducting consumer satisfaction surveys in nursing facilities is that the majority of the direct consumers, i.e., long-term care (LTC) elderly residents, suffer from some form of dementia. It is believed that as many as 50–90% of nursing home residents suffer from some form of dementia (German, Rovner, Burton, Brant, & Clark, 1992), and therefore, may not be capable of answering questions on the quality of their care, or may only be able to provide limited information. One method of circumventing the problem of interviewing residents who are cognitively impaired (for information on how to interview cognitively impaired residents, see Chapter 9 by Uman et al.) is to interview surrogates, i.e., family, appointed custodians, or concerned friends (FCF) (Kleinsorge & Koenig, 1991).

Even though FCFs often present very different perspectives from residents when evaluating care (Aharony & Strasser, 1993; Kleinsorge & Koenig, 1991; Lavizzo-Mourey, Zinn, & Taylor, 1992), nursing facilities still find it reasonable to target these surrogates for their input on the services and care received by their relatives. This is because some FCFs visit often and may be quite involved in the care provided to their relative (Zarit & Whitlatch, 1992). In surveying families as surrogates, it is important to assess the information provided by them in the context of their familiarity with the care and services provided to their relative. One indication of this is to evaluate the information in the context of the frequency of their visits.

Another critical issue in surveying families is to understand whether they are speaking about their own perception of the care provided to their relative, or whether they are attempting to capture the perspective of their relative. A simple question to this effect could be asked at the end of the survey: "Whose views are expressed in this survey?" (Strasser, Schweikhart, Welch, & Burge, 1995). Response categories to this question could range from: family member's view, and family member's perception of resident's view (it may be important to find the type of relationship, be it spouse, son, daughter, son/daughter-in-law, nephew/niece, other, or friend so that differences in the satisfaction levels of such groups can be assessed, if needed). Alternatively, the instructions can be used to ask family members to describe their own perceptions of the quality of care provided to their relatives, or their view of how their relative perceives his/her care. Despite taking such precautions, one might still be unclear as to whose opinions are being expressed in the survey, because there is literature to suggest that families/proxies cannot really separate their own views/judgments from what they "think" their relative's views are (Seckler, Meier, Mulvihill, & Paris, 1991). Even though this confusion may exist, it is still important to survey FCFs because of the reasons cited earlier, and because they might capture some aspects of care that residents might overlook.

One method of comparing similarities and differences between FCF and resident perceptions of care is to survey a cohort of cognitively alert residents and assess their views of the services and care provided to them. The views expressed by this cohort of residents can be linked specifically to the data from their families, and differences in perceptions can be analyzed. This information may provide clues as to the extent to which resident perceptions differ from those of FCFs (Lavizzo-Mourey, et al., 1992).

Even if one does not link a subset of family and resident data, it is a good idea to survey residents of long-term care facilities as well, since they are the direct consumers of such services and care. In fact, implementation of the Omnibus Budget Reconciliation Act (OBRA) in 1990 was spurred by a study conducted by The Institute of Medicine (IOM) in 1986, that found that the voices of residents are often overlooked, sidestepped, and ignored in LTC facilities (Institute of Medicine, 1986). Another study conducted by the National Citizens' Coalition for Nursing Home Reform (NCCNHR) in 1985 found that it was critical to "listen to" how nursing home residents defined quality of nursing home life and care, and called for a refocus of the survey process from a paper orientation that examined the structure and processes of care, to a resident-rights orientation (NCCNHR, 1985). Therefore, it is imperative to include the resident perspective in understanding consumer satisfaction.

A third group of consumers in the nursing facility is the short-term resident who has been discharged from an acute care setting (usually a Medicare, Part A patient). With the emergence of managed care contracts, nursing homes are likely to see a greater proportion of such patients enter their facilities. The services provided to these patients have similarities to those provided to LTC residents, but they often have a different focus. For example, some of these patients may have had an acute episode in the hospital (such as a stroke or a heart attack), but have to be prepared to go back to living either alone or with their spouse/family in the community. They may require intensive rehabilitation services, such as physical and occupational therapy. They may need to learn basic skills for coping independently in the community. It is likely that the survey for this group of consumers will have a different focus than that of the families and resident of LTC services. Since the short-term, post-acute patients may not suffer from the same degree of dementia as LTC residents, it may be possible to directly survey them rather than to survey their families or friends.

In summary therefore, three types of "consumers"—families, LTC residents and short-term residents—may be surveyed in nursing home settings. See Table 8.1 for a description of the consumer in long-term care and suggested techniques to interviews such consumers. Since one may not be able to survey all consumers, it is important to draw a sample that is representative of the population being surveyed in the LTC facility/(ies). For a summary of such issues, refer to Table 8.2.

DEVELOPING THE INSTRUMENT/S

There are numerous strategies to develop an instrument (the instrument can also be called a survey form, a questionnaire, a tool, and a measure). The easiest method is to purchase one from an agency specializing in marketing and conducting nursing home satisfaction surveys. It is advisable to ask the agency (see Chapter 6) as to whether it has tested the instrument on existing nursing home populations, evaluated its psychometric properties, tested it for reliability and validity, and refined it over the course of its experience in conducting such surveys. A facility could use such a

Table 8.1 Selecting the Consumer: Relevant Techniques to Conduct Consumer Satisfaction Surveys in Long-Term Care (LTC)

Consumers of LTC Services	Reasons for Selecting Consumer	Suggested Techniques to Survey Consumers	Advantages of Techniques	Disadvantages of Techniques	Alternatives or improvements to Techniques
1. RESIDENTS OF LTC SERVICES (a) Cognitively alert residents (b) Cognitively impaired residents	• Direct consumers of LTC services • Opinions of consumers are often ignored[2,3] • OBRA (1987) emphasized resident rights movement • Same as above	• Face-to-face interviews (with residents who have been screened for cognitive abilities based on staff judgment; MDS+ data; or a screening tool like the Mini Mental State Examination)[1] • See Chapter 9 by Uman et al.	• Interviewers can access residents who may suffer from visual or hearing impairments • Residents have opportunity to ask questions • Interviewer has opportunity to persuade residents to participate • Interviewer can observe residents in natural setting	• Expensive • Time-consuming • Difficult to schedule appointments with residents	• Train and use volunteers or students • Students may be paid, volunteer, or earn credits

Table 8.1 (*continued*)

Consumers of LTC Services	Reasons for Selecting Consumer	Suggested Techniques to Survey Consumers	Advantages of Techniques	Disadvantages of Techniques	Alternatives or improvements to Techniques
2. RESIDENTS IN SHORT-TERM REHABILITA-TION PRO-GRAMS (sub-acute or step-down from the acute or hospital setting)	• Same as above • Residents not as cognitively impaired as LTC residents • Needs may differ from LTC residents (focus on rehabilitation to community)	• Face-to-face interviews* (same as above) • Mailed questionnaire (sent within 4–14 days of discharge, allowing residents to assimilate their experience)[5] • Telephone interview* (telephoning within 4–14 days of discharge)	• Same as above • Cheap • Reduces likelihood of socially desirable answers • Respondents can answer at their own pace and leisure • Generally better response rate than mailing	• Same as above • Poor response rates (may typically range from 10–40%) • More expensive than mailing • Not efficient (may take several calls to contact resident or arrange interview) • Not appropriate for hearing-impaired	• Same as above • Increase response rates by sending a reminder notice or calling • Train and use volunteers or students with flexible schedules

Table 8.1 *(continued)*

Consumers of LTC Services	Reasons for Selecting Consumer	Suggested Techniques to Survey Consumers	Advantages of Techniques	Disadvantages of Techniques	Alternatives or improvements to Techniques
3. SURROGATES (family members, friends or legal guardians)	• 50–80% of LTC residents suffer from some form of dementia • Common to survey surrogates • Families care about the well-being of their relatives and remain involved in their care[7]	• Same as above (mail or telephone surveys are most commonly used)	• Same as above	• Discrepancies may occur between family perspective and resident perspective • Difficult for surrogates to separate their own judgements from their impressions of their relative's perspective[4] • Families are often more critical of care than patients[6]	• Use caution in interpreting results from surrogates • Specify whose opinion is being measured (i.e., the surrogate's own perspective, or their impression of their relative's perspective) • Assess differences between types of surrogates • Link data sets of a cohort of residents with their families to assess differences in levels of consumer satisfaction

* *Note.* Only a select number of survey techniques have been listed. For further survey techniques or details on the techniques shown above, please refer to Chapter 6 by Crawford.
References (complete citations are listed at the end of the chapter):
1. Folstein, Folstein, & McHugh, 1975   2. IOM 1986   3. NCCNHR, 1985   4. Seckler et al., 1991
5. Strasser & Davis, 1991   6. Strasser et al., 1995   7. Zarit & Whitlatch, 1992

generic instrument and add a few questions specifically relevant to their own nursing facility. If a facility does not find an existing instrument that addresses its particular needs, and is committed to developing its own instrument, has the resources in terms of staff time and competency, or is willing to hire a consultant to help out, then some of the following processes may be kept in mind.

As a first step, a facility can set up a multidisciplinary committee (with a project coordinator) comprised of staff and volunteers to work on developing the instrument. This committee could be responsible for reviewing the literature on consumer satisfaction with LTC services, developing and pretesting its own instrument, conducting the survey, and perhaps, even analyzing the data (see Figure 8.1). Depending on how much and what exactly a nursing facility wishes to accomplish, members of this committee could include staff/board members or volunteers who have some experience in developing and conducting surveys. One could also invite a staff member from a local university (with experience in survey methodology) to serve on the committee. Or, a facility could hire a person with expertise in survey methodology to consult on their committee, if they do not have a person with such expertise in-house.

The committee would be responsible for reviewing the literature on consumer satisfaction in long-term care (see Chapters 3 and 5, and Appendixes I–IV of this book). Since this literature may be meager, the committee can draw inferences from the literature on consumer satisfaction with acute care services. It may be necessary to consult with other facilities that have conducted consumer satisfaction surveys locally or nationally and get their perspective on what to include in an instrument. Some nursing facilities have research departments (such as Menorah Park Center for the Aging and The Benjamin Rose Institute in Cleveland, Ohio, the Hebrew Home of Greater Washington, in Washington, DC, the Hebrew Rehabilitation Center in Boston, or the Nerken Center for Geriatric Research at the Parker Jewish Geriatric Institute in New York) and may serve as good sources of information on the subject. The committee may also contact national organizations such as the American Association of Homes, Housing and Services for the Aging (AAHSA) and the local body of the American Health Care Association (AHCA). Some of these organizations may be willing to share their instruments. Since most of these instruments are copyrighted, the facility must be careful not to plagiarize items, by obtaining permission or setting up a purchase agreement, if it decides to use some items or the entire instrument. See Figure 8.1 for a step-by-step process for conducting consumer satisfaction surveys in house in long-term care settings.

Table 8.2 Research Methods: Some Relevant Issues in Conducting Consumer Satisfaction Surveys in Long-Term Care (LTC)

Method	Dfinition & Rationale	Techniques	Precautions and/or examples
1. SAMPLING	• A scientific process to select a sub-set of respondents from a larger group or the target population receiving the same services and care. (Rationale: It may be too expensive and time-consuming to survey everyone in the population).	• See below	• Avoid mixing different groups (i.e., LTC residents, short-term residents, and surrogates come from different groups or populations, and separate samples have to be drawn from each of these groups). The groups remain distinct during the entire survey process.
Probability Sampling	• Method to select a subset of the population in which each member has an equal chance of being selected.	• Need to have a population list to select from. • Can select via: *Simple random sampling:* Flipping a coin; or, drawing names from a hat or a bowl; or assigning numbers to the list and selecting only those that get selected based on a table of random numbers. *Systematic random sampling:* Every kth (e.g., 10th or 20th) person is selected from the list of the population. For example, if a sample of 100 was considered desirable from a population of 1,000 residents, the sampling interval would be 10. *Stratified random sampling:* Dividing the population into smaller sub-groups (such as dementia care units or other sub-groups of special interest) and selecting random samples from each group.	• Considered the most basic form of random sampling. Can lead to sampling biases such as over- or under-representation of certain sections of the population. • Can lead to biases if there is a method in which the population is divided (for example in units/floors), leading to over- or under-representation of the population. • Attempts to take care of the above problem, since simple random sampling might not have given equal or adequate representation to these subgroups.

Table 8.2 (continued)

Method	Dfinition & Rationale	Techniques	Precautions and/or examples
Sample Size	• Selecting a sample size that is representative of the population and large enough to examine the issues at hand.	• Generally five factors affect sample size: 1) Research hypothesis 2) Level of precision or accuracy of results desired 3) Homogeneity of the population 4) Type of sampling technique used	• It is sometimes assumed that a larger sample is more representative than a smaller one. However, calculating an appropriate sample size is more complicated.
2. INSTRU-MENTATION TESTING FOR RELIA-BILITY	• Reliability refers to the extent to which the instrument is stable and consistent in producing results over time.	• *Test-retest reliability:* A number of subjects respond to the instrument and a few days later respond to it again. The correlation between these two administrations is then calculated. The higher the correlation between the scores, the better the reliability. • *Inter-rater reliability:* Two or more inter-viewers interview the same respondent. The correlation between the scores obtained by the different interviewers is calculated. The higher the correlation of the scores of the interviewers, the better the reliability • *Internal consistency:* Identifies factors or themes around which items cluster together (using Cronbach's alpha). In one instrument, it is possible to have different factors, those items that cluster around administrative issues might form one factor, whereas those that cluster around direct-care services such as nursing and social work, could form another factor.	• The subjects interviewed during the first and second phases have to be the same. * Both interviews have to be conducted within a short time frame to avoid bias from extraneous factors such as changes in the subjects condition. • The interviewers have to inter-view the same subjects or observe the same subjects at the same time (but conduct their rat-ings independently of each other). • Factors should make conceptual and/or theoretical sense.

Table 8.2 *(continued)*

Method	Dfinition & Rationale	Techniques	Precautions and/or examples
3. INSTRUMEN-TATION TESTING FOR VALIDITY	8 Validity refers to the process of the instrument actually measuring the concepts it intended to measure.	• *Face validity:* A group of professionals or experts in the field, or a focus group of subjects evaluate whether the items "appear" to be measuring the concept in question. • *Criterion-related validity:* Whether the instrument is correlated to another criterion measuring the same/similar issues. • *Construct validity:* Whether the instrument correlates with other instruments related to it in theory and the extent to which its various theoretical dimensions are captured in the instrument being developed.	• Considered to be the most basic and therefore, most crude form of establishing validity. • The criterion against which the instrument is being measured has to be related. For example, scores on overall satisfaction with services should be highly correlated with positive referrals to others. • Some researchers are attempting to correlate quality indicators based on the MDS+ with satisfaction survey results. This has potential for establishing construct validity.

* *Note.* For further details on sampling techniques, testing an instrument for reliability and validity, please refer to any textbook on research/survey methods (including Monette, Sullivan, & DeJong, 1994, or Rubin & Babbie, 1997).

After the review of the literature is complete, a facility may want to incorporate the perspective of its particular type of clientele by ensuring that the instrument covers all areas that are important and relevant to its service recipients (Applebaum, 1989; Geron, 1998; Miller-Hohl, 1992; Riley, Fortinsky, & Coburn, 1992). Too often, surveys present the viewpoints of the researchers, or those of upper management, rather than of consumers. One method of involving consumers is via a focus group. A focus group uses a planned discussion to allow members to discuss a specific topic in their own terms (Krueger, 1994). If one is trying to develop an instrument for evaluating consumer satisfaction with LTC services, members of a focus group could be comprised of a group of nursing home residents and/or their families. It is important that members of the focus group are representative of the specific nursing home population that is being surveyed. Depending on the nature of the population, it may be necessary to ensure that different minority or racially diverse groups are represented in the focus group. Some facilities might want to use staff focus groups to understand the type of information that will be useful to staff to improve the care provided to residents. Usually a group of 8 to 10 members is optimal, and ideally, a professionally experienced person conducts the focus group to ensure that members feel free to express issues that are relevant and of concern to them (Geron, 1998). The task at hand is to remain focused on understanding the important aspects of care and services (as defined by the group) and not to get sidetracked with other issues that might emerge as a result of these discussions.

Important areas of concern to consumers can be identified using the information provided by the focus group. (See Chapter 3 by Soberman et al. on domains/areas of consumer satisfaction). Based on the combination of the information obtained from the focus group and the review of the literature, a set of questions (also called items) may be developed. In developing the questions, the focus should be on the target group to be surveyed, be it families, LTC residents, or short-term residents.

It is advisable to develop specific questions for each area, rather than developing just a single item, global measure of satisfaction in each area. Global measures include questions such as: "Overall, how satisfied are you with the services and care you are receiving?" Since satisfaction with long-term care is a complex and multidimensional concept, single, global judgments are not recommended (Geron, 1998). Multiple item measures are more sensitive and increase the chances of identifying differences between services or programs and in pinpointing the specific areas that need change (DeVellis, 1991; Spector, 1992; Stewart & Ware, 1992). Examples of multiple item measures in the area of activities could include the extent to which residents/families are satisfied with the number of activities provided, the

*7 INCORPORATE PERSPECTIVE OF CONSUMER
- Conduct focus groups with consumers (8-10 members) to identify key questions & issues to include in survey
  areas/issues important to service recipients
- Include minorities in focus group to get diverse perspectives

*8 DEVELOP FIRST DRAFT OF INSTRUMENT
- Include important questions base on literature & focus groups
- Use specific questions, rather than global measures
- Develop questions that are easy to interpret from the point of view of implementing change
- Decide on response categories for close-ended questions
- Develop open-ended questions for comments
- Keep instrument short, simple, & easy to complete

*8 PRE-TEST INSTRUMENT
- Use group/s of consumers to evaluate & critique instrument
- Identify questions that are confusing, unimportant to consumers
- Identify areas/issues that were excluded
- Or, use first year survey as pilot data
- Establish reliability & validity of instrument (Table 2)
- Refine instrument
- Judge time taken to complete instrument

*9 FINALIZE INSTRUMENT
- Select sample (Table 1)
- Pilot test refined instrument with a group of 50-100 respondents (may be necessary if a large number of facilities are involved)

*10 CONDUCT SURVEY
- Develop cover letter
- Obtain informed consent
- Select sample (Table 1)
- Mail survey / set up time for face-to-face or telephone surveys
- Use follow-up techniques to encourage non-respondents to participate (e.g. send reminder notices or make phone calls)

*11 ANALYZE DATA
- Enter information in a database program (for larger data sets, double entry is recommended)
- Handle missing information
- Run simple statistics (means & percentages)
- Crosstabulate data by unit or floor to focus on certain areas (need large number of respondents for this to be meaningful)
- Adhere to timeline for completion of survey

*12 PRESENT FINDINGS
- Report findings to Board of Trustees, Administration & staff
- Report findings & plans of action to respondents (families, surrogates, & residents)
- Use visual aids (bar graphs, pie charts)

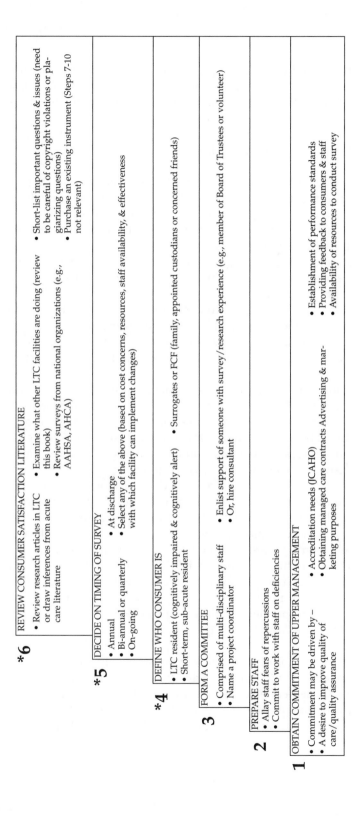

*6 REVIEW CONSUMER SATISFACTION LITERATURE
- Review research articles in LTC or draw inferences from acute care literature
- Examine what other LTC facilities are doing (review this book)
- Review surveys from national organizations (e.g., AAHSA, AHCA)
- Short-list important questions & issues (need to be careful of copyright violations or plagiarizing questions)
- Purchase an existing instrument (Steps 7-10 not relevant)

*5 DECIDE ON TIMING OF SURVEY
- Annual
- Bi-annual or quarterly
- On-going
- At discharge
- Select any of the above (based on cost concerns, resources, staff availability, & effectiveness with which facility can implement changes)

*4 DEFINE WHO CONSUMER IS
- LTC resident (cognitively impaired & cognitively alert)
- Short-term, sub-acute resident
- Surrogates or FCF (family, appointed custodians or concerned friends)

3 FORM A COMMITTEE
- Comprised of multi-disciplinary staff
- Name a project coordinator
- Enlist support of someone with survey/research experience (e.g., member of Board of Trustees or volunteer)
- Or, hire consultant

2 PREPARE STAFF
- Allay staff fears of repercussions
- Commit to work with staff on deficiencies

1 OBTAIN COMMITMENT OF UPPER MANAGEMENT
- Commitment may be driven by –
- A desire to improve quality of care/quality assurance
- Accreditation needs (JCAHO)
- Obtaining managed care contracts Advertising & marketing purposes
- Establishment of performance standards
- Providing feedback to consumers & staff
- Availability of resources to conduct survey

* Refer to text for greater details.

Figure 8.1 Suggested Steps in Conducting Consumer Satisfaction Surveys in Long-Term Care (LTC)

type of activities provided, the timing in which activities are generally held, and the courteousness of the activity staff. One could also include a generic/global question at the end of this subset of questions that measures the overall quality of the activities provided.

Strasser and Davis (1991) offer important suggestions for writing good survey questions, a few of these are discussed below.

1. Avoid leading questions; for example, "Wasn't the food excellent?"
2. Use simple language. Assume that the consumer knows very little about health care concepts, ideas, and language. For example, residents and families may not be familiar with the term "D.O.N." but would be with the term, "Director of Nursing."
3. Attempt to see things through the respondent's eyes. Try to use the language used by consumers in the focus groups so that the questions are not confusing.
4. Be specific when writing the content of the survey questions. The statement "The food was good" is more confusing and nonspecific than the statement "The food was tasty" or "The food temperature was good (hot foods were served hot and cold foods were served cold)."
5. Avoid double-barreled questions. A question must be specific and refer to only one idea. For example, a question that attempts to measure whether the activity staff were courteous and timely in providing the activities is double-barreled, it measures two concepts (courteousness and timeliness), and the analysis will not be able to distinguish which one of these was being rated.
6. Ask both positively and negatively worded questions. For example, "The activity staff were courteous," is positively worded, whereas "The social service staff were not courteous" is negatively worded. One does not need to have a 50:50 split between the positively and negatively worded questions, but a few items worded in the opposite direction to the rest is beneficial. Having both positively and negatively worded items may avoid acquiescent response bias (the desire to please on the part of the respondent). It also lowers the chances of the respondents getting into a response set pattern such as circling all the "agrees" in a questionnaire.

In addition to developing appropriate questions, one has to choose how to measure each item (i.e., choose the type of response categories in the instrument). Closed-ended questions use predetermined response categories to answer the questions, such as: "Very satisfied," "Satisfied," "Neutral," "Dissatisfied," and "Very dissatisfied" (refer to Chapter 6 by

Crawford). Open-ended questions are generally those in which there are no predetermined responses, and consumers can feel free to write in their comments to each question, such as: "What new activities would you enjoy"? Both types of questions are important in the development of a consumer satisfaction instrument, although from an analysis perspective, close-ended questions are easier to code/tabulate than open-ended questions that are more time-consuming to categorize.

For closed-ended questions, it is particularly important to develop appropriate response categories to assess the level of consumer satisfaction with an item. The literature suggests that there are problems with acquiescent response bias in most consumer satisfaction surveys, which means that generally consumers of health care services are happy with the services and positively agree with the questions (La Monica, Oberst, Madea, & Olf, 1986). It is believed that the consistently high skew of satisfaction scores could be a function of respondents giving socially desirable answers; fear of reprisal (especially if they know they will have to return to the same health care setting/provider), or could be a function of using leading questions (e.g., "Weren't you happy with the food?") or inappropriate response categories (too many or too few to chose from) (Cleary & McNeil, 1988; La Monica et al., 1986; Ventura, Fox, Corley, & Mercurio, 1982). Although, one has to provide respondents with options to express the extent of their level of satisfaction or dissatisfaction, one must be wary of providing too many options that can become confusing and tedious, especially to older consumers and their families (many of who are also elderly). On the other hand, too few options may not afford the respondent a category he/she feels comfortable with, and may skew responses to the middle category, since responders generally avoid the extreme responses. Even though Strasser & Davis (1991) recommend the use of a 5- or 7-point continuous interval scale (with a "neutral" midpoint) for assessing consumer satisfaction, this type of scaling might work with FCFs of residents in LTC and with patients in the acute care or sub-acute setting, who are younger and more cognitively alert than long-term care residents. Norton, van Maris, Soberman, and Murray (1996) found that LTC residents were most comfortable with a 3-point scale and Chernoff faces (for example, depicting happiness, sadness, or neutrality) to help with response options. Zinn et al. (1993), had success with a two-step process in which residents were first asked to give a yes/no response to each item, followed by a 4-point rating scale that evaluated the extent to which they agreed or disagreed with a particular item. For further information on closed-ended response categories, refer to Chapter 6 or to The Benjamin Rose Institute's family satisfaction instrument and other instruments descirbed in Appendices I–IV of the book.

With respect to the length of an instrument, it is desirable that it is neither so long that consumers shy away from its mere size, nor so short that it does not ask the questions that are critical to effectively evaluate different services and care provided by a facility. Deciding on what is considered "too long" or "too short" is a matter of personal judgment and experience, therefore, there are no hard and fast rules on this subject. Some facilities consider a one-page (back-to-back) survey to be optimal (be it on letter or legal size paper); others desire a more detailed survey consisting of a couple of pages. The best method to ensure that the instrument is of a reasonable length is to pretest it. Zinn, Lavizzo-Mourey, and Taylor (1993) started with an instrument that had 26 items, but based on their pilot study, observed that the ability to make meaningful distinctions deteriorated as the resident interviews progressed. To remedy this problem, they simplified the phrasing of questions and reduced the items from 26 to 10 and experienced greater success in the subsequent use of the instrument. Other instruments have had success with over 30 or 40 items (Ejaz, Hendrickson, Miranda, & Schur, 1998; Kleinsorge & Koenig, 1991).

Another approach to reducing the length of the instrument is to avoid asking demographic information on the instrument (e.g., age, race, length of stay, and health, status such as number and type of chronic illnesses etc.). Demographic information may be useful to evaluate differences in levels of satisfaction among varied consumer groups (such as minorities versus nonminorities). One method of avoiding asking these questions is to attach identification numbers to the questionnaires and link the data either manually (from resident chart records) or electronically (as with the MDS+ data) to the satisfaction survey data. It is critical that identification numbers are unique identifiers and are not duplicated in subsequent surveys to other residents, as this would impede the possibility of conducting longitudinal analyses of data. Another method suggested by Strasser and Davis (1991) is to use encoding labels that identify pertinent demographic and clinical information onto each individual instrument prior to distribution. Their research showed that despite the danger of the survey not being anonymous, their return rate was the same (in fact, slightly higher) whether the instruments were preencoded or not.

PRETESTING THE INSTRUMENT

Conducting a pretest is an essential stage in the development of a measure or the modification of an existing measure (Spector, 1992). Pretesting refers to the process of using a small group of respondents (from a similar group to which the survey is addressed) to evaluate and critique the questions in the instrument, and the time taken to respond to the survey (Geron, 1998). Consumers respond to the instrument as if they were actually participating in a survey, then they debrief the interviewers regarding questions that they found confusing, difficult to interpret, unimportant, and important but not included. They may also discuss the length of the instrument, if there appears to be problems associated with the time taken to complete the instrument. Usually, a pretest is conducted with 12 to 25 respondents. Based on the input from the pretest, the instrument is further refined and its final length decided (Geron, 1998). The participants in the pretest should not be included in the final survey to avoid exposure to the questions and resulting biases in subsequent administrations of the instruments.

After the instrument is refined, a pilot survey may be conducted if the size of the facility is very large or if numerous facilities are involved. A pilot refers to conducting the survey with a larger group of respondents than used in a pretest. A group of 50–100 respondents, similar to those who will ultimately be administered the instrument, may participate in the pilot (Geron, 1998). It is not uncommon to use the first year of conducting the survey as the pilot to get feedback from respondents regarding the instrument. This might be considered a more cost-effective method of piloting the instrument. Data from the pilot can be used to establish the reliability and validity of the instrument (see Table 8.2 for examples of techniques to establish these). Based on the results, the instrument can be further refined and items modified or deleted.

The refinement of the instrument can be an ongoing process, whether the process is conducted in-house or subcontracted. Nursing home staff can re-evaluate and reassess the instrument if they believe they need to improve it. Items with large amounts of missing information, or questions or issues with which respondents are unfamiliar, require greater scrutiny; and one has to judge whether these questions can be changed, reworded, or deleted from the survey. Once satisfied with the content and the reliability and the validity of the instrument, staff can use the instrument over time to conduct longitudinal analyses, comparing the results with subsequent administrations. If however, further refinement of the instrument is desired, staff must be aware that changing questions will make the longitudinal analyses of those items difficult.

WRITING A GOOD COVER LETTER TO ACCOMPANY THE INSTRUMENT

A cover letter that effectively explains the purpose of the study is an integral part of the protocol of conducting a successful survey. In the case of a mailed survey, this cover letter is usually sent along with the questionnaire, with the goal of addressing general questions associated with the survey. In the case of personal interviews, the cover letter is usually sent a few weeks prior to the interviewer calling respondents for conducting or setting up an appointment to conduct the actual interview. In some facilities, the cover letter and the consent form may be combined, so that the cover letter explains the survey process as well as the issues involved in obtaining informed consent and maintaining confidentiality.

Generally, a cover letter addresses some of the following issues: the purpose of conducting the survey, the importance of obtaining consumer feedback (for quality assurance with the view to target areas for improvement), and of getting honest responses; the timeframe for returning the questionnaires (usually within a few weeks from the mailing); and the name and phone number of the person responsible for conducting the survey, so that respondents can call if they have any questions. It is also advisable to include a self-addressed, stamped envelope with the questionnaire if a mailed survey is being conducted.

The cover letter may be personalized, especially if a facility has a computerized mailing system that includes titles (such as "Mr.," "Mrs.," or "Dr.") with names. There are pros and cons to using a personalized cover letter in a satisfaction survey. Some respondents might like the personal approach, while others might feel threatened by a personalized letter (since they might fear that they could be specifically targeted by staff). Therefore, some facilities use a generic greeting ("Dear Family Member," "Dear Patient") in their letter. (See example in Appendix IV).

The cover letter could be signed by a variety of people. If a facility is using an outside agency, it is probably best that they sign the letter, since it will appear to be more objective (see Chapter 6). If the survey is being conducted in-house, the administrator of the nursing facility, the executive director, the project coordinator, a member of the research team, or a board member could sign it. The decision to choose one of these should be based on the concept of promoting confidence in the survey process and by providing the guarantee that confidentiality will be maintained.

Using an updated address list is especially important when mailing a cover letter to respondents participating in a mailed survey or participating in face-to-face interviews with discharged residents. If a nursing facility has an updated, computerized list of "responsible parties" of current LTC residents, obtained either through admission records or for billing purposes, or a list of former discharged patients/residents, it may not be difficult to generate address labels for these populations. In a proxy survey, a "responsible party" of a LTC resident is usually a family member, most likely a child. It is advisable that social service staff review the list, because these lists may contain the names and addresses of multiple contact persons per resident and therefore, are not likely to be set up to identify the family member who visits the most or is most involved with the care of a resident (especially in the case of billing records). The questionnaire can be sent to the "primary" family member identified by Social Services, or in the case of those residents who do not have involved families, to their friends or guardians. These "primary" surrogates can then fill out the questionnaire in consultation with other family members or friends (the cover letter can explain this approach). From a research standpoint, the issue of bias is reduced when using this approach, since it avoids surveying multiple family members of some residents and not others (in the case of those who have only one contact listed). In one nursing home, Social service staff identified a family member who lived in another state but was considered to have greater contact with the resident (visited the facility for a weekend every month) compared to another family member who lived in town, did not visit often, and did not have a good relationship with the resident. In such cases, one has to trust the judgment of staff to ensure that the appropriate surrogate is selected, although one has to be cautious that staff do not select those who are the least critical of the care being provided to their relatives.

OBTAINING INFORMED CONSENT

Depending on the type of consumer being surveyed (families/surrogates, long- or short-term care residents), it is wise to include some consent procedures as part of the survey process. Consent procedures generally include statements verifying that participation in the survey is strictly voluntary and that nonparticipation would not affect the quality of care being provided by the nursing facility in any way; that respondents are encouraged to answer all questions, but may choose not to answer those they are uncomfortable with; that all responses would be treated in a highly confidential manner and not be revealed to the general staff; that only those responsible for conducting the survey would have access to the identifying information on respondents; and that data would be reported only in aggregate form, without names or identifying information.

In personal interviews, a short statement concerning voluntary participation and confidentiality may be read to respondents, and the respondent may sign the statement or the interviewer may sign the statement stating that he/she obtained consent from the respondent. Usually, the latter process works better with nursing home residents, who are sometimes suspicious of what they are signing, therefore, obtaining verbal consent may be adequate, since the survey process usually does not involve any invasive medical procedures. Verbal consent is also usually obtained in telephone surveys. In the case of mailed surveys, an attached consent form can be included for respondents to sign and return along with their surveys. However, some facilities do not include a separate consent form because they believe that returning the questionnaire is proof of having obtained consent to participate. It is still be important to preface the mailed instrument with a statement that participation is voluntary and that nonparticipation will not involve any negative consequences.

ANALYZING THE DATA

Data analysis (as instrument development) requires professional expertise, and depending on whether a nursing facility has staff who are trained to analyze data, the service may be contracted out to consultants. Or, a simple data-entry program like a spreadsheet, a database or a statistical software package such as SPSS could be used to enter the data manually or to scan it in to a database. One could also try to get student help from a local university. Even in this case, double data entry for a comparison of data is advisable to control for errors. If the data set is large, it might be cheaper to subcontract the data entry to a specialized firm. Such firms can be very cost-effective, fast, efficient, and accurate (since most of them double enter the data).

Once the data are entered, data analyses can begin. As a rule of thumb, one may start with analyzing the data by running simple statistics and measures of central tendency (frequencies, means, and standard deviations) for the closed-ended responses. If there are more than three response categories, the data could also be re-run by collapsing some of the different response categories into broader "Satisfied," "Uncertain," or "Dissatisfied" categories. Cross-tabulation of the data by floor/unit may be conducted by a facility to analyze differences with regard to the care provided on the floors. This, however, requires large numbers of respondents on each floor/unit for it to be statistically meaningful. In larger facilities, this could help administrative staff focus on strategies to improve the care provided on certain floors and units, or to examine why certain floors received more positive ratings than others. In one large nursing facility, negative criticism of a department was narrowed to a problem in one specific unit. Some large facilities/nursing home chains might have large data sets to conduct multivariate analyses to identify the predictors associated with overall satisfaction scores. For example, in a consumer satisfaction survey of families of dementia residents in five nursing facilities in Ohio, negative scores were associated with the perception of nurse assistants being insensitive, and having experienced negative interactions with staff in general (Ejaz, Noelker, & Wells, 1997).

Another issue to keep in mind is the issue of missing data or "not familiar with" items. In some areas, like the effectiveness of rehabilitation therapists, many LTC residents and their families may be unfamiliar with these services, either because the resident is highly mobile and ambulatory, or is bedridden and therefore, has never required the service. On the other hand, if respondents are not familiar with the social worker or with the nurse on duty, one has to re-examine whether this unfamiliarity has to be treated as an area which "needs some improvement" or that it is reflecting "some dissatisfaction" with these services. Specific decisions have to be made for each of the questions that have large amounts of "missing" or "not familiar with" data. These decisions could include whether such proportions of missing data are reasonable, whether they reflect on the service being investigated, or whether the wording of the question could be confusing. In some cases, one has to reconsider whether these questions could be deleted from the surveys in subsequent administrations.

The open-ended comments could be categorized under broad service and care areas, such as Food Services, Nursing, Social Services, and Activities. These categories can be further divided into positive and negative comments in each of the areas, with the corresponding numbers of respondents who stated that comment or a similar comment. In cases where there is confusion over what a comment means, or how it could be classified, help from a third party may be sought and a decision made to either include the comment in one of the identified categories, to place it in the general comments category, to drop it. One can also use qualitative data analysis software (such as Text Smart, NUD*IST, or Ethnograph) to appropriately analyze these data. See Appendix IV of the book for examples of how open-ended questions can be summarized.

For a general preview on conducting and analyzing consumer satisfaction data, one can refer to two interesting articles on the Web published by SPSS, entitled "Using Satisfaction Surveys to Achieve a Competitive Advantage," and "Satisfaction Survey Analysis Using Statistics: You'll Be Delighted with the Results."

PRESENTING THE FINDINGS

Different levels of statistical sophistication or in-depth coverage could be used to present the data to different constituencies. For example, the report for administrative staff may have more detailed findings compared to the report presented to residents. Each report can contain information on the close-ended data (e.g., numbers of respondents and percentages), select findings presented in bar graphs, pie charts, and figures, and information on the open-ended comments. The use of visual aids in demonstrating the findings to administrators, practitioners, and direct care staff will help convey the findings of the closed-ended responses in a concise and interesting manner. Research has demonstrated that some staff enjoy graphical presentations of the data so that they can prioritize areas needing improvement by visually eyeballing the findings (Ejaz, et al., 1998). See Appendix IV for an example of a bar graph.

A systematic protocol can be set up to present the findings. The findings may first be presented either to the executive director of a facility or to the nursing home administrator. The administrator can then set up a management meeting to discuss the findings and to prioritize and develop strategies for areas needing improvement. Families and residents could receive a newsletter that covers the major findings from the survey. In one facility, bar graphs with the positive areas were enlarged and laminated in color. They were placed in the main corridor of the facility with the goal of boosting employee morale and as advertisement for families and visitors (see Chapter 11 by Slavin and Carter for presenting the findings and developing strategic plans based on the findings).

SUMMARY

Whereas conducting a scientifically sound survey process can form the basis for significant quality improvement, an invalid survey may lead to decisions being made based on invalid data. The institute may thus make costly mistakes. Indeed, Strasser and Davis (1991) warn that most health care managers have very little idea how easy it is to design an unreliable, invalid survey, leading to large amounts of misinformation. Toward that end, we caution nursing homes to conduct satisfaction surveys only if they have the expertise to do so in-house or to contract with consultants to help them with the various stages of the process.

A CASE EXAMPLE

In a social service agency in Ohio which has a nursing facility as well as a research department, research staff along with key administrative and direct care staff from the nursing facility set up a committee to develop their own satisfaction survey for families of LTC residents, cognitively alert

LTC residents, and short-term rehabilitation patients. The process began by reviewing some preliminary pilot work done by the nursing facility in the past, as well as obtaining satisfaction instruments from a variety of agencies providing similar services in the area (Social Service staff had requested this information from hospitals, sub-acute units, and nursing homes). Research staff also conducted a literature search on the subject and reviewed journal articles and magazines in long-term care to identify important issues and items. Both practitioners and researchers exchanged relevant surveys and important articles with each other.

Following this review, the committee met to highlight important areas, questions, and issues to keep in mind while developing their own survey. All major service and staff areas in the facility were identified, and questions were developed by the research staff to suit the facility's needs. Questions in each area generally dealt with the quality of the care provided, as well as with the manner (courtesy, compassion, respect) with which the care was provided.

The latter issue was considered critical because the research department had conducted studies on the relationships between families, residents, and nurse assistants in nursing homes and had found that respect and compassion were critical elements of how quality care could be defined (Ejaz et al. 1997). Furthermore, other studies have found that families desire their relatives to be treated not as a work load, but as a person, capable of receiving personalized, sensitive care (Brannon, Cohn, & Smyer, 1990; Duncan & Morgan, 1994).

Some critical areas were subdivided to get more focused information. For example, Nursing was subdivided into professional nursing care (provided by RNs and LPNs) and hands-on, direct care (provided by nurse assistants). This division was considered necessary because having generic questions on nursing care, as some other surveys had done, would not enable the facility to distinguish between the quality of professional versus direct care services. Further, the literature emphasized the distinct role played by nurse assistants in providing the majority of care to nursing home residents, and the importance of the quality of that care (Duncan & Morgan, 1994).

With respect to response categories for rating each area, numerous strategies were reviewed by the Committee. An earlier draft of the survey assessed the extent of satisfaction with services based on a three-point Likert scale. However, in the piloting of the instrument, acquiescent response bias was evident. To avoid this, the Committee decided to use the following three response categories in each area: "No improvement needed," "Some improvement needed," and "A great deal of improvement needed." It was believed that this approach would provide respondents with the opportunity to state whether they believed improvement was needed in an area, rather than asking them about the extent to which they were satisfied. A fourth response category was also added ("Not familiar with") to enable researchers to distinguish between missing data and unfamiliarity with the services or staff (e.g., some families were not familiar with the physical and occupational therapists in a facility; others were not familiar with the dining room experience because their relatives were being tube-fed). This type of scaling eliminated a great deal of the acquiescent response bias and enhanced the variability in responses in subsequent administrations of the instrument (Ejaz et al., 1997).

Following the refinement of the instrument, directors of the different divisions were forwarded a copy of the three different survey instruments that were developed: (1) for all families of LTC residents, (2) for cognitively alert LTC residents, and (3) for short-term, sub-acute discharged patients. The purpose of involving all division heads was twofold: to get their involvement/commitment to the process, and to further refine the instruments based on their suggestions. Division heads were encouraged to share the instrument with their staff during regular meetings and to allay any fear of retaliation. Communication with staff succeeded for the most part, and further refinements were made to the instrument based on their input.

It was decided that the survey would be conducted annually and that all families of LTC residents and discharged patients would receive mailed questionnaires, whereas all cognitively alert residents would be interviewed by a student from a local university (the research department has an on-going affiliation with a local university that helps recruit students interested in gaining research experience in gerontology). Social Service staff on the different floors identified the family member that visited most often and also provided the research staff with a list of all LTC residents that were believed to be cognitively alert enough to be interviewed. The billing department provided a list of all sub-acute, discharged patients within the previous year.

The student from the university was trained by research staff in the principles of interviewing, especially with regard to elderly nursing home residents. Since the survey forms were only one page long, issues of fatigue were not expected. Approximately 35% of the family surveys were returned, only 26% of the short-term discharged patient forms were returned, and 60% of the cognitively alert residents were successfully interviewed. For subsequent administrations, it was decided to mail the short-term discharged patients their instruments within 2 weeks of discharge, rather than on an annual basis. It was further decided to send reminder postcards to nonrespondents in the mailed surveys in order to enhance response rates in future administrations. It was also decided that staff should be involved in scheduling up appointments with the student and the cognitively alert residents (rather than asking the student to "find" the residents). Many of these alert residents were involved in Activities, and it was difficult to pin them down during the day/times the student was available.

The data were entered and analyzed by the research staff. Percentages of responses for each of the closed-ended items were calculated. Following this preliminary analysis, the three response categories were collapsed to two categories: "no improvement" and "improvement needed" (the latter included responses to "some" and "a great deal of improvement") to develop bar and pie charts for visual presentation of the areas of excellence (over 75% of respondents believing "no improvement" was needed) and problematic areas (50% or more respondents believing improvement was needed). The decision to use these cut-off points was not based on any scientific calculations, but based on the administrator's request. These areas are now being tracked longitudinally to examine change over time as demonstrated by subsequent administrations of the survey.

The findings are annually presented to the administrative staff and the board of trustees and are used to develop action plans to address areas of concern. The data have revealed that many respondents are unfamiliar with a number of areas such as Rehabilitation Services, the administrative staff, and the billing department [especially in the case of Medicaid patients], and these questions are being re-evaluated for inclusion in later administrations. A shorter version of the original instrument was also successfully used with five other nursing facilities in the area. A copy of the instrument used with families of LTC residents is included in the Appendix II of this book (when mailed to families, the instrument is copied on legal-size paper and is only one page long, back-to-back). This instrument is copyrighted, and permission has to be obtained to use it in other facilities.

REFERENCES

Aharony, L., & Strasser, S. (1993). Patient satisfaction: What we know about and what we still need to explore. *Medicare Care Review, 50*(1), 352–382.

Applebaum, R. A. (1989, Winter). What's all this about quality? *Generations,* 5–7.

Brannon, D., Cohn, M., & Smyer, M. (1990). Caregiving at work: How nurses aides rate it. *Journal of Long Term Care Administration, 181,* 10–14.

Cleary, P. D., & McNeil, B. J. (1988). Patient satisfaction as an indicator of quality care. *Blue Cross and Blue Shield Association, 25,* 25–36.

DeVellis, R. F. (1991). *Scale development: Theory and applications*. Newbury Park, CA: Sage.

Duncan, M. T., & Morgan, D. L. (1994). Sharing the caring: Family caregivers' views of their relationships with nursing home staff. *The Gerontologist, 34*(2), 235–244.

Ejaz, F. K., Hendrickson, D., Miranda, S., & Schur, D. (1998). *Kethley House 1997 satisfaction survey results*. Unpublished manuscript.

Ejaz, F. K., Noelker, L. S., & Wells, L. (1997). *Predicting satisfaction among nurse assistants and families of dementia residents: A research practice partnership*. Presented at the 60th annual meeting of the Association of Ohio Philanthropic Homes, Housing and Services for the Aging, Cleveland, Ohio.

Folstein, M. F., Folstein, S. E., & McHugh, P. R. (1975). Mini Mental State: A practical method for grading the cognitive status of patients for the clinician. *Journal of Psychiatric Research, 12*, 196–198.

German, P., Rovner, B., Burton, L., Brant, L., & Clark, R. (1992). The role of mental health morbidity in the nursing home experience. *The Gerontologist, 32*(2), 152–158.

Geron, S. M. (1998). Assessing the satisfaction of older adults with long-term care services: Measurement and design challenges for social work. *Research on Social Work Practice, 8*(1), 103–119.

Institute of Medicine, Committee on Nursing Home Regulation (1986). *Improving the quality of care in nursing homes*. Washington, DC: National Academy Press.

Kleinsorge, I. K., & Koenig, H. F. (1991). The silent customers: Measuring customer satisfaction in nursing homes. *Journal of Health Care Marketing, 11*(4), 2–13.

Krueger, R. A. (1994). *Focus groups: A practical guide for applied research* (2nd ed.). Thousand Oaks, CA: Sage.

La Monica, E., Oberst, M. T., Madea, A. R., & Olf, R. M. (1986). Development of a patient satisfaction scale. *Research in Nursing and Health, 9*, 43–50.

Lavizzo-Mourey, R. J., Zinn, J., & Taylor, L. (1992). Ability of surrogates to represent satisfaction of nursing home residents with quality of care. *American Geriatrics Society, 40*, 39–47.

Miller-Hohl, D. A. (1992, January). Patient satisfaction and quality care. *Caring*, 34–39.

Monette, D. R., Sullivan, T. J., & DeJong, C. R. (1994). *Applied social research: Tool for the human services* (3rd. ed.). Chicago: Harcourt Brace College Publishers.

National Citizens' Coalition for Nursing Home Reform. (1985). *A consumer perspective: The residents' point of view*. Washington, DC: Author.

Norton, P. G., van Maris, B., Soberman, L., & Murray, M. (1996). Satisfaction of residents and families in long-term care: I. Construction and application of an instrument. *Quality Management in Health Care, 4*(3), 38–46.

Omnibus Budget Reconciliation Act (1987). Subtitle C. Nursing Home Reform. Publ. No. PL100-203. Washington DC: US Government Printing Office.

Riley, P. A., Fortinsky, R. H., & Coburn, A. F. (1992). Developing consumer-centered quality assurance strategies for home care: A case management model. *Journal of Case Management, 1*(2), 39–48.

Rubin, A., & Babbie, E. (1997). *Research methods for social work* (3rd ed.). Pacific Grove, CA:, Brooks/Cole.

Seckler, A. B., Meier, D. E., Mulvihill, M., & Paris, B. E. C. (1991). Substituted judgment: How accurate are proxy predictions? *Annals of Internal Medicine, 115,* 92–98.

Spector, P. E. (1992). *Summated rating scale construction: An introduction* (Series/ Number 07-082). Newbury Park, CA: Sage.

Stewart, A. L., & Ware, J. E., Jr., (Eds.). (1992). *Measuring functioning and well-being.* Durham NC: Duke University Press.

Strasser, S., & Davis, R. M. (1991). *Measuring patient satisfaction for improved patient services.* Ann Arbor, MI: Health Administration Press.

Strasser, S., Schweikhart, S. B., Welch, G. E., & Burge, J. C. (1995). Satisfaction with medical care: It's easier to please patients than their family members and friends. *Journal of Health Care Marketing, 15*(3), 311–321.

Ventura, M., Fox, R., Corley, M., & Mercurio, S. (1982). A patient satisfaction measure as a criterion to evaluate primary nursing. *Nursing Research, 31,* 226–230.

Zarit, S. H., & Whitlatch, C. J. (1992). Institutional placement: Phases of the transition. *The Gerontologist, 32,* 665–672.

Zinn, J. S., Lavizzo-Mourey, R., & Taylor, L. (1993). Measuring satisfaction with care in the nursing home setting: The nursing home resident satisfaction scale. *Journal of Applied Gerontology, 12*(4), 452–465.

Chapter **9**

SATISFACTION SURVEYS WITH THE COGNITIVELY IMPAIRED

Gwen C. Uman, Dennis Hocevar, Harold N. Urman, Roy Young, Maureen Hirsch, and Susan Kohler

WHY FOCUS ON "QUALITY OF LIFE" OF THE COGNITIVELY IMPAIRED?

Kane (1996) has described nursing homes as "dreaded destinations." In the minds of most people, they are associated with a miserable quality of life, regardless of the resident's cognitive condition. Studies based on observations concur that most nursing homes fall far short of providing

The authors gratefully acknowledge the support provided by the National Institute for Nursing Research (NINR): grant numbers R43-3864 and R44-3864. The authors are also grateful for the support and encouragement received from the American Association of Homes and Services for the Aging (AAHSA) for the field trial reported herein, including Evvie Munley, Susan Pettey, Suzanne Weiss, and Sheldon Goldberg. The ongoing support and expertise of the entire research team is greatly appreciated by the authors: Levon Muradyan, Research Assistant; Jennifer Roberts, Qualitative Data Processor; Shaun Zhao, Quantitative Data

an environment and care to support a life worth living (Henderson & Vesperi, 1995; Lidz, Fischer, & Arnold, 1992). Notably, the majority of these testimonials do not focus on the cognitively impaired, but one would guess their conditions are the same.

Recognizing the general perception of substandard quality of life in nursing homes, the Institute of Medicine recommended in 1985 that residents should be cared for "in such a manner and such an environment as will promote maintenance or enhancement of their quality of life" (IOM, 1985, p. 27). Soon thereafter, nursing home reform legislation [Omnibus Budget Reconciliation Act (OBRA), 1987] was enacted based on these recommendations, mandating nursing homes to ensure quality of life for residents.

Interpretative guidelines of the legislation led to implementation of a standard assessment tool that included the Minimum Data Set (MDS). The MDS includes items related to well-being, and the government's inspection process was changed to include an assessment of the "impact of facility environment, schedules, and policies and staff interactions with residents on quality of life" (Health Care Financing Administration (HCFA), 1995, Appendix P, p. 33). Clearly, there is nothing in the above regulations that legally excludes the cognitively impaired.

The civil rights theme was sounded by Kane (1991), who asserts that personal autonomy is the critical ingredient of quality of life for nursing home residents stemming from freedom as a dominant value in the United States, as outlined in the Declaration of Independence and the Bill of Rights. Nevertheless, observations of many homes and a review of the literature leads her to conclude that "few nursing home residents have control over and choice in the basic conditions of their daily life and care." Elsewhere, Kane (1991) identified routine, regulation, restricted capacity, and resource constraints as four enemies of autonomy. Collopy (1988), arguing for the need to empower the institutionalized elderly, suggests that autonomy in the aging individual be viewed as one's ability to make

Processor, and Vanessa Gamboa, Data Manager; Maria Dwight, at Gerontological Service, Inc., and David Hary, at Integrated Scientific Resources. The authors extend special thanks to the editors for their helpful and insightful guidance in the preparation of this chapter.

Drs. Uman and Urman, Mr. Young, and Ms. Hirsch are at Vital Research, LLC: 8380 Melrose Avenue, Suite 309, Los Angeles, CA 90069. For further information, contact Dr. Uman. Dr. Hocevar is at the Rossier School of Education, University of Southern California: Los Angeles, CA 90089-0031. Ms. Kohler is at Glendale Adventist Medical Center, Rehabilitation Services Department: 1502 E. Chevy Chase Drive, Suite 210, Glendale, CA 91206.

intentions known and to use resources in the environment to carry out those intentions. In other words, autonomy can be an interdependent if not an independent trait, and providers can foster residents' perception of autonomy by offering choices.

Everybody disparages the concept of warehousing in long-term care. It is both a legal precedent and a societal value that everyone deserves to experience a good quality of life, no matter what his or her level of function. For this reason, it is important for everyone to be asked to report on the quality of his or her daily life experiences. Quality can be defined as meeting customers' needs and expectations (Berry, 1991). In other words, in a consumer context, perceptions are reality. With this definition as a guide to evaluating the quality of life in nursing homes, recent literature suggests the key concept is resident satisfaction (Zinn, Lavizzo-Mourey & Taylor, 1993). The quality of daily experiences, reported by residents, as a direct measure of resident satisfaction.

The subjective nature of quality perceptions may explain why studies have found that surrogates cannot accurately represent nursing home residents' satisfaction with nursing home care, even when the resident is not cognitively impaired. Lavizzo-Mourey, Zinn & Taylor (1992) studied 152 resident-surrogate (family members or others) pairs in four non-profit nursing homes using a 26-item instrument covering the quality of physician services, nursing care, and the home environment. Correlations of residents' with surrogates' scores were low, and, therefore, the researchers concluded that no ratings could be used in lieu of residents' opinions. In another study, health-related quality of life (as measured by the Short Form-36 [SF-36]) was reported by residents and by their physicians and nurses as proxies. Berlowitz, Du, Kazis, and Lewis (1995) concluded that physicians and nurses had little insight into residents' perceived quality of life. The researchers recommended that only patient-based assessments be used in making determinations of the quality of life of the nursing home population. Although both of these studies on surrogates did not deal explicitly with the cognitively impaired, it is not unreasonable to conclude that it would be even more difficult for surrogates to report on the quality of life of the cognitively impaired.

Sheer numbers further argue for the inclusion of the cognitively impaired in any nursing home evaluation. For example, in one sample studied by the authors, a total of 4,736 residents were interviewed in 33 different nursing homes across the United States. More than two-thirds of the sample was mildly to very severely impaired, scoring from 2 through 6 on the Cognitive Performance Scale (CPS) (Hartmaier et al., 1995; Morris et al., 1994). Residents at these more impaired CPS levels continually are in the process of perceiving the environment and the people around them, and they represent the majority of the direct consumers of skilled nursing and Alzheimer's special care services in long-term care.

It is important to measure quality of life in cognitively impaired residents, not only because of their sheer numbers in long-term care, but also for the following reasons.

- Unlike the cognitively intact, who may be able to create a quality of life for themselves, the cognitively impaired are more dependent upon providers to create quality.
- It is possible that the cognitively impaired receive poor care and experience a lower quality of life compared to the cognitively intact.
- Alert residents see how impaired residents are treated and make judgments about whether they experience a good quality of life.
- Families see how other residents are treated, not just their own, and also make judgments about whether the facility will meet the future needs of their relatives.

Although there is a clear consensus that nursing home residents' perceptions of their quality of life needs to be assessed, researchers make judgments as to which residents are interviewable, quickly screening out those who are presumed to be incapable of responding accurately. For example, Lavizzo-Mourey and colleagues (1992) asked professional staff to identify eligible residents. In another study (Kruzich, Clinton, & Kelber, 1992), any resident diagnosed with Alzheimer's disease was excluded. Even the Health Care Financing Administration (HCFA) defines an interviewable resident as one "who has sufficient memory and comprehension to be able to coherently answer the majority of questions contained in the Resident Interview. These residents can make day-to-day decisions in a fairly consistent and organized manner" (HCFA, 1995, Appendix P, p. 13). The practical application of these criteria often requires subjective judgment, and usually results in disqualifying more than half of all residents. Such large disqualification rates cannot be accepted uncritically, especially in light of the numerous legal, moral, and practical arguments concerning the cognitively impaired that have been set forth in the above paragraphs.

The purpose of this chapter is to describe whether it is feasible to measure quality of life in the cognitively impaired. Toward this end, an identical methodology (i.e., an interview schedule) was used in random samples of both cognitively intact and cognitively impaired nursing home residents. The next section of this chapter focuses on the nature and psychometric characteristics of the interview schedule. The final section further describes the interview process.

THE NATURE AND PSYCHOMETRIC
CHARACTERISTICS OF THE INTERVIEW SCHEDULE

Sample and Setting

In our largest study reported here, data on a total of 5,482 residents from 82 facilities in 12 states and 3 regions of the United States (West, Plains/Midwest, and East) has been collected. Residents who participated in the studies, or their guardians, were asked for permission to release their most recent annual Minimum Data Set assessment information for purposes of: selecting a stratified random sample of residents to ensure inclusion of all cognitive levels; customizing each interview guide according to level of independence in Activities of Daily Living (ADL); and comparing satisfaction levels among different types of residents. If MDS data were not released, a generic interview guide (containing all questions) was prepared for residents whose MDS data were unavailable.

Approximately 2/3 of the residents studied were mildly to very severely impaired, scoring from 2 through 6 on the Cognitive Performance Scale (CPS) (Morris et al., 1994). The CPS is derived from items in the MDS and has respectable validity coefficients with other better known measures of cognitive status (Hartmaier et al., 1995).

Resident data were obtained through interview. The rate of completed interviews generally has been about 70%. Responsiveness to interview by CPS level in one subsample is shown in Table 9.1. In this sub-sample, 952 residents' responses could be matched with their MDS data, and 70% gave complete or partial interviews. Refusals, failures, and partial interviews came from every CPS level. However, as expected, impaired residents were less likely to complete the interview than were intact/borderline residents (see last column of Table 9.1). Nonetheless, it is important to emphasize that substantial usable data (42-80% completion rates) were obtainable at all levels of impairment except level 6 (very severely impaired).

Instrument: The Resident Satisfaction Interview (RSI)

WHAT ARE THE APPROPRIATE INDICATORS OF QUALITY OF LIFE IN THE COGNITIVELY IMPAIRED?

What are the indicators of resident quality of life? The best way to answer this question is to ask the residents themselves. Accordingly, 30 qualitative interviews were carried out at three urban nursing homes. Interviewees included both Caucasian and African American residents, and all CPS lev-

Table 9.1 Responsiveness to Interview by CPS Score

Interview status					
CPS	Refused n (150)	Failed n (74)	Partial n (60)	Complete n (668)	Completion rate
Intact/borderline (0,1)	22	4	6	295	90%
Mildly impaired (2)	10	6	9	103	80%
Moderately impaired (3)	42	11	22	193	72%
Moderately to severely impaired (4)	12	12	4	33	54%
Severely impaired (5)	20	13	11	32	42%
Very severely impaired (6)	34	28	8	12	15%

Total $N = 952$.
Note. Percentages are computed row-wise.

els were represented. The interview was unstructured and only a few open-ended questions were typically asked: "What makes you happy here?" and "What makes you unhappy?" and "What would you like to change at this facility?" Fifty-one unique responses were provided by 24 residents. Six residents were unable to compose a usable response. Not surprisingly, the usable responses primarily were provided by higher-functioning residents, and none of the residents with CPS scores of 4 or higher provided any usable quality of life indicators during the open-ended interview. Among those 24 residents who were able to describe their happiness, no association between their responses and their ethnicity and their cognitive level was noted.

Two surprises occurred during the initial interviews. The first was that only one or two residents mentioned anything about clinical care (by physicians or nurses) when asked what made them happy or unhappy at the facility, or what they would like to change. The topics that residents mentioned were largely related to everyday life experiences. The second surprising thing was that residents did not differentiate between staff roles in their descriptions. They did not identify social workers, dietary staff, housekeepers, nurses, nursing assistants, or any particular profession as they described their likes and dislikes. For these two reasons, the structure of a satisfaction instrument for residents did not include queries about clinical care, and was not divided into different types of staff.

Six themes emerged from the interviews and became the domains used to further develop the Resident Satisfaction Interview (RSI). These themes were autonomy and choice; communication; companionship; food and environment; help and assistance; and safety and security. Other researchers using similar and different methods have identified essentially the same set of quality of life themes (Abt Associates, Inc., 1993; DePoy & Archer, 1992; Uman, Urman, & Schnelle, 1996). Within each theme are a number of indicators representing a concrete, observable "event" that is desired or not desired by residents of all cognitive levels. Using this approach, residents do not rate their feeling on a vague satisfaction scale, but rather they report their perceived experiences with various aspects of their environment. Several other benefits of using concrete, observable, items accrue. By nature, they can be answered "Yes" or "No." The event, often a staff behavior, either occurs or it doesn't. The cognitively impaired are more able to understand concrete examples than abstract concepts. Finally, we were able to use the actual words and phrases that residents used in the creation of the items, thus truly activating the voice of the resident.

Forty-two observable indicators were developed into simple interview items based on the six domains identified in the qualitative interviews. Special attention was paid to the wording of items and a response format that would be easy to hear, understand, and remember. An example of two indicators for each of the six domains is given in Table 9.2. Although there has been considerable fine-tuning of the RSI over the last several years, the most recent version of the RSI includes the same six themes, and facsimiles of many of the original 42 items. The most recent version, available from the first author, has 50 scorable items, each belonging to a single theme: autonomy and choice (11 items); communication (9 items); companionship (4 items); food and environment (6 items); help and assistance (13 items); safety and security (5 items) and two overall satisfaction items.

Because the majority of the indicators were originally proposed by cognitively intact residents, it is reasonable to ask whether these indicators are equally important to the cognitively impaired residents. Accordingly, a small rating study was conducted with 23 intact residents and 69 impaired residents to assess residents' feelings about the importance of 29 different indicators. For example, residents were asked "Is it important that you know about changes in your daily schedule"? Responses were scored either yes or no, with "sometimes," "don't know," "no response," and "not applicable" being considered as a "no" response. Results shown in Table 9.3 demonstrate rather conclusively that the majority of residents, both intact and impaired, feel that all indicators are important. The only obvious difference between the two groups is that the "mobility" items appear to be more important to the intact group. For example, "Is it important to have someone take you places here?" is rated important by 100% of the intact group and only 74% of the impaired group. This 26% difference is shown in the last column of Table 9.3.

Another reasonable issue is whether or not the cognitively impaired fully understand each of the indicators. To assess this issue, six experts, all

Table 9.2 Themes and Sample Indicators

Themes	Sample Indicators
Autonomy and choice	Can you decide what clothing to wear? Does (facility name) offer a variety of activities?
Communication	Do the people who work here talk with you? Do the people here listen to what you say?
Companionship	Are you friends with anybody who lives here? Are you alone too much?
Food and environment	Is it clean here? Do you get a variety of foods here?
Help and assistance	Does somebody answer your call button right away? Do the people who work here help you walk?
Safety and security	Are your personal belongings safe here? Do the people who work here handle you gently?

with extensive interviewing experience in geriatric settings, were asked to rate the understandability of 50 indicators on a 1–4 scale (1 = very few residents understand the indicator; 4 = almost all residents understand). Results are given in Table 9.4. Naturally, all items are rated as more understandable by the cognitively intact resident, but more importantly, only 4 of 50 items were problematic, in the sense that our judges agreed that at least "some" impaired residents would not understand the indicator. These four items all had a composite rating of 2.00 or below, and are shown at the bottom of Table 9.4.

Are Assessments of the Cognitively Impaired Reliable and Valid?

RELIABILITY

Particularly in a cognitively impaired resident sample, it is possible that responses to RSI Quality of Life indicators are unreliable. That is, responses might reflect a fleeting judgment that is not likely to be replicated. To examine this potential problem, 36 cognitively intact residents and 51 cognitively impaired residents from three nursing homes were assessed at intervals ranging from 1 day to 1 week. If a resident gave the same response, coded "yes" or "no" on consecutive occasions, the indicator was considered stable. If the response changed, either "yes" to "no" or "no" to "yes," the indicator was considered unstable. Two considerations are important to mention at this point: first, "some", "don't know", "no

Table 9.3 Percentage of Residents Rating an Indicator as Important by Cognitive Level

Item	Intact	Impaired	Difference
Help getting dressed	85	98	-13
Change your wet diaper	88	97	-9
A clean place	100	97	3
Do things for yourself	96	95	1
Feel safe here	95	95	0
Have clean teeth/denture	100	92	8
Take a walk or ride	75	89	-14
Shave or comb hair	100	89	11
Privacy	87	89	-2
Get washed up	93	88	5
Know about schedule	71	85	-14
Have tasty food	91	85	6
Help going to the toilet	80	83	-3
Staff listen to you	86	82	4
Get help with eating		82	
Go anywhere you want	86	79	7
Have activities	65	79	-14
Get out of bed	76	78	-2
Be friends with staff	85	75	10
Get out of your room	80	75	5
Take you places	100	74	26
Talk to other residents	85	73	12
Get help right away	68	72	-4
Get away	95	72	23
Be friends with residents	95	72	23
Given supportive touch	74	71	3
Choose what to do	95	69	26
Have a dry pad at night	50	65	-15
Staff talk with you	58	58	0

response", and "not applicable" were coded as "no" on both occasions to simplify the analysis; and second, it is impossible to separate random measurement error from true instability in this analysis. Because of the second consideration, the reliability coefficients reported herein are underestimates of the true reliability. Nonetheless, these analyses are very instructive, in that they provide an unbiased assessment of the extent to which cognitive impairment might be associated with spontaneous judgment.

Table 9.5 shows the percentage of stable responses for each of the two groups. As expected, the intact resident responses are more stable than the impaired group on most indicators (29 of 39), but more importantly, the impaired group demonstrated a substantial amount of stability. Specifically, on 28 of 39 indicators, the impaired group had stability coefficients in the moderate range or higher (70%). These results suggest that the cognitively impaired group were for the most part not giving responses that could be described as unstable; rather, they appear to be reporting accurately their experiences. Further, the stability coefficients for the cognitively impaired group, while clearly lower than the cognitively intact group overall, were generally very close in magnitude to the cognitively intact group. Thus, for a large majority of the cognitively impaired group, overall stability equaled or even sometimes exceeded that of the typical intact resident.

VALIDITY

A bottom-line issue is whether or not the responses elicited using the RSI inventory and concomitant procedures are valid for the cognitively impaired population. That is, do the results obtained provide an accurate and useful portrayal of quality of life in this potentially difficult-to-assess subgroup? Much of the evidence for validity already has been described in the prior section of this chapter, but this evidence is for the most part content validity. Specifically, Table 9.6 addresses the validity issue more directly.

The data in Table 9.6 are based on 257 resident interviews in three different nursing homes. Approximately, one quarter of the sample was classified as cognitively intact according to the CPS criteria described earlier. Responses to 40 RSI indicators were solicited and coded using the following scale: yes, no, some, don't know, no response and not applicable. For the present analysis, a response of "yes" (coded 1) was taken to indicate that a resident was satisfied fully with a particular indicator. Any other response (coded 0) was taken to indicate that a resident was not fully satisfied. Table 9.6 shows the percentage satisfied on each of the indicators broken down by the intact and impaired subgroups.

At present, the main issue is whether or not the responses of the cognitively impaired are valid. One way to assess this issue is to examine the extent to which the responses of the cognitively impaired agree with those of the cognitively intact group. If the responses of both groups coincide, then the only reasonable conclusion is that the responses are valid, or at least, the responses of the impaired group are no less valid than the responses of the intact group. As shown in Table 9.6, the responses for the two groups were for all practical purposes the same. That is, the indicators that generated the highest satisfaction rates (e.g., "Is it clean here?") and the lowest satisfaction rates (e.g., "Help taking a walk") were for the

Table 9.4 Experts' Average Understandability Ratings by Cognitive Level

QOL indicator	Intact	Impaired	Differences
Decides when to go to bed	4.00	3.33	.67
Staff smiles at resident	4.00	3.33	.67
Supportive touch	4.00	3.33	.67
Environment clean	4.00	3.33	.67
Time to finish meal	4.00	3.33	.67
Overall satisfaction	3.83	3.33	.50
Gets as many baths as desired	4.00	3.17	.83
Talks with other residents	4.00	3.17	.83
Help with make-up and hair	4.00	3.17	.83
Help with shaving	4.00	3.17	.83
Staff relieves pain	3.83	3.17	.66
Recommend to a friend	4.00	3.17	.83
Staff gets angry with resident	3.83	3.17	.66
Decides when to eat	3.83	3.00	.83
Goes outside	3.67	3.00	.67
Alone too much	3.75	3.00	.75
Food right temperature	3.60	3.00	.60
Kept awake by noise	3.83	3.00	.83
Variety of food	3.60	3.00	.60
Help getting dressed	3.80	3.00	.80
Physically safe	3.83	3.00	.83
Privacy	4.00	3.00	1.00
Decides what to wear	4.00	2.83	1.17
Goes to activities	4.00	2.83	1.17
Resident understands staff	3.67	2.83	.84

most part identical for the two groups. There was somewhat of a tendency for the cognitively impaired to be less satisfied with certain indicators (e.g., "Do you get help washing up?"; "Do the staff help you get dressed?"), but this tendency is likely due to the fact that the impaired group has a greater array of hard-to-meet physical needs. It is not surprising that the less-functioning would be less satisfied when their needs were greater.

Because the cognitively impaired and cognitively intact residents were in the same homes, one would guess that for the most part the experiences of residents would have a lot in common. Table 9.6 shows that this is exactly the case. Further, if the procedure for assessing the two groups was somehow haphazard in the impaired group, any concordance between the satisfaction rates reported in Table 9.6 would be virtually impossible. Clearly, Table 9.6 provides compelling evidence that responses of the cognitively impaired to the RSI are valid.

Table 9.4 *(continued)*

Staff listens to resident	4.00	2.83	1.17
Help walking	3.67	2.83	.84
Handles you gentle	3.67	2.83	.84
Help moving in wheelchair	3.60	2.80	.80
Decides when to get up	3.83	2.67	1.16
Change diaper often	3.83	2.67	1.16
Help with oral care	4.00	2.67	1.33
Help with toileting	4.00	2.67	1.33
Someone to solve problems	3.67	2.67	1.00
Belongings secure	3.83	2.60	1.23
Variety of activities	3.83	2.50	1.33
Staff tells daily schedule	3.67	2.50	1.17
Friends with other residents	3.33	2.50	.83
Decides when to bathe	3.33	2.33	1.00
Friends with staff	2.83	2.33	.50
Help eating	3.67	2.33	1.34
Can be alone	3.67	2.17	1.50
Goes off campus	3.17	2.17	1.00
Staff talks with resident	3.33	2.17	1.16
Answer call light right away	3.50	2.17	1.33
Ask for help more than once	3.40	2.17	1.23
Volunteers do things with resident	3.17	2.00	1.17
Staff spends time	2.83	1.83	1.00
Food fresh	2.80	1.80	1.00
Staff turnover	3.67	1.33	2.34

METHODS FOR CONDUCTING SATISFACTION SURVEYS WITH THE COGNITIVELY IMPAIRED

Beyond the design of questions that cognitively impaired persons are able to respond to, four key factors determine to what extent satisfaction information can be elicited from this important subgroup of consumers: interviewer selection, interviewer training and supervision, resident selection, and interview techniques.

Selecting Interviewers

Selecting the right interviewers contributes to successful interviews of cognitively impaired residents. Ideally, interviewers should be mature and have enough life experience to establish short-term relationships with

Table 9.5 Percent of Residents Providing Stable Responses by Cognitive Level

Item	Intact	Impaired	Difference
Handles you roughly	77	93	-16
Get enough food	94	87	7
Like the food	71	85	-14
Understands the staff	80	84	-4
Help with toileting	82	83	-1
Feel safe here	100	83	17
Ever upset the staff?	77	82	-5
Is it clean here?	94	80	14
Staff understands you	91	80	11
Help clean teeth/dentures	88	78	10
Greeted with a smile	71	78	-7
Change your wet diaper	73	77	-4
Talks to other residents	80	76	4
Can be alone	71	76	-5
Help you eat	83	75	8
Do things for yourself	89	74	15
Get away from the facility	83	74	9
Likes the facility	86	74	12
Help getting dressed	89	73	16
Go whenever you want to	65	72	-7
Go where you want to	77	71	6
Help washing up	89	70	19
Supportive touch	71	70	1
Get medicine on time	89	70	19
Staff spends time with you	72	70	2
Enough showers/baths	74	70	4
Stopped from going places	74	70	4
Friends with residents	74	70	4
Handles you gently	88	69	19
Help shave/comb hair	86	66	20
Go to activities	71	67	4
Friends with staff	54	66	-12
Told about schedule change	88	85	3
Gets help right away	75	65	10
Staff talks with you	74	64	10
Privacy when changing	81	61	20
Staff listens to you	77	56	19
Has activities you like	83	57	26
Choices about what to do	54	54	0

Table 9.6 Percent of Residents Satisfied on Each Indicator by Cognitive Level

Item	Intact	Impaired	Difference
Is it clean here?	97	94	3
Staff understands you	95	90	5
Feels safe here	98	90	8
Get enough food	97	89	8
Staff handles you gently	85	89	-4
Ever upset the staff?	86	89	-3
Get medicines on time	94	86	8
Understands the staff	88	85	3
Can be alone	81	84	-3
Like the facility	81	82	-1
Do things for yourself	90	81	9
Go where you want in home	88	81	7
Privacy when changing	90	81	9
Help getting dressed	95	80	15
Greeted with a smile	79	79	0
Change your wet diaper	94	79	15
Handles you gently	88	78	10
Staff listens to you	79	77	2
Talks to other residents	80	74	6
Help shave/comb hair	88	73	15
Has activities you like	79	73	6
Enough showers/baths	70	72	-2
Go where you want to	85	69	16
Help with toileting	56	69	-13
Go to activities	75	67	8
Go whenever you want to	65	65	0
Help washing up	83	63	20
Friends with residents	78	63	15
Gets help right away	67	61	6
Like the food	48	61	-13
Supportive touch	62	60	2
Friends with staff	66	60	6
Told about schedule change	53	58	-5
Help with wheelchair	63	56	7
Choice about what do	62	53	9
Staff spends time with you	68	51	17
Help clean teeth/denture	50	50	0
Get away from the facility	66	44	22
Staff talks with you	38	43	-5
Help taking a walk	47	38	9

residents that are based on trust and mutual respect. The outcome of such a dynamic is a sensitive and credible recording of resident perceptions. Personal characteristics needed for success are:

- A genuine interest in older people
- The willingness to suspend disbelief, i.e., to believe that each resident has something important to say about his/her daily life experiences (Van Maris, Soberman, Murray, & Norton, 1996)
- The understanding that it is the interviewer's role to try to elicit each residents' perceptions
- A positive energy that is reflected in animated facial expressions and varied vocal inflection
- The willingness to conform to the requirements of a structured interview schedule.

An example of an interviewer who is willing to suspend her disbelief follows:

"I saw this man on the Alzheimer's unit for a couple of days. He was disheveled and everyone, including the nurses, avoided him. I was hoping he wouldn't be on my list. Then one day, I came to his interview guide, so I took a deep breath and I approached him and asked him if he would answer some questions for me. He turned out to be just wonderful. He had been an engineer, he was willing and able to answer questions, and was very enjoyable. I don't know why everyone avoided him. From then on I realized more fully how important it was to believe in every resident, regardless of how he looks."

Whether hiring is done face-to-face (as in a local project) or over the phone (as in a nationwide project), the hiring interview provides an opportunity to discuss the role of the interviewer, and to explore experiences that have potential impact on the resident interview process. Successful applicants report that they are energized by resident interviews, while unsuccessful trainees, often those who have recently lost a loved one, say that they become depressed.

Training and Supervision of Interviewers

In a structured interview, each interviewer is responsible for delivering each question with exactly the same emphasis, in the same tone of voice for each resident. Potential interviewers are provided with materials before the 2-day training session in a nursing home. The training curriculum is structured for maximum trainee participation. Short periods of didactic material are alternated with essential interactive activities. Group debriefing and feedback sessions that provide opportunities for clarification of techniques and recording of resident responses follow a resident demonstration interview by a skilled interviewer. Trainees are then paired with experienced interviewers who mentor them and are responsible for debriefing each training interview. Practice and feedback are provided with residents of various cognitive levels and who exhibit various behaviors, such as wandering, agitation, lack of attention, crying, and somnolence.

Although role-playing is not used in the training process, because there is no substitute for experiencing actual residents in the interview situation, videotape of interviews with residents is shown and critiqued. Trainees also participate in a "hearing test" to sensitize them to how residents may interpret words and to teach them that repeating the same word again is not effective. They are exposed to residents with various levels of cognitive impairment where they practice techniques to deal with agitation and lack of attention under the supervision of an experienced interviewer.

Supervision involves intermittent on-site observations of interviews with feedback, and audiotaping the interview of a randomly selected resident. The audiotapes are listened to for correspondence between the resident's oral answers and the answer the interviewer recorded. Interview guides are randomly checked for completion and accuracy. Interviewers receive positive and corrective feedback as needed on an ongoing basis. Duration of interviews and proportion of refusals and "failures" are tracked for each interviewer. Inter-rater agreement exceeds 90% for each indicator, regardless of residents' cognitive status.

Refresher training is provided regularly to ensure that the structured interview has not been inadvertently altered over time by the interviewers. Interviewers' skills are again observed and a videotaped resident interview is used to test for accuracy of recording resident responses. Interviewers function quite independently in the nursing home, thus this type of refresher provides a lively forum to discuss the questions, challenges and satisfactions associated with face to face interviews.

Resident Selection Criteria

The interviewer is supplied with Resident Satisfaction Interview guides to bring to the nursing home. To avoid having interviewers make undue assumptions about residents, the cognitive status of the residents is not known to the interviewers. Instead, a short behavioral Screening Interview Schedule (S.I.S.) is used to determine whether a resident is able at that time to participate in the interview process. The major criterion for inclusion is the ability of residents to communicate that they know their name. If unable to answer this question, the resident is thanked and the interview terminated. Once they have identified themselves, the ability to respond "yes" and "no" to at least one of the screening questions is required for the interview to proceed. The interviewer is not responsible for interpreting or filtering the resident's responses. One example of a screening question is, "Did you get something to eat today?" If the resident says "no" and the interviewer saw breakfast trays, the recorded response is still "no" and the resident's response is accepted as his or her perception. If the resident passes the S.I.S., the interviewer proceeds with the interview and continues to have the option of ending the interview if the resident is unable to continue.

Cognitive status, including attention span, ability to understand, and short-term memory can often be partially compensated for by using simple techniques described in the next section. Although visual and auditory deficits are not unique to the cognitively impaired elderly, these deficits do augment the apparent cognitive impairment of residents, making it all the more important to compensate for sensory losses while interviewing.

Interviewing Techniques for the Cognitively Impaired

Although there are few interviewing techniques specific to the cognitively impaired, interviewers need to apply a set of techniques consistent with structured interviewing to all residents. The techniques are summarized in Table 9.7.

Environmental manipulation is essential (Clark, 1994). Extraneous stimuli must be minimized, so it is important to ask the resident's permission to turn off the radio or television. In order to add the voice of a hearing and cognitively impaired resident to the satisfaction data, interviewers must use supplemental strategies. The use of simple electronic sound amplifiers with lightweight stereo headphones can often compensate for hearing loss in those residents not using hearing aids. The resident may then perform at a much higher level than the CPS score would suggest. Likewise, glasses should be found, cleaned off, if necessary, and worn by residents so all visual cues will be available to them. Vision will be enhanced if natural or artificial light is not glaring on the resident's face. The mouth and whole face of the interviewer should be kept visible at all times to further maximize cues. Good interviewing technique demands that resident and interviewer are sitting at eye level with one another. An additional environmental control is advisable with the cognitively impaired, and that is the minimization of distraction caused by movement such as hallway activity that the resident might see

Table 9.7 Recommended techniques to interview the cognitively impaired

Purpose	Technique
Gain the resident's attention	Approach slowly.
	Be visible when approaching.
	Establish and maintain eye contact.
	Prepare the resident for what you will talk about whenever possible.
	Use common gestures and facial expressions when appropriate.
	Use the resident's name often to gain or redirect attention.
	Be pleasant and smile.
Manipulate the environment	Face resident, 2–3 feet away.
	Check whether hearing aids are working.
	Offer use of amplification device for unaided residents with hearing loss.
	Check for "extras" to enhance communication: glasses, dentures, adaptive devices, or personal items.
	Make sure light is on your face.
	Avoid glare on your face or the resident's face.
	Speak with the resident at eye level.
	Look at the resident when you speak.
	Place resident away from open doors where there is visible traffic.
	Minimize background noise—turn off TV and radios.
Articulate clearly	Choose familiar, common words.
	Use low-pitched speech, without exaggeration.
	Use alternative phrases to convey meaning.
Compensate for cognitive losses	Use short, concrete sentences.
	Request yes/no answers.
	Use one-step questions; avoid conditional phrases and clauses.
	Give extra time for processing and responding, using silence and pauses.
	Avoid questions about the timing or duration of events.

during the interview. Also unique to the cognitively impaired is the comfort they find in a familiar environment with familiar people. Thus removing sources of noise and view of activities and providing for privacy is sometimes at odds with the resident's comfort level in remaining in familiar surroundings and among friends. The interviewer may have to effect a compromise in the environment at times, balancing the resident's need for familiarity with the interviewer's responsibility to reduce stimuli and provide privacy for the interview.

Establishing rapport with cognitively impaired residents involves making and maintaining eye contact while reading questions and recording answers, and speaking very clearly and with enthusiasm to emphasize the meaning of each question (Brady, McLean, & McLean, 1995). Clear articulation of familiar words using a low-pitched tone of voice enhances understanding. In contrast to the cognitively intact, by whom conversational banter is enjoyed and understood, the cognitively impaired become confused and flustered when presented with a flurry of words. It is necessary to use short sentences without extraneous words that cause confusion. Furthermore, it is not advisable to ask about the specific timing or duration of events (Bolinger & Hardiman, 1989; Lovelace, 1990) because cognitively impaired residents may become upset, agitated, or exhibit signs of embarrassment and loss of self-esteem if they perceive that they don't know the answers. With the cognitively impaired, it is necessary to pause and wait for a response longer than one would wait for a cognitively intact resident's answer. The use of silence after a question has been asked allows residents to process the question and decide on their answer. Residents' facial expressions will usually reveal evidence of confusion, calling for the use of structured alternative wording or prompting after the initial pause.

Establishing and maintaining attention with the cognitively impaired is perhaps the most important factor in obtaining a successful interview. Their minds wander; and they may physically wander, as well (Cohen-Mansfield & Billig, 1986). Residents who are physically agitated and tend to pace or wander can be interviewed if approached at a time of day when they are calmer (Hasselkus, 1992). Some residents can be successfully interviewed if the interviewer walks or paces with the resident. The nursing staff can tell interviewers when the best times are for certain residents. Interviewers can also observe, in the course of their work day, when a given resident is sitting and looks calm, and can take that opportunity to try an interview (Sternberg, Whelihan, Fretwell, Bielecki, & Murray, 1989). Verbal cues, such as use of the resident's name and physical touch (if the resident doesn't object to that) can also be used to gain or redirect attention, just as they are for garrulous cognitively intact residents. Some residents, on the opposite end of the spectrum, seem to be too somnolent to be interviewed. Staff can be very helpful by telling interviewers when a given resident is usually most alert. Snack time at a facility has often rescued a waning interview—the punch or popcorn has perked up residents who were starting to doze off, a situation that rarely occurs with the cognitively intact.

Wandering away or appearing somnolent may alert the interviewer that the resident is suspicious about talking to a stranger or answering sen-

sitive questions. Some cognitively impaired residents seem to have no pro-
tective filtering mechanism, and will freely and loudly report negative
aspects of daily life, even when staff or roommates are overhearing. Others
may be so suspicious or frightened of retribution that they will not talk to
the interviewer (Hull & Griffin, 1989). Occasionally this reluctance can be
overcome by having a trusted staff member personally introduce the interviewer to the resident, and explain that the resident will be helping by
answering questions and that their answers are confidential. Beyond this
introduction, it is inappropriate to pressure the resident to participate.

In summary, it is important to recognize that most residents can be
interviewed when careful steps are followed in the measurement process.
Careful selection and training of interviewers, appropriate selection of residents and use of interview techniques that attempt to compensate for
reduced vision, hearing, and cognition will enhance the potential for successful resident interviews. For complete confidence in the validity of the
information received, the measurement process must be clearly defined
and monitored. When these four major conditions are met, it is possible to
obtain satisfaction data from residents across a range of cognitive levels.

REFERENCES

Abt Associates (1993). *Evaluation of the LTC survey process.* Boston: Abt Associates.
Berlowitz, D. R., Du, W., Kazis, L., & Lewis, S. (1995). Health-related quality of life
    of nursing home residents: Difference in patient and provider perceptions.
    Journal of the American Geriatrics Society,43, 799–802.
Berry, T. (1991). *Managing the Total Quality Transfromation.* New York: McGraw-Hill.
Bolinger, R., & Hardiman, C. J. (1989). Dementia: The confused-disoriented com-
    municatively disturbed elderly. In R. H. Hull & K. M. Griffin (Eds.),
    Communication disorders in aging (pp. 61–77). Newbury Park, CA: Sage.
Brady, N. C., McLean, J. E., & McLean, L. K. (1995). Initiation and repair of inten-
    tional communication acts by adults with severe to profound cognitive dis-
    abilities. *Journal of Speech and Hearing Research, 38,* 1334–1348.
Clark, W. (1994). General principles of management In: R. C. Hamdy, J. M. Turnball,
    W. Clark, M. M. Lancaster (Eds.) *Alzheimer's Disease: A Handbook for Caregivers,*
    2nd ed. St. Louis: Mosby.
Cohen-Mansfield, J., & Billig, N. (1986). Agitated behaviors in the elderly: I & II.
    Journal of the American Geriatrics Society, 34, 711–727.
Collopy, B. J. (1988). Autonomy in long-term care: Some crucial distinctions.
    Gerontologist, 28, (Suppl.) 10–17.
DePoy, E., & Archer, L. (1992). The meaning of quality of life to nursing home res-
    idents: A naturalistic investigation. *Topics in Geriatric Rehabilitation, 7,* (4), 64–74.
Hartmaier, S. L., Sloane, P. D., Guess, H. A., Koch, G. G., Mitchell, C. M., & Phillips,
    C. D. (1995). Validation of the Minimum Data Set Cognitive Performance Scale:

Agreement with the Mini-Mental State Examination. *Journal of Gerontology, 50A*,(2), M128–M133.

Hasselkus, B. R. (1992). The meaning of activity: Day care for persons with Alzheimer Disease. *The American Journal of Occupational Therapy. 49*(3), 199–206.

HCFA, (1995). *State Operations Manual: Provider Certification: Transmittal No. 274, Appendix P*, p. 13, 33.

Henderson, J. N., & Vesperi, M. D. (Eds.). (1995). *The culture of long-term care: Nursing home ethnography.* Westport, CT: Bergin & Garvey.

Hull, R. H., & Griffin, K. M. (1989). *Communication disorders in aging.* Newbury Park, CA: Sage.

IOM. (1985). *Improving the quality of care in nursing homes.* (Report of the Committee on Nursing Home Regulations). Washington, DC: National Academy Press.

Kane, R. A. (1991). Personal autonomy for residents in long-term care: Concepts and issues of measurement. In J. E. Birren (Ed.). *The concept and measurement of quality of life in the frail elderly.* (pp. 315–334). New York: Academic Press.

Kane, R. A. (1996, July). *Assuring quality of life in nursing homes: Regulatory strategies.* Paper presented at "Improving quality of life for nursing home residents: The challenge and the Opportunities" Symposium, Health Care Financing Administration Health Standards and Quality Bureau Center for Long-term Care, Baltimore, MD.

Kruzich, J. M., Clinton, J. F., & Kelber, S. T. (1992). Personal and environmental influences on nursing home satisfaction. *The Gerontologist, 32*(3), 342–350.

Lavizzo-Mourey, R. J., Zinn, J., & Taylor, L. (1992). Ability of surrogates to represent satisfaction of nursing home residents with quality of care. *Journal of the American Geriatrics Society, 40*, 39–47.

Lidz, C. W., Fischer, L., & Arnold, R. M. (1992). *The erosion of autonomy in long-term care.* New York: Oxford University Press.

Lovelace, E. A. (Ed.). (1990). *Aging and cognition: Mental processes, self-awareness, and interventions.* New York: North-Holland.

Morris, J. N., Fries, B. E., Mehr, D. R., Hawes, C., Phillips, C. Mor, V., & Lipshitz, L. A. (1994). MDS Cognitive Performance Scale. *Journal of Gerontology: Medical Sciences, 49*, M174–M182.

OBRA (Omnibus Reconciliation Act) (1987). U.S. Congress. Public Law, 101–508.

Sternberg, J., Whelihan, W., Fretwell, M., Bielecki, C. & Murray, S. (1989). Disruptive behavior in the elderly. *Clinical Gerontologist, 8*(3), 43–56.

Uman, G. C., Urman, H. N., & Schnelle, J. (1996). *Long-term care customer satisfaction methodology.* Washington, DC: Department of Health and Human Services Public Health Services, 1 R43 NRO3864-01.

Van Maris, B., Soberman, L., Murray, M., & Norton, P.G. (1996). Satisfaction of residents and families in long-term care: Lessons learned. *Quality Management in Health Care, 4*, 47–53.

Zinn, J. S., Lavizzo-Mourey, R., & Taylor, L. (1993). Measuring satisfaction with care in the nursing home setting: The Nursing Home Resident Satisfaction Scale. *The Journal of Applied Gerontology, 12*(4), 452–465.

Chapter 10

EMPLOYEE SATISFACTION AND OPINION SURVEYS: A CASE STUDY

Jon R. Zemans and Gwenn Voelckers

Effective human resource management is one of the most important factors in running a successful long-term care facility. A positive work climate has a direct and positive affect on customer service, which in turn, has a direct and positive effect on resident satisfaction.

To be recognized for service superiority, facilities must have motivated employees. And, to have motivated employees, managers must first understand employee needs. That was experienced first-hand by Wesley-on-East, a senior living and nursing home community in Rochester, New York. (Wesley-on-East will hereafter be referred to as Wesley.)

The organization observed, over time, the important relationship between employee morale and the satisfaction of employee needs. Given the strong correlation, it has been committed to identifying those needs, and has successfully done so with the administration of a series of Employee Opinion Surveys, beginning in 1985.

REASONS TO CONDUCT A SURVEY

There are forces driving health care organizations to measure employee satisfaction, and multiple factors have contributed to the growing interest in survey outcomes. The key forces driving this interest are described below. A comprehensive discussion of the specific benefits that an organization may realize from satisfaction measurement is provided by Schweikhart and Strasser (1994).

Continuous Quality Improvement

The adoption of Continuous Quality Improvement (CQI) by long-term care organizations has reinforced the fundamental importance of understanding and meeting the needs and expectations of customers. Moreover, CQI has led health care managers to the realization that multiple customer groups exist, including patients, patients' family members, friends, physicians, payors, and employees. Satisfaction data provides health care organizations engaged in CQI efforts with a better understanding of how various customers perceive the quality of their experience with an organization.

The Assertive Employee

Labor force demands for responsive, higher-quality management and working conditions have landed squarely on the shoulders of health care providers. First experienced in manufacturing, the demands crept into health care, initially in hospitals and ultimately (inevitably) into long-term care settings. Evidence of this trend toward heightened awareness and intolerance of "perceived" injustices in the workplace range from the renewed interest in unionization to pervasive feelings of "entitlement" among some employee groups. Satisfaction measurement, then, is a primary vehicle through which employees can transmit their "voice."

Heightened Competition

Increased competition among long-term care providers for increasingly scarce human resources has motivated providers to seek new ways to satisfy and retain current employees and attract new ones. By assessing employees' expectations and perceptions, employee satisfaction data can help an organization understand what its labor force thinks, wants, and is likely to do in response to organizational change. This knowledge gives an organization a competitive edge.

Accreditation Requirements

The fundamental role of employee satisfaction in quality management and assurance is perhaps most clearly revealed by accreditation mandates of the Joint Commission on Accreditation of Healthcare Organizations, which requires hospitals and long-term care facilities to have formal complaint management systems.

Human Resource Management

Running any successful operation requires effective human resource management. Criteria for the esteemed Malcolm Baldrige National Quality Award emphasizes the value of developing and utilizing the full potential of the work force through employee participation, quality leadership, and personal and organizational growth. Optimizing the potential of the work force can be better accomplished with a comprehensive picture of how the work force views itself and its environment. Seen as a management tool, an Employee Opinion Survey can help diminish the risk of many difficult decisions.

IDENTIFYING A SURVEY INSTRUMENT

Convinced that measuring employee satisfaction was not only desirable, but essential, Wesley set its sites on identifying a reliable survey instrument. After researching several options, the organization elected to work with its local Industrial Management Council (IMC), an employer association formed in 1916 to provide human resource services to its members.

The IMC Employee Opinion Survey provides a personal and confidential opportunity for employees to communicate their needs and opinions directly to top management. Using this survey also gives an organization access to national norms, which provides a sound basis for comparison and interpretation of results. It is a reliable survey instrument and proven method of gathering quantitative and qualitative data.

Through information obtained from the Employee Opinion Survey, Wesley positioned itself to:

- Evaluate problematic situations that can lead to low productivity, absenteeism, and poor morale;
- Assess training needs;
- Uncover avenues for improving employee morale and company productivity;

- Compare its organization's responses to those obtained by similar employer associations throughout the United States (national norms);
- Evaluate overall effectiveness of an organization's human resource program;
- Identify internal trends and alert managers to potential problems; and
- Most importantly, provide the basis for corrective action.

Survey Design

The IMC's Employee Opinion Survey is a written questionnaire which asks employees to agree or disagree with 60 qualitative statements. It measures employee opinions confidentially in eight major areas—those which have the greatest impact on an organization's effectiveness. Below are sample statements associated with each of eight major "quality factors:"

1. TOP MANAGEMENT

- I always feel free to speak to anyone in top management.
- In my opinion, top management here could operate the organization more efficiently.

2. WORK AND SAFETY CONDITIONS

- I am not supplied with proper safety equipment.
- My work is pleasant—I am not pushed for more than I can do.

3. SUPERVISORY EFFECTIVENESS

- My supervisor gives praise where praise is due.
- I have been well-trained on all jobs to which I have been assigned.

4. PAY AND BENEFITS

- My rate of pay is fair and equitable for the job I am doing.
- Employee benefits are not adequate.

5. COMMUNICATION AND RECOGNITION

- Our management keeps us informed about new plans and developments.
- We are encouraged to make suggestions for improvements in our work.

6. JOB SECURITY AND PROMOTION

- If layoffs should occur, the organization would be fair in its layoff system.
- My abilities and skills aren't used by this organization.

7. EMPLOYEE RELATIONS

- My co-workers are cooperative and work well together.
- I am pleased to tell others where I work.

8. SURVEY RESULTS COMPARED TO NATIONAL NORMS

- I do not believe any good will come from taking part in this survey.
- I think top management here will use the results of this survey to our best interest.

The IMC survey also contains a three-part employee comment section which allows participants to expand and clarify their thoughts, providing important subjective information. Employees are asked what they like and dislike about their employment with the company and what improvements they would recommend to make the organization a better place to work.

The IMC, in cooperation with similar employer associations across the United States, has the ability to deliver the same program to all types of businesses and thereby has access to national normative data which provides a sound basis for comparison and interpretation of results. No other survey has as large or as current a data base. Over 200,000 employees have participated in the survey, and the current normative data is based on over 50,000 employees in over 400 companies.

SURVEY METHODOLOGY

While Wesley selected a written questionnaire for surveying purposes, there are other methods for gathering information. Cost, quantity, and quality of data; expected participation rates, ease of administration and tabulation; and other factors enter into an organization's choice of survey instrument. An organization's goals, budget, and timetable will influence the survey method and scope, i.e., all employees or a sampling.

Briefly described below are several survey methods and their advantages and disadvantages. Because Wesley chose a written questionnaire, the pros and cons of this survey method are examined in more depth at the end of this section.

Face-to-Face Interviewing With a Questionnaire

This survey method requires a personal interview with each survey participant. It works well when a questionnaire is especially lengthy or complex, and when participants need to look at samples, concept statements, or other visual material.

Advantages:
- The answering of questions is strictly controlled.
- The "relationship" between the interviewer and participant may result in higher-quality responses.

Disadvantages:
- Cost. This survey method is very labor-intensive.
- Lack of confidentiality.

Telephone Interviews

Telephone interviewing has become a major method of gathering survey data, primarily because it is more cost-effective than face-to-face interviewing.

Advantages:
- Greater speed and lower cost than face-to-face interviews.
- Computer-aided interviewing makes it more efficient.

Disadvantages:
- More impersonal than face-to-face.
- Participants may easily refuse to be interviewed.

Focus Group Interviews

Focus group interviews bring six to ten people and a moderator together for a round-table discussion of a topic.

Advantages:
- The give and take during discussions may generate interesting insights.
- Survey process may be completed in a short time frame.

Disadvantages:
- Participants tend to say what is acceptable to other participants.
- Lack of confidentiality.

Written Questionnaire Through The Mail

This survey method enables the organization to survey a good sample through the mail. Typically, a questionnaire is transmitted by a cover letter that addresses why the survey is being conducted and how the addressee was selected.

Advantages:
- Mail surveys are less expensive than face-to-face, telephone, or focus group interviews.
- Confidentiality.

Disadvantages:
- Absence of an interviewer to explain complex instructions.
- Lack of control over the sequence in which questions are answered.

Written Questionnaires Administered on Site

This survey method has been used six times by Wesley with good success. Employees were given advance notice of the survey and encouraged by both management and union leadership to use this opportunity to tell management what they think of their working terms and conditions.

Meeting rooms and times were designated for survey administration in small groups. Employees could choose where and when to complete their surveys.

Advantages:
- Large number of employees can be surveyed.
- Everyone responds to the same question format.
- Maximum level of confidentiality is achieved.
- Significant amount of data can be efficiently summarized and analyzed by computer.
- Fewer staff are required to administer the survey.
- Interviewer bias is controlled.
- Employees at multiple sites can easily participate.
- This method is generally less expensive to conduct than other survey methods.
- Standardized questions allow for comparison of results from one survey to the next (internal trends).
- Standardized questions allow for comparison with norms.

Disadvantages:
- Employees may interpret questions differently.
- If lengthy, employees may not complete entire survey.
- Employees often do not read instructions carefully, and this can lead to poor data quality.
- The scope of employee response is limited by the design and content of the survey instrument.
- Response rate for "absentee" surveys is hard to calculate.

SURVEY ADMINISTRATION

After identifying the survey methodology and the Employee Opinion Survey "consultant," Wesley proceeded with survey administration.

Pre-Survey Activity

Wesley and the IMC jointly defined employee groups for comparison purposes. Since 1985, Wesley has refined these employee groups by further segmenting the work force for survey purposes.

Initially, the organization divided the work force into five groups: leadership, professional/technical, office/clerical, nursing assistants, and support services. The multi-disciplinary groups (e.g., support services, which contained maintenance, food service, and housekeeping personnel) were, as one would anticipate, more difficult to assess, given the inability to attribute responses to particular employee segments.

As Wesley's experience with the survey process evolved, so did the definition of employee groups. In its most current survey conducted in 1997, eight survey groupings were established, i.e., nursing administration, certified nursing assistants, clerical, maintenance, food service, environmental services, social work, and management personnel.

The more-tightly defined, homogenous employee groups made it easier to interpret survey results and determine satisfaction levels on a more precise basis. The value of the process was enhanced.

With each survey administration, Wesley management worked with the IMC to develop specific subjective statements tailored to its needs to strengthen and customize the survey. Sample agree/disagree statements used on previous surveys included:

- I support this organization's emphasis on superior customer service.
- I am not given the training that I need to deliver superior customer service.
- If you have any concerns or questions regarding the building expansion program at Wesley, please indicate below.

Survey Administration

A successful Employee Opinion Survey is in part measured by the participation rate. Wesley took these measures to secure the participation of its employees:

- The organization selected a survey instrument that could be completed anonymously.
- Management personnel were informed of the objectives of the Employee Opinion Survey and were brought on-board early on in the process.
- The cooperation of union leadership was secured—a necessary early step in the implementation process.
- The IMC was engaged to conduct the survey. An impartial representative facilitated the administration of the survey in small-group sessions.
- The survey was administered on-site in each of Wesley's three facilities and on all three shifts. Refreshments were served.
- Ample and varied forms of communication (e.g. memos, posters, verbal encouragement) were used to encourage participation.
- Supervisors were instructed to actively promote the participation of their employees.

• Employees who were not scheduled to work on the day the survey was administered were given an opportunity to complete an absentee survey by mail. The IMC arranged for collection of the survey questionnaires from those employees.

Obstacles to Full Employee Participation

Wesley worked diligently to overcome the obstacles to full employee participation. Wesley identified fear and apathy as key deterrents: fear of speaking without reprisal, and apathy toward management's commitment to doing anything constructive in response to the survey results.

The organization addressed the issue of fear by guaranteeing confidentiality. Wesley promoted the survey as an anonymous way for employees to express their opinions, "without signing their names." The use of an IMC facilitator for survey administration also reinforced the confidential nature of the process. Upon completion of the survey, the employee handed the survey to the IMC facilitator. Wesley management never saw the raw data.

Apathy was addressed over time by management's commitment on the front end of the survey process to share the results with employees and then doing exactly that. Further, Wesley was deliberate about addressing any "soft spots" identified through the survey. Action plans were developed with the input of employees. Managers were held accountable for plan implementation. Over time, the fear and apathy subsided, and a growing trust and respect for management took its place. This byproduct of the survey process has had positive and lasting consequences.

SURVEY TABULATION AND
PRESENTATION OF RESULTS

The IMC provided Wesley with the results of the "60 agree/disagree" employee responses compared against the national database norms. This data was presented by the employee group as well as by the total organization.

On request, the IMC will analyze the results and will provide a written report and recommendations to management. It will also schedule a presentation and provide summary overview of the results to management, if asked. As an additional option, the IMC will conduct employee focus groups to communicate the survey results, determine reasons for the survey response, and obtain employee input regarding potential solutions to specific issues (search for causes and solutions). Wesley did not engage the IMC for this purpose, electing instead to conduct these meetings itself.

Results Presentation

Table 10.1 depicts internal trend compared to national norms since Wesley first conducted the Employee Opinion Survey in 1985.

Each of the eight quality factors is identified in the left column. The numbers of responses below the norm for each of the years Wesley conducted the survey are in the center section, numbers of total responses 10 percentage points or more below the norms are in the right section. The number 41 in the bottom row, far left corner of the center section told the organization that in 1985, 41 combined (total) responses to the 60 subjective statements were below the national norm. Shift over to the right section, bottom row, same year, and note that of the 41 responses, 25 were 10 percentage points below the norm. Clearly, Wesley was hurting in 1985. While its new management team was aware of employee dissatisfaction, it needed specifics, which is why it conducted an Employee Opinion Survey. The negative results in this baseline year were fully anticipated.

By 1987, the number of total responses below the norms had decreased to 13 of 60, only 4 of which were 10 percentage points or more below the norms. Improvement in employees overall opinion of the 8 quality factors is clearly evident. The 1990 results continue this trend, having eliminated all responses 10 percentage points or more below the norms. It can be easily seen in Table 10.1 that the 1993 survey reflected the best result, having reduced to one response below the norms.

While a quick scanning of the results of all the participants reveals no responses 10 percentage points or more below the norms in the March, 1993 survey, such is not the case 4 years later in March, 1997. And a comparison of the responses for each of the 60 subjective statements of the 1993 and 1997 surveys shows deterioration in seven quality factors and no movement in one. What happened?

Between 1993 and 1997 two major events took place: the State of New York undertook aggressive cost-reduction measures, which forced Wesley to downsize, and then, 2 years later, the organization undertook a significant renovation and expansion project which disrupted the day-to-day operation of the facilities for several years.

These two items of analysis were provided by Wesley management and speak for themselves. A less apparent result was revealed with IMC assistance in the analysis. Specifically, in the 1997 survey, "supervisory effectiveness" was rated very positive to norms, while the opinion of "top management" was significantly negative. The IMC analysis suggests that the first-line supervisors were ineffective in delivering top management's message and in functioning as managers. Instead, they were behaving more like friends, confidants, and fellow-commiserators.

Table 10.1 Overall comparison to National Norms

Quality Factors	Number of total responses below the norms						Number of total response 10 percentage points or more below the norms					
	11/85	5/87	5/90	3/93	3/95	3/97	11/85	5/87	5/90	3/93	3/95	3/97
Top management	8	2	0	0	7	7	5	0	0	0	1	4
Work and safety conditions	4	1	0	0	0	3	3	0	0	0	0	1
Supervisory effectiveness	4	0	0	0	0	0	1	0	0	0	0	0
Pay and benefits	4	4	4	0	5	6	2	4	0	0	0	1
Communications and Recognition	5	1	0	0	1	4	3	0	0	0	0	1
Employment security and promotion	7	3	0	1	6	6	5	0	0	0	4	2
Employee relations	6	2	0	0	1	5	5	0	0	0	0	0
Survey results	3	0	0	0	4	4	1	0	0	0	2	2
Total	41	13	4	1	24	35	25	4	0	0	7	11

A comprehensive action plan was developed in response to the March, 1997 survey, with emphasis on management training for first-line supervisors.

This analysis would probably not have been made without the assistance of the IMC and their broad base of experience.

Figure 10.1 is a graphic depiction of survey results for the company as a whole in 1997. The center column of numbers represent the national norm for each statement. The numbers that comprise this column correspond with each of the 60 numbered statements on the survey instrument, and have been grouped under the appropriate quality factor. If the number is "boxed," Wesley's result hit the norm right on the head.

Any result which appears to the right of center is positive. Anything which appears to the left of center is negative. One can now clearly see how employee perceptions of top management and supervisory effectiveness differ. This disparity prompted Wesley to dig deeper, and the IMC analysis revealed an opportunity to bolster the management skills of first-line supervisors.

Figure 10.2 is a graphic depiction of the results of the food service group. Its visual impact is very different from the company-wide graph, and reveals at a glance the profile of this particular employee group. This graph is one of the eight groups chosen by Wesley. Each graph depicts the unique perceptions of each employee group. The food service group profile is more evenly balanced in many respects than the company as a whole, although these employees tend to hold relatively strong positive and negative feelings. Supervisory effectiveness is perceived as mixed, as is the perception of top management. These employees are part of the service and maintenance organized labor unit, yet the response to statement 49 under employment security and promotion indicates that their confidence in their union may be flagging. The statement (49) spoke to whether employees could be fired for petty things. This led management to review the union contract more aggressively and to develop and promote a common understanding of the meaning of "petty things."

Figure 10.3 is startling. This graph depicts survey results for Wesley's housekeeping group. What's interesting is that this group is managed by the same executive that manages food service. The group is also a part of the organized labor unit. One of the values of the survey is that this executive now knows which group needs more attention and can better prioritize her action plans.

POST-SURVEY ACTIVITY

Sharing the results of the Employee Opinion Survey with employees and others is the next step in this process. It is an important—if not critical—

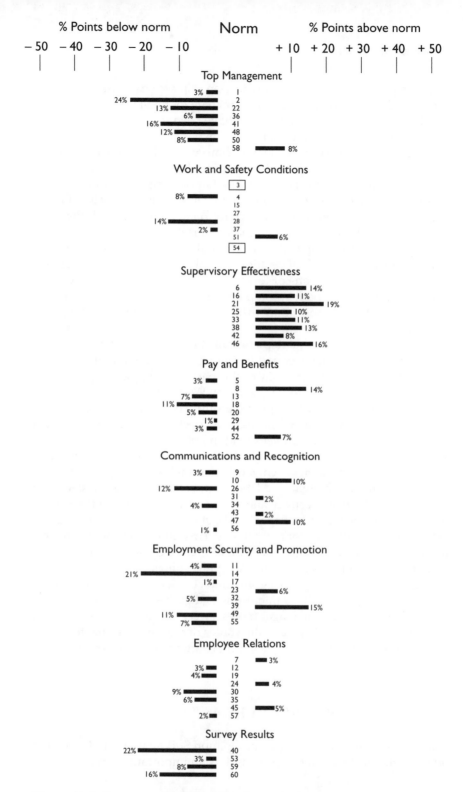

Figure 10.1 Company-Wide Results Compared to Norms

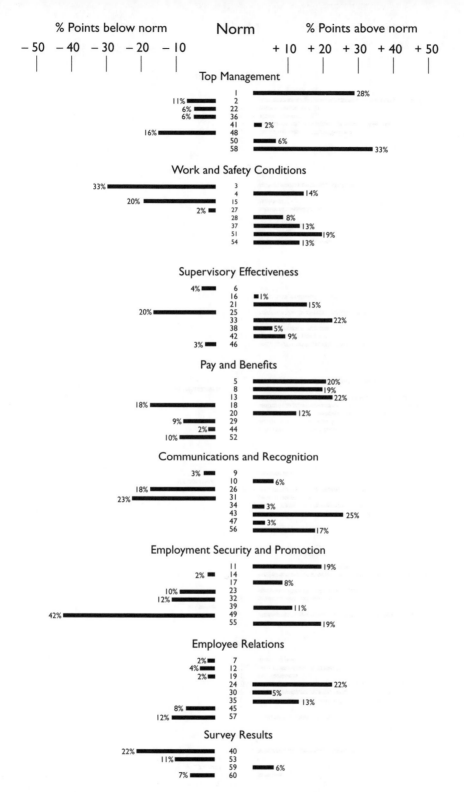

Figure 10.2 Food Service Results Compared to Norms

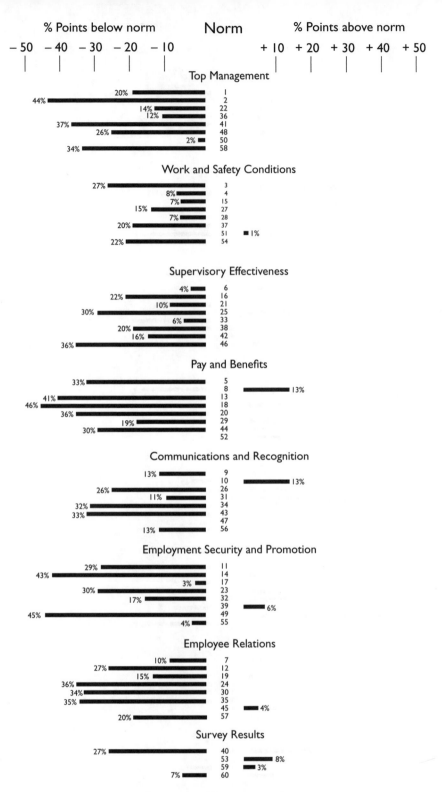

Figure 10.3 Housekeeping Results Compared to Norms

step if management is to preserve its integrity and keep its promise to share the results—good or bad.

Sharing the results is also important because it gives management additional insight into what motivated employees to respond as they did; sharing the graphs and written comments in small-group sessions sparks lively discussions, and can inspire creative solutions for survey-identified problems.

The causes, solutions, priorities, and suggestions that result from these small-group sessions are captured and summarized in writing for middle managers. It is the responsibility of the middle managers to digest the survey data, narrative comments, and small-group summaries, and to recommend action plans designed to address problem areas. These action plans then go to the Executive Team, which reviews; revises, if necessary; and approves them for implementation.

These action plans then become the responsibility of the managers to implement according to an agreed-upon schedule. Wesley's performance approval system called Results Management is used to track a manager's success, or lack thereof, in implementing action plans.

This series of steps following the receipt of the Employee Opinion Survey results is an effective way to demonstrate management's desire to involve employees in a problem-solving capacity. And, when done well, it can result in improved morale and increased employee "ownership" in the quality of their work experience.

TIMETABLE

The Employee Opinion Survey cycle typically takes 16 weeks from start to finish:

Week 1: Survey is administered to employees.

Week 7: Survey results are tabulated, interpreted, and returned to management.

Week 9: Management personnel have reviewed survey results and scheduled small-group sessions to find "causes and solutions."

Week 12: Small-group sessions have occurred and key points have been summarized in writing.

Week 15: Middle managers have drafted action plans for review by Executive Team.

Week 16: Executive Team has reviewed, revised, and approved action plans for implementation.

COST

The cost of Employee Opinion Surveys will vary depending on the survey instrument and research consultant you use. The cost of the IMC Employee Opinion Survey averages $15 per employee. This includes the pre-survey work, the survey administration itself, results tabulation and interpretation, and the post-survey work. The IMC recommends that management re-survey within 2 years of the initial survey and every other year thereafter to assess progress and determine internal trend.

CONCLUSION

Wesley now has internal trends for the eight quality factors, by employee work group, as well as comparisons to current national norms. Our results over time reflect management initiatives and the impact of external forces. The results have been critical in establishing focused action plans and a baseline during hard times. Along with other quality measurement tools, these Employee Opinion Surveys have provided grist for our continuous quality improvement program, at a reasonable cost.

The effort has paid off. Our motivated work force can take the credit for clean health department surveys, high levels of resident and family satisfaction, and accreditation by the Joint Commission on Accreditation of Healthcare Organizations.

REFERENCES

Schweikhart, S. B., & Strasser, S. (1994). The effective use of patient satisfaction data. *Topics in Health Information Management, 15*, 49–60.

Chapter 11

USING SATISFACTION SURVEYS IN LONG-TERM CARE AN ADMINISTRATOR'S PERSPECTIVE

Warren Slavin and Patricia Carter

INTRODUCTION

The long-term care industry is facing an era of unprecedented change. A service provider can pick up any of the numerous professional journals or publications and the message is the same. Medicare and Medicaid are undergoing transformation, federal elderly housing programs are under increased scrutiny, managed care is seen as the panacea for controlling costs, government oversight and regulatory requirements continue to demand more time and effort, and competition continues to escalate as other service delivery models emerge along the chronic care continuum. This list of changes is constantly evolving at a rapid pace. An industry that was once viewed as custodial care for the elderly is being propelled into the next century by an array of services, specialties, and funding scenarios that were unthinkable just a decade ago.

At the Hebrew Home of Greater Washington, a 558-bed long-term care facility, we have identified the emergence of a very different customer in

the wake of these changes. Our consumers are more educated and knowledgeable regarding the type and quality of services they want in their
senior years. Patients, families, and payers are demanding choices that will
provide cost-effective quality care in a residential-type setting and defer
nursing home placement for as long as possible. Our current customers,
in contrast to their predecessors, are helping to define service excellence.
This new era, where the customer, not the provider, defines service excellence makes it imperative that we keep in constant communication with
those who may seek our services and develop an ongoing method of
obtaining knowledge about their needs and wants for senior care. The successful organizations will be the ones who provide excellence in customer
service and satisfaction.

In this chapter, we will address what process the Hebrew Home has
developed and implemented to gain knowledge about our customers
and their satisfaction with our services. An overview of the role of the
customer, our organization's philosophy , and the utilization of customer
satisfaction data as part of our strategic planning and continuous quality improvement process will be provided. However, the core of the
chapter will focus on disseminating the results of the survey, reviewing
examples of the deployment process, and discussing our lessons learned.
The critical point to this chapter is that if you are not going to devote the
time and resources to productively utilizing the resident/family satisfaction data collected, then do not bother developing and implementing
a survey.

UNDERSTANDING THE CENTRALITY
OF THE CUSTOMER

The customer plays an essential role in the design of services and their
continued improvement. Focusing on the needs and wants of the customer is central to the success of any organization. Today's customers
demand quality service. Quality customer service requires that customer
needs be diagnosed and understood and programs and services developed to meet these needs. The long-term care organization must know
its customers and potential customers to make these determinations. The
long-term care market is very competitive, and the customer can select
an organization from a whole host of providers and settings. The key is
to differentiate your organization from the others by delivering service
excellence.

CUSTOMER KNOWLEDGE AND ITS
LINK TO SERVICE EXCELLENCE

At the Hebrew Home, we believe that establishing and maintaining a system for continuous quality improvement (CQI) is vital for the provision of service excellence. Planning services, establishing standardized measurements of quality, utilizing industry benchmarking and monitoring process outputs are all essential tools for CQI. However, if service excellence is defined by the customers, the toolbox would not be complete without information on how theses customers define quality. Gaining information about what delights the customer and then doing something with this knowledge can help an organization to improve service quality and meet its goals. Determining what the customer defines as quality is not an easy task, but it is crucial. It is an ongoing evolution that is never satisfied. Complacency in the marketplace must be continually guarded against if an organization is to be successful. Thus, given the importance of customer knowledge, more and more long-term care service providers are asking their customers for their opinions on their services and gathering data on what satisfies or dissatisfies them.

SETTING THE STAGE AT THE HEBREW HOME

Considering Essential Elements

Developing and conducting a resident and family survey is just the first step. Asking the right questions in the right way will be for naught if the organization is not prepared to receive and to take action on the data. At the Hebrew Home of Greater Washington, we identified several elements that were essential for productive use of survey results. These elements included the following:

1. *The results of the resident/family satisfaction survey* needed to be seen by staff as essential information that would assist them in day-to-day operations and not as superfluous data that was not related to performance. The key is for staff to understand how to apply the information about customers' needs and wants to their hands-on work. To accomplish this, the process of utilizing the data had to be integrated into the formal objective setting process, linked to the organizational goals, and integrated with the performance appraisal process.

2. *A commitment to defining and understanding service excellence* needed to be articulated and confirmed throughout the organization. As part of

the performance improvement process, customer service had to be recognized as an ongoing organizational priority with the allocation of time and financial resources.

3. *The process has to be data driven* and the survey information correlated with other fact-gathering processes within the organization. This was accomplished by educating the staff and board on how to interpret the data and working cooperatively to reach consensus on what the data was telling us about our operations.

4. *The dissemination of the survey results* to departments had to be positive and conveyed within the quality improvement philosophy of the organization. The data obtained had to be interpreted as a means of helping us identify opportunities for improvement and not as a report card for punitive action.

Developing an Infrastructure

The Hebrew Home of Greater Washington's strategic quality planning approach provided the structure to utilize the results of the customer satisfaction survey. The keys to the success of our process are the involvement of all employees, the refinement of work processes, and the serious consideration and integration of customer needs. Our planning/deployment methodology is: (1) customer-driven, (2) participative, (3) data-driven, (4) outcome-and process-oriented, and (5) designed with a feedback loop, referred to as the Stewhart Cycle, Deming Cycle, or PDCA cycle (see Figure 11.1).

The first step in our organizational process was to establish, through our planning process, broad organizational goals. These goals serve as the focus for all subsidiary planning efforts. The goals identified through our planning process focused on improvement in customer satisfaction, service delivery, financial performance, and competitive market position. These goals are broad and generic to most long-term care organizations, however, the crucial step in the process is the deployment of the goals and establishing tasks specific to the organization.

Deployment, as we defined it, is the conversion of goals into actionable operational plans. The methodology is based on a process designed by the Juran Institute. A graphic display of this deployment process is depicted in Figure 11.2. This deployment process subdivides the goals into objectives. The objectives and specific tasks to achieve them are developed by the departments. As part of our planning process, the departments further delineate resources needed, responsibility, and anticipated outcomes. Specific examples of how the resident/family satisfaction results were utilized within this framework will be discussed later in the chapter.

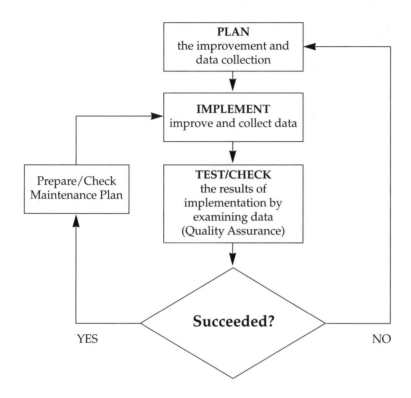

Figure 11.1 Planning/deployment methodology.

DEPLOYING THE RESIDENT/FAMILY
SATISFACTION SURVEY RESULTS

Understanding the Data

Once the results of the survey are obtained the information has to be digested and understood by senior management. All new data regarding the organization is reviewed and analyzed to ascertain its relevance to the strategic goals. The presentation of the data is an important issue. The quality of the data obtained from the customer satisfaction survey and the ease by which the organization can utilize the data, depends on how it is summarized and presented. A reliable questionnaire will be of little practical use to the facility if the data cannot be understood. (See example of presentation of data in Appendix IV, section c).

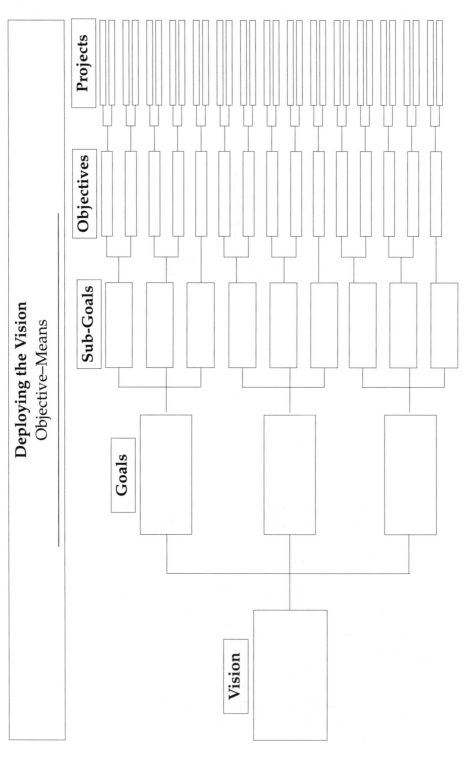

Figure 11.2 Steps in deploying the vision

The first step to understanding the information is a meeting with senior management and the consultant to review the findings and ensure consensus on the interpretation of the data. Once this is completed, the senior management group needs to review the key findings in conjunction with the existing strategic plan and goals, identify the priorities for the organization, and develop a plan for the dissemination of the material to department heads and the board. A sample of our communication action plan is included in Table 11.1. The survey will provide a large volume of data and it is imperative that it be managed and focused in relation to the organization's goals and objectives. Once these tasks are completed, an educational session is held with the department heads and the information on their individual areas is distributed to them.

Presentation of Survey Results

At the Hebrew Home the results of the survey were disseminated at a department head meeting according to the following agenda.

INTRODUCTION

This included such items as: (1) a brief background on the survey and review process for obtaining data, (2) a review of how the data fits into organizational strategic planning and CQI process, (3) a comparison and contrast with the prior survey results, if not the first survey, (4) an explanation of how rising expectations can make it difficult to move the satisfaction scores in a positive direction and how improving in one area may focus attention on other facets of care, and (5) a sharing of information from the customer survey consultant on others experiences with changing the rating scores , percentage that is reasonable to expect, length of time to affect change, etc.

OVERVIEW OF ORGANIZATION-WIDE RESULTS

Review the facility's overall satisfaction rating with the group. Highlight how likely the families and residents are to recommend the facility to others and what aspects of care most highly correlated with overall satisfaction. This information will assist the department heads in evaluating their individual department's ratings in relation to the whole organization and help them prioritize issues within their areas that have the most impact on customer satisfaction.

Table 11.1 1997 Resident/Family Satisfaction Study Time Line for Communication/Action

Results from survey received	Aug.–Sept.
Present information to senior management	Oct. 8
Form and implement task force to plan time line and presentations	Oct. 15 and 22
Present to department head. Distribute report	Oct. 30
Departments analyze data and submit improvement objectives to CEO/COO (use 1998 planning/ deployment objective form)	Nov. 20
Senior Management Group reviews and approves objectives	Nov. 25
Presentation to Board of Governors	Dec. 3
Distribute copies of report to attendees	
Mail copies to those not attending and to Oversight Committee	Dec. 4
Presentation to Oversight Committee	Dec. 10
Brainstorm and reach consensus on priority issues	
Schedule follow-up meeting to present department objectives	
Letter to families	
Presentation to Family Forum	Dec./Jan.
Oversight Committee meeting	Dec./Jan.
Review departmental 1998 objectives that address survey results and identified priorities	
Home Happenings (newsletter for staff) issued	Jan. 1998
Home Front article (community paper)	Feb./Mar. 1998
Insert for admission's packet	
Mini-survey at Family Forum to check key improvement issues	Mar. 1998
Mini-surveys with discharged residents by volunteers/admissions	Mar. 1998
Updates on improvements due with quarterly CQI/QA report	April 15, 1998
Reviewed by Performance Improvement Committee per CQI policy and procedures	
Continued Monitoring (PDCA)	
CQI quarterly report dates	July 15, 1998
	Oct. 14, 1998
	Jan. 13, 1998

HOW TO READ AND INTERPRET RESULTS

- Statistically significant differences (show sample data page)
- Correlations (review list from survey results)
- Regressions (show sample chart on overall satisfaction)
- Sample department chart; Show one department as example (review with that department head prior to sharing with group)
- Relate data from survey to departmental CQI/QA and planning process and link to organization's strategic direction

DISTRIBUTION OF DOCUMENTS (save until the end so staff are not reading report during educational session)

- Consultant's report, verbatim comments, and data for overall satisfaction and departmental information

SUMMARY

The department heads are instructed to review the information with their staff, identify areas of excellence and those in need of improvement, and develop objectives to address improvement areas. The department heads do this using the planning/deployment structure of the organization that we discussed earlier in the chapter. The departments' objectives are documented on the broad organizational deployment form and they are reviewed and approved by their immediate supervisor and the senior management team. Once approved the objectives are reviewed and monitored as part of the facility's ongoing PDCA cycle and CQI/QA process.

DEPLOYMENT PROCESS/ILLUSTRATED EXAMPLE

Table 11.2 provides an example of an objective deployed from the resident/family satisfaction survey utilizing our deployment process. One of the broad organizational goals of the Hebrew Home is to become a service-driven organization. We defined this as improving our quality of service, enhancing our customer focus, and improving our customer-friendliness. One area, from the survey, that related to this broad organizational goal was the ratings received for the Activities and Dietary departments.

Table 11.2 Hebrew Home of Greater Washington Annual Report: Status Of 1996 Objectives and Projects

Goal: Become a Service Driven Organization

Objective activities department	Supporting projects	Target completion date	Projected outcome	completion date	Status — Actual outcome / results
To better educate and communicate with families about the Activities Department	Send letters to family members on each unit twice a year—January and June	First set of letters mailed first week of February. Second set will be mailed at the end of June.	Families will learn more about activities program on each unit, and about taking their family members to programs off the units.	Feb. '96 July '96	Goal met. Letters mailed to all units (with the exception of the rehab units in Wass.) Very little feedback from families. Letters will be sent only once in '97 (in February) to keep families informed about the changes in the department: new staff members, new programs.
	Write an annual *Home Front* article talking about the department's philosophy and goals, and residents' rights	Article with pictures to appear in March 1996 Home Front.	Potential customers, community members and families will learn about the department's mission, its objectives in enhancing quality of life.	March '96	Goal met. The article (with pictures) has become a valuable teaching tool and is distributed to new families at the "welcome brunch" held quarterly.
	Plan two family/resident activities-one floor or unit in each building	April 1996-2nd floor in SK and 5W in Wass.	Families will feel more connected to the Home in a "good time" atmosphere. Again, will learn about our program first-hand.	April 14 - 5W in Wass. April 30 - 2nd floor in SK	Goal met. Both events were *extremely* successful. Many families attended each event, and the feedback was excellent. As a result, 5W, 5N, 4N, 1E, 2E, 2S, and 4E will have family/resident events in '97.

Table 11.2 *(continued)*

Objective activities department	Supporting projects	Target completion date	Projected outcome	completion date	Status Actual outcome / results
To better educate and communicate with families about the Activities Department	Create a pictorial collage of residents participating in activities which will be displayed on each unit twice a year.	End of May 1996 End of November 1996	Families and other visitors will see pictures of residents "in action" on each floor.	May '96 Nov. '96	Goal met. Pictures were displayed in SK corridors, and in the tower rooms in Wasserman. The Wass. location was poor - very few people noticed the pictures. We'll rethink locations for the future.
To increase the variety of programs offered to better meet the residents' needs.	Plan a 4–6 session course to be offered in both buildings (for intact residents).	"Women in Judaism," April 1996 "Election 1996" -October 1996	Intact residents will have opportunity to meet away from their units - increased socialization	Mar. 27, 3 sessions in April.	Twenty-five intact residents attended all four sessions of the course. Outstanding feedback. Election '96 never happened due to resignation of a therapist.
	Train volunteers to conduct regularly scheduled art tours in the Wasserman Building (for intact and impaired residents).	Training in May and June	We will use resources in our own building to expand residents' horizons at whatever level they function	June '96	Goal partially met - 3 volunteers were trained to conduct tours, but program was never implemented due to illness and resignation in the department.

Table 11.2 (continued)

Objective activities department	Supporting projects	Target completion date	Projected outcome	Status	
				completion date	Actual outcome / results
	Plan 4 trips using the Ring House bus (for intact residents).	April, May, September, October	Residents will have the opportunity to get out in the community - a request they made in the customer satisfaction survey	April, May, Sept., Oct. '96	Goal met. Ten residents enjoyed traveling to Washington or Sugarloaf Mountain (each trip). Four trips are scheduled for '97.
To increase the variety of programs offered to better meet the residents' needs.	Work with teams on 3 West and 4 East to develop a calendar of full-day programming with all disciplines participating in residents' stimulation.	Starting January 1996 - refinements throughout the year	More positive structured stimulation for Alzheimer's / behavior residents. We will be more competitive with other facilities providing full-day programs for these populations.	Ongoing process.	Goal met. The biggest changes occurred on 4E at mid-year, and still continues. Nurses on 3W and 4E conduct groups weekly. Family feedback - especially on 4E - very positive. Continued refinements in '97.
	Develop a more structured 1:1 program and a better documentation tool - to be piloted on 3 North and 3 South	Tool developed in January 1996 - assessment of pilot in December 1996	To provide consistent stimulation for residents who will not or cannot participate in groups.	Throughout the year	Goal met. Particularly successful on 3N - a heavy-care unit: Residents participate in groups in the morning, nap in the afternoon, and enjoy 1:1 visits in their rooms. Activities therapist and assistants document each visit.

Table 11.2 (*continued*)

Objective activities department	Supporting projects	Target completion date	Projected outcome	Status	
				completion date	Actual outcome / results
	Increase the number of programs offered on Sundays in each building - 6-8 groups in each building	Starting January 1996	Sundays will be more like any day of the week - residents will receive more stimulation	Ongoing	Goal met. An activities assistant works in each building on Sundays and conducts seven groups. Therapists conduct two groups or oversee a special Social Hall event. Residents are receiving more stimulation. Sunday is more like any other day of the week.
	To create a summer day camp program in Wasserman. Utilize the Day Care Room and Tyser Garden.	Starting June '96	Residents will benefit from a complete change of atmosphere and routine	Aug. '96	*Extremely* successful. *WASHINGTON JEWISH WEEK* wrote a lovely article about the program. Each unit (not the rehab center) went to "camp" twice in the course of the summer. Will be repeated in 1997.

Table 11.2 (continued)

Objective activities department	Supporting projects	Target completion date	Projected outcome	Status	
				completion date	Actual outcome / results
Implement Aladdin Heat-on-Demand System	This is a state-of-the art heated pellet system to assure greater temperature retention for resident hot foods	September 1996	Increase temperature retention of hot foods on resident trays. Increase resident perception of food flavor and overall quality.	August 1996	Implementation was uneventful. Results were dramatic and immediate. Objective measuring tools have revealed significant heat retention up to 40 minutes from service. Positive perceptual differences have been noticed since the inception of the system.
Improve dining atmosphere for residents	Establish interdisciplinary quality improvement team	June 1997	Improved resident satisfaction with the dining room experience.	June 1997	Team completed. Root causes of resident dissatisfaction identified through quality improvement process. Action plan developed and implemented. Satisfaction to be monitored informally and through results on the next customer survey.

The Hebrew Home's Activities Department was shown to be highly rated by the family members both on an overall basis and on specific elements. Nearly three quarters (74%) of families were highly satisfied with the activities department overall (rating a 6 or 7 on a scale from 1 to 7 with 7 being extremely satisfied) and 93% rating the department 5, 6, or 7. Of those respondents who were less than fully satisfied with the Hebrew Home's Activities Department, they expressed the need for more appropriate activities for relative's intellectual level (33%), better information to residents about available activities (31%), staff encouragement for residents to participate in activities (28%), and provision of more activities (17%). In summary, the data indicated families felt they did not know enough about activities available for the residents, and they also perceived that there was not a wide variety of programs offered to meet the residents' needs.

In the examples shown on the deployment forms in Table 11.2, the activity department's objectives were developed to respond to the data from the resident/family satisfaction survey. The Activities Department deployed these objectives after analyzing the data from the survey and brainstorming as a department on projects to address the improvement area identified. As the deployment form indicates, these objectives supported the Home's broad organizational goal to become a service-driven organization. This illustrates how the Home integrated the resident/satisfaction survey information. The objectives developed by the departments to address improvement areas are tracked and monitored within this framework.

One of the lowest-rated areas of the Hebrew Home was the Food Services or Dietary Department. Based upon the correlation analysis, food, however, was not a key factor in overall satisfaction with the facility, but nevertheless presented us with an area that needed to be evaluated and analyzed for improvement. A closer look at the data provided insight into specific areas of dissatisfaction and helped us focus on items to increase customer satisfaction. Among specific aspects of the food service, family members were most satisfied with the menu variety offered in the dining room (47% rated it a 6 or 7 and 80% rated it a 5, 6, or 7). Respondents were less than satisfied with the atmosphere in the dining room (40% rated a 6 or 7 and 69% rated a 5,6, or 7). Menu variety and the atmosphere in the dining room are the only aspects of the food service that were even slightly important to families, so the information indicated that attention to these issues could improve overall satisfaction with the food service. The aspect of the food that displeased the most residents was the temperature when served to them.

After the Dietary Department had thoroughly reviewed the information as a team, the department developed several objectives to address improvement areas highlighted by the data reviewed. (See Table 11.2) This included the investigation and implementation of the Aladdin Heat-on-Demand System to provide greater temperature for the residents' food which would also improve overall perception of taste. These were two key characteristics tied to resident satisfaction with food service. A quality assurance monitoring system to evaluate the temperature of food was initiated prior to the new system and continued after implementation. A significant increase in heat retention to 40 minutes was verified, and informal random solicitation of the residents' opinions indicated that satisfaction with the food was improving. A second initiative implemented was the formation of a quality team task force to examine and provide an implementation plan to improve the dining experience as perceived by the residents and families. Since several disciplines impact on the atmosphere in the dining room, the team was composed of representatives from the Dietary, Nursing, and Social Work Departments as well as residents. The results of the second Hebrew Home resident/family satisfaction survey indicated that the Dietary Department's efforts were successful. In summary, the elements of the deployment process are:

- Subdivided broad goals
- Specific objectives
- Assigned responsibility and target date
- Identified projects/actions
- Identified resource needs
- Allocation of resources
- Measurable outcomes
- Monitoring and evaluation process

EXPERIENCE

The Hebrew Home has been through two cycles (4 years) of its resident/satisfaction survey process. Our experiences have taught us a lot about the practical application of satisfaction data to improve customer service and care. We have learned that the effort expended in preparing the organization to focus on and understand a customer-driven organization is essential for the successful utilization of resident/family satisfaction surveys. With the development of a sound infrastructure, including a solid deployment methodology such as the Juran Institute's Strategic Quality Planning process, service improvement efforts can be productive. However, even with the Home's well-developed deployment process, there are pitfalls. We are still learning ways to improve the integration of the data into our quality/planning efforts and how to determine improvement efforts that will have the most positive impact on resident/family satisfaction. This will probably be an ongoing evolution for the organization.

PITFALLS

Some of the obstacles encountered and lessons learned include:

INTERPRETATION OF DATA

What does the data really tell us about satisfaction with our services and products? Truly understanding and interpreting the data is not an easy task. The satisfaction ratings are tied to broad topics. In order to get specific data, the questionnaire would be too long to be functional. Therefore, it is difficult to narrow the focus to manageable improvement projects and or ones that will target the customers needs and/or wants and make significant impact on satisfaction scores.

The Activities Department's objective deployment process described earlier and depicted in Table 11.2, is an example of this lesson. The Activities Department thought they had adequately identified objectives that would result in increased customer satisfaction. However, on the subsequent wave, satisfaction with activities actually decreased slightly. This prompted further analysis of our data interpretation. In doing this, we have identified some improvement efforts that might help us better focus our efforts. We believe there is a need to communicate throughout the year with families and residents regarding the results of the survey, the projects we have implemented in regard to their responses, and their perception of how we are doing. We have not designed the instruments and/or other methods of obtaining feedback between surveys. However, we believe that the listening posts already exist within the organization that can be used to receive immediate feedback on our improvement efforts and allow us to make adjustments periodically as appropriate. These listening posts include such media as the resident councils, family forums, welcome program, and discharge follow-up calls. This will hopefully help us focus on what features of our services matter most to the customer and determine what really is the root cause of their dissatisfaction. If our improvement projects are not increasing satisfaction, we can get immediate feedback and make adjustments with the users' input. In addition, this increased communication with our customers we believe will further enhance their understanding of our commitment to service excellence and the value we place on their input. This alone may increase overall satisfaction.

INTEGRATION OF DATA

The resident/satisfaction data cannot stand alone. Initial interpretation needs to be correlated with the other listening posts, as mentioned above, and the data that is obtained through the departments, ongoing CQI monitoring of quality indicators. This can further assist the organization in prioritizing improvement needs and in identifying trends and or common themes that need to be addressed throughout the organization.

RECOGNITION OF CHANGE

The only constant in today's long-term care environment is change. Our organizations are challenged to provide high-quality care and caring in the face of extreme pressures from many sources. Added to this is the challenge of dealing with increasingly demanding consumers. For many organizations, the knowledge that they must become increasingly customer-driven and must strive consciously and conscientiously for service excellence is a real change in focus. The recognition of this change is coming at a time of many other changes in the delivery of eldercare. Management of these changes in the context of the organization is critical. "Focusing on the customer is essential for advancing the organization. It's only once you have laid that foundation that the organization will be able to respond to change rapidly as it needs to." (Buzzell, & Gale, 1987.)

TIME LAG

We have experienced a real time lag between the time improvements are made and they are perceived and acknowledged by the customer. This can be demoralizing to staff who have worked hard to implement improvement projects, only to see satisfaction scores stay the same, increase slightly, or decline despite their efforts. Realistic expectations need to be conveyed and established with the departments both as a group and individually as they evaluate their specific ratings. The consultant can assist the organization here by relating the time it takes to impact scores and the degree of change that can be expected based on their statistical history with other surveys. In our consultant's experience, it takes a minimum of 6 months to a year before the changes that are instituted have any impact on the scores at all. In the case of the long-term care institution, it may take even longer, since typically the families are not interacting with the organization on a daily basis. Therefore, improvement efforts may not be readily recognized by the majority of families unless they are very dramatic and continually highlighted in the facility.

COMMUNICATION

Communication with the board, department heads, staff, residents, families, and the community is important. However, communication with department managers and staff is the most critical. These players are key to accepting the need for change and implementing it. It is important to share successes and discuss frustrations and roadblocks. This strengthens organizational alignment and fosters a supportive and learning culture which is imperative to meet the challenges in today's long-term care market.

CONCLUSION

In summary, the resident/family satisfaction survey is a valuable tool for achieving service excellence in the long-term care organization. However, it is only one tool, and it can not stand alone. Its value can only be realized through the careful planning of its development, implementation, and integration throughout the organization. This is not a simple task and it is not a one-time event. Just as the resident/family satisfaction survey is ongoing so is the evolution of how to interpret and use the data to realize the desired outcomes. Increasing customer knowledge is continuous and requires a systematic approach that puts the customer first and aligns the organization's resources and processes to heighten customer satisfaction. The winners are organizations that have learned that the best way to become externally focused and internally aligned is to focus their organization on the customer. The externally focused, internally aligned organization will dominate the future. Put even stronger, it is the only kind of organization that may survive the future. (Forum Corporation, 1992.)

REFERENCES

Buzzell, R., & Gale, B. (1987) GE Medical Systems ASIA. (Ed.), The PIMS principles (pp.). New York City: Free Press.

Forum Corporation. (1992) *Leading the customer focused company: Lessons learned from listening to the voices of leaders.* Boston, MA: Author.

Chapter 12

INTEGRATING SATISFACTION SURVEYS AND OTHER SOURCES OF INFORMATION ON QUALITY OF LONG-TERM CARE

David R. Zimmerman and Barbara J Bowers

As a source of information in assessing the quality of long-term care, satisfaction surveys are a relative newcomer. The growing popularity of satisfaction surveys is a welcome development because it reflects a long overdue recognition that the consumer—in this case the resident, or alternatively a family member—is a credible source of information on quality of care, and quality of life in long-term care.

As satisfaction surveys take their place along with other sources of information in measuring the quality of long-term care, it is essential to examine how these various sources relate to each other, as well as the larger and more important questions of how each source contributes to the measurement of both quality of care and quality of life. Addressing these two questions guides our discussion throughout this chapter. Along the way, we offer a new organizing framework for understanding quality, what each source contributes to this understanding, and what insights, collectively, these various sources provide about quality in long-term care. We do this by exploring the conceptual history and evolution of quality reviews in long-term care, and specifically, addressing the use of MDS data for this purpose.

Understanding quality and how it has been measured takes us on a curious and quite circuitous journey. In general, discussions of quality in long-term care (Davis et al., 1997; Grant et al., 1996; Grau et al., 1995; Katz et al., 1993; Kleinsorge & Koenig, 1991; Kosberg, 1974; Kruzich et al., 1992; Maithiasson & Anderson, 1997; Meister & Boyle, 1996; Parasuraman et al., 1998; Pearson et al., 1993; Spalding, 1989) have reflected—explicitly or implicitly—the following assumptions:

1. Quality is a multidimensional concept.
2. Multiple sources of information must be brought to bear on assessments of quality.
3. Quality of life and quality of care are the primary divisions of quality.
4. Quality of life is conceptually and empirically distinct from quality of care.
5. Information sources related to quality of care and quality of life are generally distinct.
6. Quality of care is primarily, if not exclusively, the domain of clinicians and can therefore only (credibly) be assessed by professionals (as opposed to residents and family members).
7. Quality of life, on the other hand, is primarily the domain of the resident and family and must therefore be evaluated through resident and family participation; further, this domain should be tapped.
8. Satisfaction surveys are the primary means of assessing quality of life.

In the course of our discussion in this chapter, we address these assumptions, sometimes confirming our agreement with them and in other cases rejecting or amending them.

CONCEPTUAL FRAMEWORK

It is generally assumed that quality in long-term care is a multidimensional concept. Beginning with Donabedian's description of quality as comprised of a structure, process, and outcome triad (Donabedian, 1980) and proceeding through the last two decades, the complexity of quality in long-term care, and the resulting challenges to its measurement, have been well established. A variety of taxonomies to categorize the dimensions of quality are evident in the frameworks on which regulatory and accreditation quality assurance initiatives are based. While the specific elements of these taxonomies have been described using different terms, a reasonable summary of the taxonomies is that they have generally included the following "domains" or elements of quality:

1. Medical/clinical status and related interventions
2. Functional status and related care, including:
   - Physical functioning, such as mobility, ambulation, toileting, eating
   - Cognitive functioning, typically including memory, orientation, capacity for decision-making
   - Emotional status, typically including mood (depression), behavioral symptoms, spiritual needs
3. General well-being, including:
   - Preserving resident rights;
   - Maintaining independence in decisions and life patterns,
   - Maintaining integrity of finances,
   - Being treated with respect,
   - Maintaining dignity;
   - Maintaining privacy;
   - Interacting with other residents; and
   - Engaging in meaningful activities

While there can be reasonable debate about which specific dimensions and measures should be included in each domain, as well as how they should be organized into a taxonomy of care, the more important questions are:

1. How do the dimensions and measures relate to each other?
2. What are the appropriate sources of information for each one?
3. What do they tell us about quality?

Answering these questions, in turn, requires one to address additional questions:

1. Are the general categories identified above independent, or related to one another, and if related, how? (for example, are they complementary, or in competition with each other?)
2. How does quality of life relate to quality of care?
3. Do the three domains require separate, the same, or overlapping data sources?
4. How can the data sources best be tapped (collected, integrated, interpreted) to arrive at credible and useful assessments of quality?
5. Do the data sources match the questions they are used to address?

SOURCES OF INFORMATION ON THE
OF LONG-TERM CARE

As pointed out earlier, a variety of sources have been employed to assess the quality of long-term care. Typically used sources can be categorized as follows:

- Records, including medical records, billing records;
- Opinions of residents (limited to a narrow range of topics);
- Opinions of family members or others supporting the resident (limited to a narrow range of topics);
- Opinions of and information from staff; and
- Direct observation of care by an external assessor

These sources have provided the foundation for the diverse set of quality of care assessments that have been employed to monitor quality over the past decade. Below we provide a summary of those examples, and then focus in more detail on the use of resident assessment data as a source of information.

The federal and state survey processes, as part of a nursing home's compliance with federal certification and state licensing obligations, have been employed for more than two decades to gather data on the quality of care in nursing homes. The survey processes are built around a multidimensional set of quality indicators. At least in intent, the survey process utilizes each of the sources of information on quality delineated above. Surveyors are instructed to examine resident medical records, interview residents and family members, and converse with facility caregiver staff in order to arrive at conclusions about the quality of care and life of the residents. In addition, an important part of their on-site activities is the direct observation of resident care, as well as the interaction between residents and staff members.

The broad-based approach of the survey process reflects the fact that the survey is intended to evaluate all aspects of the quality of care and life of residents. There have clearly been efforts to link quality of life and quality of care from the resident's perspective (Davis et al., 1991; Kane & Kane, 1988; Kruzich, Clinton, & Kelber, 1992; Spalding, 1985). The importance of resident expectations in determining satisfaction has also been acknowledged (Davis, 1991; Parasuraman, Zeithaml, & Berry, 1988). What has not been done adequately, we suggest, is to examine how quality indicators (as clinical measures) relate to quality of life and how expectations are generated. These two questions have important implications for understanding the results of quality of care or quality of life measures, as well as knowing what to do with them.

For example, Kruzich et al. (1992) documented a relationship between "personal and environmental influences" and resident satisfaction measures. What is still needed is a way to examine how these influences relate to quality of life, as well as how clinical outcomes relate to the personal and environmental influences. The Kruzich study still keeps these elements separate.

Another example of quality of care assessment that involves multiple sources of information is the set of ombudsman programs throughout the United States. The ombudsman programs, mandated by federal law, have provided the closest approximation to a "consumer perspective" on quality, in the sense that the ombudsmen are supposed to represent the interests and perspective of the nursing home consumer, both residents and family members. While many of the specific ombudsman activities are initiated by complaints filed by consumers, the approach taken to investigating the complaints can and usually does incorporate a variety of information sources and collection strategies.

Over the past decade, "administrative data", or "program records", have also been used to analyze quality of care. The earliest source of administrative data to be used was claims data, i.e. the information available on reimbursement for services rendered under federal or state Medicare or Medicaid programs. Two major problems with claims data are the lack of information on residents not funded through Medicare and Medicaid, and the fundamental differences in information available from one state to the next, reflecting important state-to-state differences in the Medicaid program itself.

More recently, another form of program records—resident assessments, in the form of the Minimum Data Set—has emerged as a source of information with which to evaluate quality of care. The MDS is a federally mandated resident assessment instrument, used in combination with a series of Resident Assessment Protocols, or RAPs, as a way of organizing and documenting the status of residents, and the consequent decisions about needed care interventions, on many different dimensions. As of June, 1998, all nursing homes are required to submit MDS data on all residents to the state survey agency. The MDS provides information on both the outcomes and processes of care in individual nursing homes, especially as a mechanism to target further review.

The MDS Quality Indicators

Under funding from the Health Care Financing Administration as part of the Multistate Nursing Home Case Mix and Quality Demonstration, researchers at the Center for Health Systems Research and Analysis at the

University of Wisconsin-Madison) have developed a set of quality indicators based on MDS data (Zimmerman, et al., 1995). The quality indicators (QIs) were developed through a systematic process involving extensive review of research literature, interdisciplinary clinical input, empirical analyses, and field testing by staff at the University of Wisconsin-Madison.

Initially, a set of 175 quality indicators in 12 domains was developed. The initial set of QIs was reviewed by several national clinical panels representing the major disciplines involved in the provision of nursing home care. The clinical panels provided a rigorous critique, assisted in refining or deleting proposed QIs, and suggested new QIs.

CHARACTERISTICS OF THE QIS

The QIs can best be described by identifying their major characteristics along several dimensions:

Resident/Facility Level QIs. At the resident level, QIs are defined either as the presence or absence of a condition. Additionally, the resident level QIs can be aggregated across all residents in a facility to define facility-level quality indicators and assess the facility level of quality. These facility-level QIs can be used to compare any given facility with others or with nursing home population norms at the state or multistate level.

Process and Outcome QIs. The QIs were designed to cover both processes and outcomes of care and to include both prevalence and incidence types of measure. Process indicators represent the content, actions, and procedures invoked by the provider in response to the assessed condition of the resident. Process quality includes those activities that go on between health professionals and residents. Outcome measures represent the status of residents, i.e., whether the resident improved, remained the same, or declined.

Risk Factors. Some QIs require adjustment for risk. For these QIs we developed risk factors to identify resident characteristics that are associated with the likelihood of experiencing the process or outcome of care indicated by the QI. For instance, residents with desensitized skin are expected to have a greater likelihood of developing pressure sores than are residents without desensitized skin. We used a categorical approach to risk adjustment, which entails assigning each resident to either a high- or low-risk group depending on whether risk factors are present.

THE PRESENT SET OF QI'S

Through the clinical review and analytic process described, the number of QIs was reduced to a more operationally feasible set of 31 indicators. The QIs were then pilot-tested and refined to yield the set of 30 indicators that was used in the Case Mix and Quality Demonstration. These QIs are presented in Table 12.1.

The 30 QIs have been converted to a form that is consistent with the current version of the MDS (version 2.0). Because of differences in the content of various versions of the MDS and quarterly supplement, in most states only 24 of the full set of 30 QIs can be defined and used.

QIs are the basis of a major national project to provide feedback to nursing home providers that can be used to develop quality improvement initiatives. In the project, CHSRA utilizes the MDS information to provide participating facilities with reports of comparative QI information on individual QIs at the facility level and at the individual resident level. The reports and supplementary information assist participating facilities in their ongoing problem identification and internal quality improvement activities. More than 600 facilities nationwide are now participating in the CHSRA QI provider initiative projects.

The QIs are also being incorporated into HCFA's national MDS automation system. This system is being implemented to assist all nursing homes in the United States in meeting new federal requirements to submit MDS information on all residents to their respective state agencies. CHSRA staff members are developing and testing the software that will be used to provide QI reports to both state survey agencies and each facility in each state.

The MDS and "Quality of Life"

One of the major issues surrounding the implementation of the MDS has been the extent to which it adequately covers what has commonly come to be known as "quality of life". The MDS has been criticized for not providing adequate information on this aspect of care. To some extent this criticism is well-founded, since many elements of "quality of life"—such as privacy, dignity, respect from caregiver staff—are not captured on the MDS instrument. However, some important quality of life elements are addressed in the MDS. Some examples of quality of life areas covered on the MDS are presented in Table 12.2.

Despite the fact that the MDS does provide information—both directly and indirectly—about quality of life, there remains the general perception that the instrument has more to contribute to the measurement of a resident's clinical, medical, and functional status than his or her well-being, or other dimensions more closely associated with "quality of life". Satisfaction surveys, on the other hand, are sometimes thought to better tap these "quality of life" dimensions.

WORKING TOWARD AN ALTERNATIVE FRAMEWORK OF QUALITY

As we return to the central questions in this chapter—how do sources of information on quality relate to each other, and what does each contribute—we begin by asserting that the above distinction between the potential contribution of the MDS and satisfaction surveys is an inaccurate one, and that the inaccuracy stems from a misconception about the relationship between quality of care and quality of life. As an alternative, we propose a framework that acknowledges and emphasizes the inextricable relationship between quality of care and quality of life, that establishes quality of life as the paramount category, and that treats quality of care as one element (often a very important one in this population) of quality of life.

Quality of Life and Quality of Care

Misunderstandings about the relationship between quality of life and quality of care stems from the commonly held assumption—which we introduced at the beginning of the chapter—that the two concepts are conceptually (and empirically) distinct. This misunderstanding takes on even greater significance when—as is frequently the case—quality of care and quality of life are mistakenly viewed as being in competition with each other. Maintaining the distinction between them leads to several important misperceptions, including an inability to see the impact of quality of care, both outcomes and processes, on quality of life. An example of how this would work is that enhancing quality of care involves interventions that address clinical, medical, or sometimes functional problems of the resident, while enhancing quality of life more often refers to matters involving psychosocial status, or general "well-being". This is in contrast to the more integrated view we are proposing, which explores how clinical, medical, and functional problems, and the interventions related to them, affect

Table 12.1 Quality Indicators Used in Demonstration Facility and Resident Reports

Domain		Quality Indicators	Process / Outcome	Risk Adjustment
Accidents	1.	Prevalence of any injury	Outcome	No
	2.	Prevalence of falls	Outcome	No
Behavioral &	3.	Prevalence of problem behavior towards others	Outcome	Yes
emotional patterns	4.	Prevalence of symptoms of depression	Outcome	No
	5.	Prevalence of symptoms of depression with no treatment	Both	No
Clinical management	6.	Use of nine or more scheduled medications	Process	No
Cognitive patterns	7.	Incidence of cognitive impairment	Outcome	No
Elimination &	8.	Prevalence of bladder/bowel incontinence	Outcome	Yes
continence	9.	Prevalence of occasional bladder/bowel incontinence without a toileting plan		
	10.	Prevalence of indwelling catheters	Both	No
	11.	Prevalence of fecal impaction		
Infection control	12.	Prevalence of UTIs	Process	Yes
	13.	Prevalence of antibiotic/anti-infective use	Outcome	No
Nutrition & eating	14.	Prevalence of weight loss	Outcome	No
	15.	Prevalence of tube feeding	Process	No
	16.	Prevalence of dehydration	Outcome	No
Physical functioning	17.	Prevalence of bedfast residents	Outcome	No
	18.	Incidence of decline in late-loss ADLs	Outcome	Yes
	19.	Incidence of contractures	Outcome	Yes
	20.	Lack of training/skill practice or ROM for mobility dependent residents	Both	No

Table 12.1 *(continued)*

Domain		Quality Indicators	Process / Outcome	Risk Adjustment
Psychotropic drug use	21.	Prevalence of antipsychotic use in the absence of psychotic and related conditions	Process	Yes
	22.	Prevalence of antipsychotic daily dose in excess of surveyor guidelines	Process	No
	23.	Prevalence of antianxiety/hypnotic use	Process	No
	24.	Prevalence of hypnotic use on a scheduled basis or PRN greater than two times in last week	Process	No
	25.	Prevalence of use of any long-acting benzodiazepine	Process	No
Quality of life	26.	Prevalence of daily physical restraints	Process	No
	27.	Prevalence of little or no activity	Outcome	No
Sensory function / communication	28.	Lack of corrective action for sensory or communication problems	Both	No
Skin care	29.	Prevalence of stage 1-4 pressure ulcers	Outcome	Yes
	30.	Insulin dependent diabetes with no foot care	Both	No

Note: From Zimmerman D. R., Karova S. L., Arling G., Ryther-Clark, B., Collins T., Ross R., Sainfort F. (1995). Development and teaching of nursing home quality indicators. *Health Care Financing Review 16*(4), 107–127.

Table 12.2 Example Quality of Life Measures From the Minimum Data
Set (MDS)

Depression

Depression without treatment

involvement in activities

  • Social engagement

Physical restraints

Unsettled relationships

Participation in assessment/care planning

Pain

Dignity/privacy

---

quality of life. Obviously, then, quality of life assessments require the use
of data on clinical processes and outcomes (MDS) as important but insufficient elements.

Unfortunately, the artificial division between quality of life and quality of care results in an equally regrettable division between the sources of
information, with implications for how respondent perspectives are
reflected in those sources and used to inform quality assessments. There
appears to be a formidable, if not impenetrable, wall between the sources
of information for more clinical and functional domains and those that are
approved to tap the domains related to "well-being". Program records,
administrative data, and clinical professional assessment are often the
source of the former, while the latter are typically reserved as the bailiwick
of the resident or family member. This leads to a situation in which the
clinical and functional domains are restricted to reliance on the clinical professional perspective, while the well-being and psychosocial domain often
relies only on the consumer perspective, primarily through satisfaction
surveys.

As we have noted earlier, this view of the distinction between quality
of life and quality of care is inaccurate and undermines our achievement
of both. In fact, quality of life and quality of care are inextricably related,
both conceptually and empirically. Following from this belief, we suggest
that a more useful expression of the two concepts is that, at any point in
time, the quality of life of nursing home residents—just like that of any
other population—is a function of a multitude of factors, including but not
limited to the quality of the care they receive. The distinction between
nursing home residents and the rest of the population lies in the fact that
the former are more impaired and therefore more dependent on care-

givers—and the outcomes of their care—in order to maintain an acceptable quality of life. This, in turn, means that the relative importance of the quality of care in determining their quality of life is considerably greater—and the quality of that care therefore makes a much larger contribution—to nursing home residents' overall quality of life than is the case in the general population. Another important difference is that nursing home residents rely heavily on paid caregivers for social interaction, as well as many other important aspects of their lives that are not directly related to care delivery and outcomes. In other words, the things that define nursing home residents' quality of life are primarily driven by professional caregivers, by both the quality of the technical care they receive and the quality of their relationships with those who provide care. Their quality of life is therefore inextricably linked with caregiving processes and outcomes.

This expression of the relationship between quality of life and quality of care has a critical corollary. Quality of life needs to be viewed as the overarching concept, in the sense that it is the ultimate foundation on which to base assessments of how well nursing homes perform in delivering care to residents. Quality of life includes quality of care, rather than the reverse. Quality of care is a significant, and sometimes even a dominant, factor in the quality of life for nursing home residents—but quality of life cannot be subordinate to quality of care. When it is there is a danger of competition between these two "separate" domains. Quite the contrary, the quality of care provided nursing home residents needs to be defined primarily in terms of its impact on their quality of life. This, in turn, means that the quality of care—as it affects quality of life—should be defined broadly to include all the domains of quality of life, including its impact on the functional, emotional, clinical, and all other dimensions of resident status.

Resident Perceptions and Expectations

In order to have an adequate understanding of the relationship between the quality of care and the quality of life of a nursing home resident, it is necessary to consider the context in which these quality assessments are being done. The framework offered here integrates the perceptions of residents, including their expectations about the outcomes and processes of care with quality of life in general. More to the point, a resident's satisfaction with care simply reflects the match between resident expectations and resident experiences. In the course of our studies in nursing homes, we have identified the influence of context on resident expectations for care, and consequently on their assessments of satisfaction. We are suggesting, therefore, that resident expectations should also be assessed in order to determine how to interpret resident satisfaction. Satisfaction in this context of low expectations has a very different meaning than the same conclusion in the context of high expectations.

PRIOR KNOWLEDGE

Residents' prior knowledge about what life is like in a nursing home influences their expectations and consequently their expressed satisfaction. Residents were sometimes observed to express high levels of satisfaction while describing low quality of life. The explanation for this disparity is found in the low resident expectations that matched well with the experience that the quality of life and care was as good as could be expected. Very few residents expected either high quality of care or a high quality of life, which served to maintain a low standard against which to measure their nursing home experiences.

AGE-/HEALTH-DRIVEN EXPECTATIONS

Satisfaction was also mediated by what residents (as well as families, and facility staff) believed was reasonable to expect for someone of that age and impairment level. Thus, interpreting poor clinical outcomes or poor quality of life as primarily related to advanced age and general health status also led to high levels of satisfaction. It is important to make explicit what residents, family, providers, and the industry perceive as reasonable expectations on LTC settings. This is a question that is generally sidestepped in many current quality of life assessments.

NURSING HOME EXPERIENCE

In many cases resident expectations had been molded by the experience of living in the nursing home. This was particularly true of perceptions about the quality of food, response time to requests, and the quality of the interaction between residents and providers. In some instances, experiences created new categories of expectations, while in other instances, expectations about preexisting categories were altered. For example, residents might enter the nursing home believing that any medical problem would be addressed primarily by facility staff initiating contact with the physician. Through experience they might learn that much of the physician contact is actually initiated by the family and negotiated between family and the physician. Family expectations about who initiates physician contact, and whose responsibility it is to monitor medical/clinical problems, might shift as a consequence of nursing home experience. Thus, a lack of physician staff contact becomes the expectation. The consequence is that staff failing to contact the physician is not seen as a problem, and hence does not reflect negatively on satisfaction.

IMPORTANCE OF CONDITION, STATUS, OR TREATMENT

Residents bring to the satisfaction assessments notions about the importance of their functional status, medical condition, and treatment received influencing the context within which assessments are made. Nowhere is this more evident, for example, than in the interpretation of indicators like the MDS QIs.

The QIs can provide an important index of how clinically effective the care is in any given facility or for any given resident, including the impact of the condition on the quality of a particular resident's life. They cannot, however, reveal the importance of a particular clinical condition or its treatment for any given resident. We are suggesting that, in addition to any "objective" quality measure that the MDS QIs might offer, their significance must also be understood in relation to how they affect the resident's quality of life. In other words, the impact of decubitus ulcers, restraints, weight loss, and incontinence are important objective measures of quality but are mostly important through their effect on the resident's quality of life. Incontinence, and its meaning. Weight loss is, in itself, an important clinical indicator, but must also be viewed in terms of its meaning for quality of life rather than separate from it. The reasons leading to weight loss, and the consequences of not being able to eat, be it the pleasure of food or the social aspects of "dining", are quality of life issues related to this particular QI. Weight loss must be seen as part of this larger issue of quality of life. Thus, the QI represents an important, but not in and of itself a sufficient, criterion for assessing quality of life.

RESIDENT PHYSICAL, COGNITIVE, EMOTIONAL, AND CLINICAL STATUS

An undeniable corollary to the above point is that a resident's status in terms of the physical, cognitive, emotional, and clinical elements that define his or her overall situation will also have a profound effect on perceptions about quality of life and care. How one assesses a resident's "status" on a particular dimension, and how one defines and prioritizes the "importance" of a dimension to the resident's "well-being," is to some extent dependent on the resident's status on other dimensions. For example, if a resident is severely impaired clinically or functionally, the dimensions of well-being may be more constrained—or defined differently—by virtue of this impairment. This is not necessarily to say that some elements of care (or quality of care) lose their significance simply because of the existence of this impairment—quite the contrary; it could be that elements of well being such as interpersonal relationships may become even more important in the presence of such impairments and restrictions.

In combination, these contextual elements require a contingency perspective in the interpretation of how a resident perceives quality of life and quality of care. This contingency notion—and the complexity it introduces—profoundly complicates measurements of quality. Most importantly, it means that the definition and measurement of quality of care cannot be divorced or abstracted from the set of perceptions and expectations that the resident brings to the process.

THE UNDERDEVELOPMENT OF QUALITY OF LIFE

For whatever reason, the quality of life domain—at least as it has been traditionally conceptualized—remains relatively undefined. It is not clear whether this underdevelopment is a reflection of the belief that "quality of life" and "well-being" are so unique, idiosyncratic, or personal that a global standardized taxonomy is inappropriate (i.e., it runs too high a risk of missing what is truly significant to an individual), or whether it is simply that an ability to describe the concepts remains beyond the reach of our conceptual tools.

Whatever the reason, more work needs to be done to develop the quality of life and well-being domains. The accomplishment of such an objective is beyond the scope of this chapter. However, we have identified a few parameters that we think need to be integrated into such a taxonomy. They are based on interviews with nursing home residents who participated in several research projects conducted by both authors over the past several years. The order of presentation does not reflect an order of importance, as the order of importance necessarily varies with the situation.

Fear of victimization

Residents, as well as those considering a nursing home admission, expressed fear of being victimized by the nursing home and its staff. There is, for many, an expectation that they will be treated badly and that they may experience physical and emotional abuse. This fear of victimization, as well as any actual abuse, undermines the residents' sense of well-being. Actual abuse, of course, is clearly a crucial quality of life issue and must be addressed firmly and directly. Fear of victimization, however, is also an important quality of life issue that is rarely tapped through questions about actual experienced abuse, nor necessarily through satisfaction surveys, since it often requires an extended relationship and a great deal of trust to facilitate disclosure.

Social isolation

This is an area related to quality of life in a nursing home that we will address only briefly as an example of how quality of care and quality of life assessment can benefit from an integrated view. One group that is rarely the focus of special study or attention is the group of residents with severe, multiple sensory deficits. Residents with multiple sensory impairments were particularly likely to express feelings of isolation, although these comments were not confined to those with sensory impairments. Lack of meaningful interactions with others in the environment related to sensory impairment can also lead to extreme feelings of social isolation, undermining quality of life. Introducing resident expectations is also important when exploring the integration of quality of care with quality of life. Residents experiencing sensory deficits often understood their isolation to be the inevitable consequences of aging and illness when, in fact, a great deal could be done in most cases to create social links. Lack of awareness of possibilities to address these problems acted to keep expectations low and, consequently satisfaction with care high.

Reciprocity

Related to an opportunity to develop and sustain meaningful relationships is the expressed desire, of many residents, to be useful, to serve, to do good for others, in short to participate in a reciprocal relationship rather than being only the recipient of services . Many residents described the inability to give to others, or to do something useful as an impediment to a quality existence. Feelings of worthlessness, having nothing useful to give, lacking the capacity to be useful or helpful led residents to believe that reciprocity was not possible, hence, not expected.

Respect

Confirming another parameter often stressed as critical to quality of life, we also found a strong desire to be treated with respect, to be listened to, and to be taken seriously.

Discomfort

Residents with severe physical limitations tended to focus on bodily discomforts and tasks that they could not carry out without help. Their sense of well-being and quality of life seemed much more focused on bodily tending and physical comfort than on relationships. This observation raises important questions about the relationship between resident status and the relevant quality of life domains. It also demonstrates the danger in separating quality of life from quality of care.

It might be creative to develop items that measure resident/family satisfaction with such issues. Again links can be established with these items and relevant QIs. For example, how an assessment of a resident's perception of reciprocity of relationship (feeling useful, to serve and to do good) might be linked to a QI such as depression or involvement in activities. Perhaps, these could be stated as suggested linkages in a table format. Or, a creative use of Table 12.2 may be to link some of its key concepts with items tapping resident/client satisfaction.

SUMMARY AND IMPLICATIONS

The main points of our discussion can be summarized quite straightforwardly.

1. The multidimensional nature of quality of long-term care requires a complex conceptual framework within which to measure and assess it.
2. Satisfaction surveys are a welcome addition to the arsenal of information sources on quality, in part because they reflect acceptance of the long overdue notion that the resident and family member is a credible source of information about quality.
3. The traditional view of quality of life and quality of care is inaccurate in that it is based on the notion that the two concepts are conceptually and empirically distinct, and that they often are in conflict with each other.

4. This inaccuracy has led to a situation in which specific sources of information are often confined to excessively narrow roles in measuring quality. In particular, information from resident assessments is often relegated to restrictive duty only to capture clinical and functional aspects of care, while satisfaction surveys and other sources of resident perception are reserved only for examining issues about quality of life and well-being.

5. Resident perception is an essential element in assessing any dimension of the quality of care, including clinical outcomes and their significance for resident experience and quality of life.

6. Quality of care can be accurately and adequately assessed only if:
   - It is assessed in the context of its impact on quality of life;
   - It takes into account the expectations of the resident and the experience relative to that expectation; and
   - It takes into account all relevant perspectives, including both the resident/family member and the health care professional providing the care.

What are the implications of these points for the future of satisfaction surveys, and the other sources of information, in the quest to adequately measure quality of long-term care? Perhaps the most important implication is that satisfaction surveys, already an important tool in the kit as a testament to the credibility of the consumer, have an even more important and more comprehensive role to play. But with that potential comes a critical challenge: unless satisfaction surveys are prepared to take on a more expanded role, their utility will be reduced and their relevance heavily compromised. In the integrated quality of life-quality of care framework we are proposing, resident and family member information tools must be able to tap not only narrowly defined satisfaction with care, but all the relevant dimensions of resident perceptions that lead to defining quality of care. They have a clear, expanded role to play in capturing the resident perception on all dimensions of care quality, both outcome and process, as those dimensions affect quality of life.

Another important implication is that the conceptual framework within which to view quality of life and quality of care needs to be reformulated. The new framework must recognize that quality of life and quality of care are inextricably linked, with quality of life the overarching concept and quality of care a critical factor in defining quality of life across all its dimensions—particularly for an impaired population such as nursing home residents.

Still another implication is that more emphasis must be placed on the expectations which residents bring to assessments of satisfaction. This increased emphasis must focus on both the context within which the expectations are formed and the role of caregivers in that process.

The final implication is that the same, expanded role we have outlined for satisfaction surveys is awaiting other sources of information on quality. Those sources that directly or indirectly tap clinician and provider perspectives should not be restricted to measuring technical or clinical aspects of care, since those technical and clinical elements have a profound effect on quality of life as well.

There is, quite urgently, a need for more work in both conceptual and empirical camps to provide a more accurate and comprehensive framework within which to define quality of life and care, to more fully tap the variety of information sources on both concepts, and to ensure that we adequately include and integrate both the resident and the caregiver perspective in that process.

REFERENCE

Davis, M. A., (1991). On nursing home quality: A review and analysis. *Medical Care Review, 13*, 295–98.

Davis, M. A., Sebastian, J. G., & Tschetter, J. (1997). Measuring quality of nursing Home Service: Residents' Perspective. *Psychological Reports, 81*, 531–42.

Donabedian, A., (1980). *Explorations in quality assessment and monitoring: The definitions of quality and approaches to its assessment (Vol. 1).* Ann Arbor, MI: Health Administration Press.

Grant, N. K., Reimer, M., & Bannatyne, J. (1996). Indicators of quality in long-term care facilities. *International Journal of Nursing Studies, 33*, 469–78.

Grau, L., Chandler, B., & Saunders, C. (1995). Nursing home residents' perceptions of the quality of their care. *Journal of Psychosocial Nursing, 33*, 34–41.

Kane, R. A., & Kane, R. L. (1988), Long-term care: Variations on a quality assurance theme. *Inquiry, 25*, 132–46.

Katz, S., Ford, A. B., Moskowitz, R. W., Jackson, B. A., & Jaffee, M. W. (1993). Studies of illness in the aged: The index of ADL: A standardized measure of biological and psychosocial function. *Journal of the American Medical Association, 185*, 914–19.

Kleinsorge, I. K., & Koenig, H. F. (1991). The silent customers: Measuring customer satisfaction in nursing homes. *Journal of Health Care Management, 11*, 2–13.

Kosberg, J. I. (1974). Making institutions accountable: research and policy issues. *The Gerontologist, 14*, 510–519.

Kruzich, J. M., Clinton, J. F., & Kelber, S. T. (1992). Personal and environmental influences on nursing home satisfaction. *The Gerontologist, 32*, 342–50.

Mattiasson, A., & Andersson, L. (1997). Quality of nursing home care assessed by competent nursing home patients. *Journal of Advanced Nursing, 26*, 1117–24.

Meister, C., & Boyle, C. (1996). Perceptions of quality in long-term care: A satisfaction survey. *Journal of Nursing Care Quality, 10*, 40–47.

Nyman, J. A. (1988). Improving the quality of nursing homes: Are adequacy-based or incentive-oriented policies more effective. *Medical Care, 26,* 1158–1171.

Parasuraman, A., Zeithaml, V. A., & Berry, L. L. (1998). SERVAQUAL: A multi-item scale for measuring consumer perceptions of service quality. *Journal of Retailing, No. 64,* 12–36.

Pearson, A., Hocking, S., Mott, S., & Riggs, A. (1993). Quality of care in nursing homes: From the resident's perspective. *Journal of Advanced Nursing, 18,* 20–24.

Spalding, J. & Frank, B. (1985). Quality care from the residents' point of view. *American Health Care Association Journal, 11*(4), 3–7.

Zimmerman, D. R., Karon, S. L., Arling, G., Ryther-Clark, B., Collins, T., Ross, R., & Sainfort, F. (1995). Development and testing of nursing home quality indicators. *Health Care Financing Review, 16*(4), 107–127.

Chapter 13

ETHICAL ISSUES IN CONDUCTING CUSTOMER SATISFACTION SURVEYS IN LONG-TERM CARE INSTITUTIONS

Perla Werner, Farida Ejaz, and Jiska Cohen-Mansfield

INTRODUCTION

Ethics is a field of study that deals with concepts and principles about what is right and wrong. Several researchers have discussed the main ethical issues in long-term care facilities (Elander, Drechsler, & Persson, 1993; Moody, 1983), such as: 1) conflict of interests and divided professional loyalties, 2) paternalism versus autonomy, 3) confidentiality versus beneficence, and 4) the allocation of limited resources versus getting maximum benefits. The planning and implementation of customer satisfaction surveys in nursing homes is accompanied by similar as well as unique ethical issues.

This chapter takes these four principles and examines them in light of the planning and implementation of customer satisfaction surveys in nursing homes. First, issues surrounding each ethical dilemma, including making decisions as to what the ethical controversy or problem actually is, are presented. Second, several suggestions and alternatives to solve the dilemmas are suggested.

Conflict of interests and divided professional loyalties in conducting satisfaction surveys

Although customer satisfaction surveys are increasingly being used in long-term care institutions, administrators may be guided by different rationales for their use. It is important to distinguish between two general purposes of customer satisfaction surveys: marketing, and monitoring quality of care (Cleary & McNeil, 1988).

The use of customer satisfaction surveys as a marketing tool is linked to the growth of a consumer-centered approach in the health-care system. In this view, long-term care organizations are seen as providers of services, and their success depends upon meeting the consumer's preferences. This approach has been reinforced by the introduction of managed care, which imposes a marketplace model on health care delivery.

As a marketing tool, customer satisfaction surveys might have little influence on the quality of care per se. Their aim is to provide information regarding the relationship between financial outcome and cost to the purchasers of long-term care services (either managed care systems, or the individuals about to choose a nursing home). One fundamental question related to this issue is that, if the main purpose of customer satisfaction surveys is to be a marketing tool, which customer are they trying to satisfy: the residents and their families, or the managed care company? Is the satisfaction of the patient indeed the goal that long-term care institutions are trying to achieve, or is it only the means by which they are trying to make a financial gain in a highly competitive environment?

Using satisfaction surveys exclusively as a marketing tool may result in serious ethical violations, such as deception and denial. For example, isolated or under-represented remarks of consumers may be used to market a facility that has numerous problems with its quality of care. Confronted by the need to remain competitive and attractive, those using the marketing approach may report only positive comments as "grateful testimonials" of the services and ignore the overall reality in the facility. As stated by Kane (1998), in an effort to satisfy present and future customers, customer focus may be "perverted into customer appeasement" (p. 237).

Customer satisfaction surveys can, however, be guided by other principles besides marketing. As early as two decades ago, Donabedian (1980) had stated that "client satisfaction is of fundamental importance as a mea-sure of the quality of care because it gives information on the provider's success at meeting those client's values and expectations which are mat-ters on which the client is the ultimate authority" (p. 25). In this view, sat-isfaction by itself is a positive outcome of health care, and the aim of customer satisfaction surveys is to monitor, promote, and enhance services and ensure quality of care. This is especially important in long-term care, where quality of care is closely related to quality of life and life satisfac-tion (Grant, Reimer & Bannatyne, 1996; Meister & Boyle, 1996).

As a solution to the conflicts surrounding these different rationales for implementing satisfaction surveys, a compromise may be achieved whereby, the aims described above are not necessarily incompatible with each other. Customer satisfaction surveys may indeed serve as a source of data for the creation of responsible marketing strategies while at the same time using the information to enhance services. In today's highly compet-itive market conditions, health facilities are being evaluated not only in terms of cost, but also in terms of service quality. Indeed, the best organi-zations put quality first, and marketing success comes as a necessary byproduct. The aim of satisfaction surveys could be used to successfully attain both goals.

Autonomy versus paternalism

One of the underlying principles of a consumer-centered approach is to increase the involvement and motivation of the patients in the delivery of health services. This involvement is expected to give patients a feeling of empowerment and authority and to make the delivery of health services a more democratic and accountable process (Avis, Bond & Arthur, 1995). One of the main ethical dilemmas for administrators and researchers is whether this principle is feasible in long-term care institutions. The major-ity of patients in nursing homes are in a situation in which, given their functional and cognitive limitations, they do not have much choice and/or are unable to express their preferences.

Faced with the inability to obtain direct information from the patients themselves regarding their satisfaction, substituted judgment is often used as a method to respect the autonomy and right to decide of cognitively impaired residents (Seckler, Meier, Mulvihill, & Cammer-Paris, 1991). According to this method, information is collected from other sources, such as family members and staff members (Meister & Boyle, 1996), who are required to represent the point of view of the resident as closely as possi-ble were the resident be able to express the resident opinion and prefer-ences. This technique, however, has conceptual and methodological limitations. Conceptually, patients' satisfaction has been defined as an attitude, i.e., an emotional reaction to the structure, process, and outcome of health services (Cleary & McNeil, 1988). As such, satisfaction differs from the objective aspects characterizing the care, and the dilemma is whether other persons can indeed adequately assess the resident's experience. Satisfaction may sometimes be more related to caring behaviors, such as a smile or the touch of a hand, than to formal delivery of care such as the administration of medications.

Further, studies examining proxy ratings of satisfaction with quality of care (Lavizzo-Mourey, Zinn, & Taylor, 1992; Showers, Simon, Blumenfield, & Holden, 1995) found little support for accuracy or adequacy of caregiver substituted judgement. Knox and Upchurch (1992) in a survey of 134 residents, 50 administrators, and 208 nursing home employees, showed that as much as 70% of the time administrators do not understand what values are of importance to residents. Similar results were recently reported in a Canadian study assessing the perceptions of quality of care by staff members, families, residents, and families of deceased residents in nursing homes (Meister & Boyle, 1996).

Given these findings, the question is whether customer satisfaction surveys that rely exclusively on substituted judgement do indeed promote the principle of empowerment and autonomy of the residents, or do they reinforce abdication of the residents' autonomy to the preferences and priorities of their caregivers.

Another ethical issue affecting residents' autonomy relates to the paternalistic view that some of the caregivers may adopt. Mandated by the OBRA regulations of 1987 and 1990, some nursing home facilities conduct customer satisfaction surveys under the guise of promoting resident's rights. However, when it comes to actually "listening" to the voice of the direct consumer, i.e., the long-term care residents themselves, they may decide to ignore the residents' point of view under the justification that residents are not competent to make their own decisions involving health care. Although "patients may not always know the services they need, or the health services they want" (Avis, 1997, p. 30), ignoring their preferences and attitudes conflicts with the ethical principle of autonomy and self-determination.

As a solution of the conflicts arising from the principles of autonomy versus paternalism, long-term care institutions can attempt to interview cognitively impaired residents. If appropriate techniques are used, some cognitively impaired residents can be interviewed successfully, thereby providing their point of view (Simmons et al., 1997; see also Chapter 9 by Uman et al.). Although these methods may result in small samples, it allows residents with some form of dementia to express their opinions

(Post & Whitehouse, 1995) and therefore strengthens their autonomy and independence.

One successfully documented effort to interview cognitively limited residents was suggested by Grant et al. (1996) in a study aimed at examining indicators of quality in long-term care facilities. These researchers used Critical Incident Technique as the method to obtain information from elderly persons with mild cognitive impairment. The participants (residents, relatives, and nursing staff members) were asked to provide descriptions of two incidents, one reflecting the situation they liked the best and one reflecting the situation they liked the least, concerning the care received. Although according to the authors, this qualitative approach allows obtaining direct information from residents suffering from mild cognitive impairment, no data were presented regarding the validity of the method.

Van Maris, Soberman, Murray, & Norton (1996) found that relying on thoroughly trained volunteers for screening the cognitive capacity of the residents to be included in a customer satisfaction survey proved to be a more reliable method than relying on staff members. First, they found that the volunteers successfully interviewed 30% of the residents defined by staff members as cognitively impaired and unable to be interviewed. Secondly, residents felt more confident discussing quality care issues with volunteers than with staff members, on whom they depend for daily care needs.

Besides attempting to successfully interview some cognitively impaired residents, most long-term care facilities will need to interview family members or proxies, especially for those residents for whom they fail to get reliable responses. Other problems may arise when choosing the family member or proxy to respond to the survey. The person designated legally as the decision maker may not be the person most actively involved in the daily care of the resident, and consequently may not be the most appropriate source of information. Additionally, since satisfaction scores are related not only to the characteristics of the provider and its setting, but also to the characteristics of the individual responding, the selection of the family member may affect the score obtained. A solution to the problem of selecting only one family member per resident is to try to interview more than one member to reduce potential biases, and get more reliable and objective indicators of the quality of care being provided to the resident.

Confidentiality versus beneficence

Anonymity requires that the identity of the respondents be separated from the information they provide, so that researchers, administrators, and staff members are not able to associate particular information with particular participants. Confidentiality requires that even if the information can be identified by the researchers as pertaining to a particular participant, it will not be revealed publicly. Most surveys are confidential, but not anonymous to research staff.

Often, ethical issues arise as a consequence of the conflict between assuring confidentiality and the beneficence issue. Since the concept of beneficence entails doing the best for the resident (Goldstein, 1989), some of the ethical questions confronting those conducting satisfaction surveys include: Should patterns of wrongdoing be revealed? Should we whistle-blow on colleagues who are abusing or negating the elderly person? Elder abuse law in certain states requires that if a resident is being mistreated, researchers have to report the case. In such cases, researchers have to inform respondents that they are liable to report cases of abuse. The case of elder abuse, however, is an extreme example, there are countless others that deal with the conflict of attempting to maintain the confidentiality of the respondents and revealing that information to administrators to introduce changes needed to assure adequate care.

In the nursing home environment, where residents are attached to and dependent on their caregivers, it is of utmost importance to assure the anonymity and confidentiality of the data collected in a customer satisfaction survey. Residents and family members may be highly distressed if they find that the information they provided anonymously and confidentially was revealed to their caregivers. As Strasser and Davis (1991) have pointed out, there is need to be extremely careful in protecting the respondent's anonymity and confidentiality. All staff members (both those involved in the care and those involved with its administrative aspects) have to be informed and trained regarding the importance of assuring these ethical principles. Failing to secure respondents' trust regarding the anonymity and confidentiality of their information may result in the provision of biased answers, as well as deteriorating and mistrustful relationships. Therefore, in such cases, it is prudent to give a lower value to the principle of beneficence in light of upholding the principle of confidentiality by assigning it a higher value.

A solution to ensuring confidentiality, in cases where respondents are few in number or can easily be identify, is to camouflage the information so that respondents can not be identified; or to conduct analyses only for groups larger than 50. In cases where information might be accessible, it is prudent to carefully store the data in secure places (Strasser & Davis, 1991). Another suggestion is to use individuals, such as students, who are not regularly involved in the care of residents (Bliesmer & Earle, 1993).

Allocation of Limited Resources Versus Getting Maximum Benefit

Although conducting a survey in-house may be a cheaper option than contracting it to outside consultants, there are ethical issues associated with such decisions as well. Undoubtedly, when residents and/or family members are interviewed by staff members of the institution, they may fear reporting negative attitudes because of the reprisal this might have on the level and quality of care received. Indeed, most satisfaction surveys show medium to high levels of satisfaction. Given these limitations, an ethical solution may be to have an outsider conduct the interviews, such as a paid firm or consultant, as well as trained students or volunteers (Van Maris et al., 1994).

Another issue related to that of the allocation of limited resources is that of accepting low response rates without attempting to increase these rates, since doing so might be more expensive on the part of the institution conducting the survey. However, the drawback to this is that low response rates may not reflect the opinions of the majority of the consumers. Indeed, several researchers (e.g., Aharony and Strasser, 1993) state that the respondents tend to be those customers who are either extremely satisfied or extremely dissatisfied with the quality of care received.

Allyson Ross Davis, in a recent interview with Kennedy (1996) criticized those organizations that feel comfortable with low response rates because of marketing a positive image. The first ethical obligation is, therefore, to try to increase the response rate.

There is also need to try to complement the information received through the surveys with other sources, so as to reflect the perceptions of those residents who are not represented in them. Customer satisfaction surveys are one of the essential, but not unique, components of any evaluation of health care services. Several ways to complement satisfaction surveys have been suggested, including the use of informal survey techniques such as collecting unstructured data from volunteers, visitors, and staff members; and attendance by administrators in patients' care conferences (Rasmussen, 1992). Qualitative evaluations cannot be ignored, however, considerations of proper sampling, reliability, and validity issues need to be taken into consideration.

Another issue of conflict between limited resources and getting maximum benefit from the survey is the issue of not having the time, energy, or resources to do anything about the results. To use the results of the survey to change policies or practices may be more costly and complex than conducting them. Therefore, some facilities may decide not to use the findings to implement change. However, not acting upon survey results, besides negating the main raison d'être of a survey, also violates an implicit contract with customers. It is the administrator's ethical obligation to make sure that the results of the survey are implemented and are not left unused (Strasser & Davis, 1991). Customer satisfaction surveys are not an end in themselves. They are not used to satisfy legislators and auditors only. As stated by Slavin and Carter in Chapter 11, results of customer satisfaction surveys have to be interpreted and used within a larger framework of quality assessment and quality improvement.

Even if not all the issues brought up by the respondents in the survey can be addressed, there is need to relate to them. As stated by Hohl (1994), there is not always need to "react," but there is always need to "respond". Therefore, the responsibility of the administrators does not end with conducting the survey effectively. The administration has an ethical responsibility that the results be presented clearly and without bias, in that both positive and negative findings are reported objectively. All staff members have to be able to understand the findings and their relevance so that they are given feedback to help them improve quality (Soberman, Murray, Norton, van Maris, & Tasa, 1997).

The latter issue is the crux of the ethical obligation to understand the meaning and relevance of the findings to implement quality improvement projects. Ignoring or using the data derived from the survey only to describe the findings, without integrating them as part of a strategic plan, is an ethical violation of the goal and mandate of satisfaction surveys. Therefore, understanding the results goes beyond a simple description of the findings to examine correlates and patterns among the data so that appropriate action can be taken to tackle the problem identified.

Finally, the interpretation of survey results may confront researchers and administrators with additional dilemmas, such as interpreting appropriately the root of dissatisfaction expressed in a certain domain or by a segment of the population. For example, lower satisfaction levels in any specific unit or domain may be related to inadequate level of performance in this area, to unrealistic or inappropriate expectations in this area, to one or a few very difficult and disturbed customers, or to another reason. Therefore, different and alternative explanations should be taken into account while interpreting the survey's results.

Interpreting the results of the survey independently may also lead to unethical conclusions. Indeed, satisfaction scores should be interpretable in comparison to other surveys of a similar nature. The results for one segment of the population surveyed can be compared to those of others surveyed. Responses to satisfaction in one domain can be compared to those in another domain.

The way to avoid ethical problems when interpreting general satisfaction scores is to compare the responses of a survey to that of a previous survey or to identical surveys conducted in different nursing homes. The absolute scores derived from a satisfaction survey are relatively meaningless unless benchmarked against other survey results. Therefore, stating that "the majority of our residents are satisfied with all our services" does not convey very meaningful information about the satisfaction with a specific nursing home.

SUMMARY AND CONCLUSIONS

This chapter dealt with a few ethical conflicts in conducting consumer satisfaction surveys. These included conflict of interests and divided professional loyalties, paternalism versus autonomy, confidentiality versus beneficence, and the allocation of limited resources versus getting maximum benefits.

When confronted with any ethical issue, there are several important steps to take: First, it is important to frame the issue. This includes making an initial decision as to what the ethical controversy or problem actually is, and how it relates to the main philosophy or mission of the organization. Second, it is important to discuss and evaluate the alternatives. Finally, there is the need to make decisions.

Team decision-making, based on collaborative models, may be the best way to resolve ethical dilemmas. Although ad hoc ethic rounds can address ongoing issues (Robbins, 1996), an ethics committee can serve as a formal mechanism to deal with ethical conflicts or questions arising during the process of conducting customer satisfaction surveys. Since ethical committees in long-term care facilities are usually interdisciplinary and include representatives of the residents and/or their families, they are the most effective way to discuss and solve a wide range of problems from different perspectives. Ethical committees may be also effective in introducing a change in policy, if needed. Thus, even though ethical dilemmas may create tension and uneasiness, if treated adequately, these dilemmas may also become a positive force in introducing change and optimizing the process of conducting productive customer satisfaction surveys. Ethical dilemmas may increase the concern about residents' outcomes and the degree of personal responsibility, and may be a reflection of the professional commitment of those involved in the process of conducting satisfaction surveys to improve the well-being of the residents.

REFERENCES

Aharony, L., & Strasser, S. (1993). Patient satisfaction: What we know about and what we still need to explore. *Medical Care Review, 50*(1), 353–382.

Avis, M. (1992). Patient's choice. *Nursing Times, 88*(30), 29–30.

Avis, M., Bond, M. & Arthur, A. (1995). Satisfying solutions? A review of some unresolved issues in the measurement of patient satisfaction. *Journal of Advanced Nursing, 22,* 316–322.

Beck, C., & Chumbler, N. (1997). Planning for the future of long-term care: Consumers, providers, and purchasers. *Journal of Gerontological Nursing, 23*(8), 6–13.

Bliesmer, M., & Earle, P. (1993). Research considerations: Nursing home quality perceptions. *Journal of Gerontological Nursing, 19*(6), 27–34.

Cleary, P. D., & McNeil, B. J. (1988). Patient satisfaction as an indicator of quality care. *Inquiry, 25,* 25–36.

Donabedian, A. (1980). *Explorations in quality assessment and monitoring: Vol. 1: The definition of quality and approaches to its assessment.* Ann Arbor, MI: Health Administration Press.

Elander, G., Drechsler, K., & Persson, K. W. (1993). Ethical dilemmas in long-term care settings: Interviews with nurses in Sweden and England. *International Journal of Nursing Studies, 30*(1), 91–97.

Goldstein, M. K. (1989). Ethical care of the elderly: Pitfalls and principles. *Geriatrics, 44*(3), 101–106.

Grant, N. K., & Bannatyne, J. (1996). Indicators of quality in long-term care facilities. *International Journal of Nursing Studies, 33*(5), 469–478.

Hohl, D. (1994). Patient satisfaction in home care/hospice. *Nursing Management, 25*(1), 52–54.

Kane, R. (1998). Assuring quality in nursing home care. *Journal of the American Geriatrics Society, 48,* 232–237.

Kennedy, M. (1996). Designing surveys for maximal satisfaction: An interview with Allyson Ross Davies. *Journal on Quality Improvement, 23*(5), 369–373.

Knox, B., & Upchurch, M. (1992). Values and nursing home life: How residents and caregivers compare. *The Journal of Long-Term Care,* Fall, 8–10.

Lavizzo-Mourey, R. J., Zinn, J., & Taylor, L. (1992). Ability of surrogates to represent satisfaction of nursing home residents with quality of care. *Journal of the American Geriatrics Society, 40,* 39–47.

Meister, C., & Boyle, C. (1996). Perceptions of quality in long-term care: A satisfaction survey. *Journal of Nursing Care Quality, 10*(4), 40–47.

Moody, H. R. (1983). Ethical dilemmas in long-term care. *Journal of Gerontological Social Work, 5*(1–2), 97–111.

Post, S. G., & Whitehouse, P. J. (1995). Fairhill guidelines on ethics of the care of people with Alzheimer's disease: A clinical summary. *Journal of the American Geriatrics Society, 43,* 1423–1429.

Rasmussen, J. C. (1992). Communicating with residents, families and staff. *Journal of Long-Term Care Administration, 20*(3), 11.

Robbins, D. A. (1996). *Ethical and legal issues in home health and long-term care: Challenges and solutions.* Gaithersburg, MD: Aspen.

Seckler, A. B., Meier, D. E., Mulvihill, M., & Cammer-Paris, B.E. (1991). Substituted judgement: How accurate are proxy predictions? *Annals of Internal Medicine, 115,* 92–98.

Showers, N., Simon, E. P., Blumenfield, S., & Holden, G. (1995). Predictors of patient and proxy satisfaction with discharge plans. *Social Work in Health Care, 22*(1), 19–35.

Simmons, S. F., Schnelle, J. F., Uman, G. C., Kulvicki, A. D., Lee, K. O., & Ouslander, J. G. (1997). Selecting nursing home residents for satisfaction surveys. *Gerontologist, 37*(4), 543–550.

Soberman, L. R., Murray, M., Norton, P. G., van Maris, B., & Tasa, K. (1997). Satisfaction of residents and families in long-term care: III. Dissemination of results. *Quality Management in Health Care, 5*(3), 63–71.

Strasser, S., & Davis, R. M. (1991). *Measuring patient satisfaction for improved patient services.* Ann Arbor, MI: Health Administration Press.

Van Maris, B., Soberman, L., Murray, M., & Norton, P. G. (1996). Satisfaction of residents and families in long-term care: II. Lessons learned. *Quality Management in Health Care, 4*(3), 47–53.

APPENDIXES

ASSESSMENT OF SATISFACTION: SUMMARY OF PUBLISHED SCALES

Jean Kruzich and Jiska Cohen-Mansfield

This summary includes multidimensional measures specifically designed to assess nursing home residents' and their family members' perceptions of the facility where they reside or visit. While instrument names are similar, the measures reflect a good deal of variation in the domains addressed, number of items representing various subscales, and psychometric support. In some cases, measure domains represent dimensions residents and family members identified as crucial to their satisfaction, while others are based on professionals' view of what is important (Cleary & Edgman-Levitan, 1997). The context for development of satisfaction measures reflect multiple disciplinary priorities and viewpoints. Researcher's in business have developed satisfaction measures originally developed for use in retail and industrial samples (Parasuraman et al., 1988), while Spalding's study (1985) of nursing home resident views of quality of care and the larger health care literature on patient satisfaction provided the basis for other instruments detailed below.

Table I.1: Selected Measures Used to Assess Nursing Home Satisfaction of Residents and Family Members

Author study	Instrument name	Domains	No. of items	Response options	Item range	Respondent sample size	Facility sample size	Reliability
Davis, Sebastian, & Tschetter (1997)	Nursing Home Service Quality Inventory	1. Staff and environmental Responsiveness 2. Dependability and trust 3. Food-related services anD resources 4. Personal control	32	Strongly Disagree to Strongly Agree	1–7	103 residents	23	Coefficients for the subscales ranged from .68 for Personal control to .93 for Responsiveness.
Van Green (1997)	Measure and Discuss Intervention	1. Contact with personnel 2. Service 3. Food 4. Participation 5. Residents together 6. Feeling at home 7. Activities	49	Yes! to No!	1–5		9	Cronbach's alpha for subscales around .80
Higgs, MacDonald & Ward (1992)	The Institution Among Elderly Patients in Hospital Long-stay Care (developed by authors)	1. Relations with staff 2. Autonomy 3. Amenities 4. Privacy 5. Social environment	39 +2	Agree or Disagree + 2 open ended about 3 least and 3 best things	1–2	291	61 wards	

Table I.1: (continued)

Author study	Instrument name	Domains	No. of items	Response options	Item range	Respondent sample size	Facility sample size	Reliability
Koenig & Kleinsorge (1994)	Customer Satisfaction Instrument (based on Kleinsorge & Koenig, 1991a, b)	1. Nurse/aide 2. Empathy 3. Communications 4. Dietary 5. Housekeeping 6. Home issues 7. Global	24	Strongly agree– strongly disagree	1–5	319 family members	11	Alpha coefficients for subscales ranged from .60 for Home issues to .87 for Housekeeping.
Kruzich, Clinton, & Kelber (1992)	Nursing Home Satisfaction Scale (Revised version of McCaffree & Hawkins, 1976, Nursing Home Satisfaction Scale, adapted by Kane, Riegler, Bell, Potter & Koshlanc, 1982)	1.Nursing staff interest and competence 2.Food 3.Resources 4.Personal control	17	Disagree unsure/ DK agree	1–3	289 residents	51	Coefficients for subscales ranged from .46 for Personal control to .75 with a scale reliability coefficient of .80.

Table I.1: *(continued)*

Author study	Instrument name	Domains	No. of items	Response options	Item range	Respondent sample size	Facility sample size	Reliability
Lavizzo-Mourey, Zinn, & Taylor (1992);	Nursing Home Resident Satisfaction Scale for Surrogates	1. Physician services 2. Nursing services 3. Enviornment/other services	26	Not so good– very good	1–4	152 surrogates	4	Chronbach alpha for subscales ranged from .79 for Environment to .92 for Nursing; .91 for total scale. Test-retest and inter-rater reliability as well as item-scale correlations also available
Zinn, Lavizzo-Mourey, & Taylor (1993)	and The Nursing Home Resident Satisfaction Scale		11			168 residents		Chronbach alpha for subscales ranged from .69 for Physician to .79 for Nursing

Table I.1: *(continued)*

Author study	Instrument name	Domains	No. of items	Response options	Item range	Respondent sample size	Facility sample size	Reliability
Mattiasson & Andersson (1997)	McCaffree and Harkin's (1976) Satisfaction with Nursing Home Scale (modified version)	1. Security 2. Attention 3. Social relations 4. Activities 5. Routines	21	Important/ unimportant Satisfactory/ unsatisfactory	1–4 1–4	60	13	
Meister & Boyle (1996) based on Bleismer & Earle (1993)	Satisfaction Survey	1. Interpersonal aspects of care 2. Technical aspects of care 3. Attributes of the setting	15	Always–Never	1–5	Number not stated	1	
Norton, van Moris, Soberman, & Murray (1996)	Long-Term Care Resident Evaluation Survey	1. Living environment 2. Laundry 3. Food 4. Activities 5. Staff 6. Dignity 7. Autonomy	60	Yes sometimes no	1–3	127 residents/ 145 family members	1	Coefficients for subscales ranged from .39 for Activities to .81 for Staff.

Table I.1: (continued)

Author study	Instrument name	Domains	No. of items	Response options	Item range	Respondent sample size	Facility sample size	Reliability
Pablo (1975)	Patient Satisfaction Scale	1. Overall satisfaction 2. Security 3. Adequacy of care 4. Food, bed, and activity 5. Availability 6. Interpersonal sensitivity	68	Very satisfied–very dissatisfied	1-3 1-4 and yes-no	77 residents	1	
Pearson, Hocking, & Riggs (1993)	Resident Satisfaction Schedule		15	Agree Disagree Undecided	1374			
Steffen & Nystrom (1997)	Satisfaction with Service Quality (Based on items from Parasuraman et al. (1986) Quality Measure of Customer Satisfaction)	1. Responsiveness 2. Reliability 3. Assurance 4. Empathy 5. Tangibles	22	Strongly disagree–strongly agree	1-7	416 family members	41	Inter-item reliabilities for subscales ranged from .74 for Tangibles to .90 for Empathy.

Table I.1: (*continued*)

Author study	Instrument name	Domains	No. of items	Response options	Item range	Respondent sample size	Facility sample size	Reliability
Uman & Urman (1997)	Authors devised instrument, no name	1. Help and assistance 2. Communication with staff 3. Autonomy and choice 4. Companionship 5. Food and enviornment 6. Saftety and security	42	Yes/No	1–2	257 NH residents	3	
Wilde, Larsson, Larsson, & Starrin (1995)	Quality from the Patients' Perspective (QPP)	1.Medical-technical competence 2.Physical-technical conditions 3. Identity orientation 4.Sociocultural atmosphere.	40	Do not agree At All–Fully Agree Of Little Importance–Of Very Great Importance	1–4 1–3	111 nursing home residents	1 nursing home; 3 other settings	Cronbach alpha ranged from .44 to .91

REFERENCES

Bleismer, M., & Earle, P. (1993) Research considerations: Nursing home quality perceptions. *Journal of Gerontological Nursing*, June: 27–34.

Cleary, P. D., & Edgman-Levitan, S. (1997). Health care quality: Incorporating consumer perspectives. *Journal of the American Medical Association, 278*(19), 1608–1612.

Davis, M. A., Sebastian, J. G., & Tschetter, J. (1997). Measuring quality of nursing home service: Resident's perspectives. *Psychological Reports, 81*, 531–542.

Higgs, P. F., MacDonald, L. D., & Ward, M. C. (1992). Responses to the institution among elderly patients in hospital long-stay care. *Social Science Medicine, 35*(3), 287–293.

Kane, R. L., Riegler, S., Bell, R., Potter, R., & Koshland, G. (1982). *Predicting the course of nursing home patients: A progress report*. Santa Monica, CA: RAND.

Kleinsorge, I. K., & Koenig, H. F. (1991a). The health care quality quagmire: Some signposts. *Hospital & Health Services Administration, 35*(1), 39–54.

Kleinsorge, I. K., & Koenig, H. F. (1991b). The silent customers: Measuring customer satisfaction in nursing homes. *Journal of Health Care Marketing, 11*(4), 2–13.

Koenig, H. F., & Kleinsorge, I. K. (1994). Perceptual measures of quality: A tool to improve nursing home systems. *Hospital and Health Services Administration, 39*(4), 487–503.

Kruzich, J. M., Clinton, J. F., & Kelber, S. T. (1992). Personal and environmental influences on nursing home satisfaction. *The Gerontologist, 32*(3), 342–350.

Lavizzo-Mourey, R., Zinn, J. & Taylor, L. (1992). Ability of surrogates to represent satisfaction of nursing home residents with quality of care. *Journal of the American Geriatrics Society, 40*, 39–47.

Mattiasson, A-C., & Andersson, L. (1997). Quality of nursing home care assessed by competent nursing home patients. *Journal of Advanced Nursing, 26*, 1117–1124.

McCaffree, K. M., & Harkins, R. B. (1976). *Final report for Evaluation of the Outcomes of Nursing Home Care*. Seattle, WA: Battelle Human Affairs Research Centers.

Meister, C., & Boyle, C. (1996). Perceptions of quality in long-term care: A satisfaction survey. *Journal of Nursing Care Quality, 10*(4), 40–47.

Norton, P., van Maris, B., Soberman, L., & Murray, H. (1996). Satisfaction of residents and families in ling-term care: I. Construction and application of an instrument. *Quality Management in Health Care, 4*(3), 38–40.

Pablo, R. Y. (1975). Assessing patient satisfaction in long-term care institutions. *Hospital Administration in Canada, March*, 24–32.

Parasuraman, A., Zeithaml, V., & Berry, L. (1988). *SERVQUAL: A multiple-item scale for measuring customer perceptions of service quality*. *Journal of Relailing, 64*, 12–40.

Pearson, A., Hocking, S., Mott, S., & Riggs, A. (1993). Quality of care in nursing homes: From the resident's perspective. *Journal of Advanced Nursing, 18*, 20–24.

Spalding, J. (1985). *A consumer perspective on quality care: The residents' point of view*. Washington, DC: National Citizen's Coalition for Nursing Home Reform.

Steffen, T. M. & Nystrom, P. C. (1997). Organizational determinates of service quality in nursing homes. *Hospital and Health Services Administration, 42*(2), 179–191.

Uman, G. C., & Urman, H. N. (1997). Measuring consumer satisfaction in nursing home residents. *Nutrition, 13*, 705–707.

Van Green, V. M. C. (1997) The measure and discuss intervention: A procedure for client empowerment and quality control in residential care homes. *The Gerontologist, 37*(6), 817–822.

Wilde, B., Larsson, G., Larsson, M., & Starrin, B. (1995). Quality of care from the elderly person's perspective: Subjective importance and perceived reality. *Aging: Clinical and Experimental Research, 7*, 140–149.

Zinn, J. S., Lavizzo-Mourey, R., & Taylor, L. (1993). Measuring satisfaction with care in the nursing home setting: The nursing home resident satisfaction scale. *Journal of Applied Gerontology, 12*(4), 452–465.

Table I.2. Selected measures used to assess staff job satisfaction and burnout in the nursing home.

Source	Description/ purpose	Study design	Satisfaction measure used	Measurement domains	No. of Items	Response options	Item range	Reliability
Astrom, Nilsson, Norberg, Sandman & Winblad, 1991	A study of the relationship between burn-out, empathy, and attitudes towards demented patients	60 nursing staff at a psychogeriatric clinic and somatic long-term care clinic in Umea, Sweden were asked to parti-cipate in structured interviews. They were selected on the basis of high and low scores on empathy and burn-out in a previous questionnaire study.	Experience of work with demented patients	1. Experience of feedback at work 2. Care organization 3. Satisfaction of own expectations 4. Satisfactory contact with the patient 5. Satisfaction with the expectations of others 6. Satisfaction with environment	21	Minimal to Maximal	1–5	
			Pines et al. burnout (Pines, Aronson, & Kafry, 1981)		21	Never to Always	1–7	see Pines et al., 1981; test-retest r = .66; internal consistency $r > .60$
Brannon, Cohn, & Smyer, 1990	A study to assess the aggregate need for and feasibility of job redesign interventions in nursing homes	A total of 338 nurse's aides from 21 nursing homes in Pennsylvania participated.	The Job Diag-nostic Survey (Hackman & Oldman, 1980)	*Job Perceptions:* 1. Skill variety 2. Task identity. 3. Task significance 4. Autonomy 5. Feedback *Work Context: satisfaction with* 1. Supervisors 2. Pay 3. Co-workers 4. Job security				

Table I.2. (*continued*)

Source	Description/ purpose	Study design	Satisfaction measure used	Measurement domains	No. of Items	Response options	Item range	Reliability
Dunn, Rout, Carson, & Ritter, 1994	A study to examine staff stress and its relationship to coping mechanisms and demographic characteristics	112 nursing staff in 11 nursing homes in the UK completed the questionnaires which were mailed to 12 nursing homes in the UK with a potential sample of 365.	Stressor check list (Dunn et al., 1994)	1. Differing expectations about how patient care should be carried out 2. Management factors 3. Not getting adequate support from other staff 4. Feeling inadequately trained to deal with emotional and practical demands of the job 5. Home-work conflicts	44	No stress to Extreme stress	1–5	
		Job satisfaction scale (Warr, Cook, & Wall, 1979)			15		1–7	
Grau, Chandler, Burton, & Kolditz (1991)	An examination of the relationship of institutional loyalty to job-related factors, including satisfaction	In groups, 219 nursing assistants from day, evening, and night shifts in not-for-profit homes completed a questionnaire administered by research team with no affiliation with the facility	Subscales 1,2, & 3 from Grau et al. (1992); Subscale 4 from Work Environment Scale (Moos, 1974); Subscale 5 adapted from Sheridan et al. (1984); Subscale 6 from Organizational Commitment (Porter et al., 1974).	1. Job tasks 2. Job benefits 3. Adequacy of resources to do job 4. Social climate 5. Facility administration 6. Institutional loyalty.	40	Agree Strongly to Disagree Strongly	1–4	Coefficients for subscales ranged from .70 for Job resources to .84 for Job tasks.

Table I.2. (continued)

Source	Description/ purpose	Study design	Satisfaction measure used	Measurement domains	No. of Items	Response options	Item range	Reliability
Helmer, Olson, & Heim (1993)	Study aimed to analyze factors correlated with high turnover	Facility administrations in 40 nursing homes were mailed 600 surveys. They distributed and returned completed surveys from 246 nursing assistants (response rate of 41%).	Authors created a Likert-type scale.	1. Pay / benefits 2. Interaction / organizational factors 3. Task requirements 4. Job status 5. Autonomy	17	Not At All to Very Much	1–4	
Holtz, 1982	A study to investigate the degree to which the 10 factors identified by the Motivation-Hygiene Theory are reported as being important to a stable staff of nurse's aides who have worked in Level II and III nursing homes for 12 mos. or more.	Three nursing homes in 3 different Massachusetts cities and towns were used. 31 staff members were administered the questionnaire.	The authors devised a questionnaire that asks 2 questions for each of the 10 variables from the Herzberg's motivation-hygiene theory.	1. Supervision 2. Interpersonal relationships 3. Responsibility 4. The work itself 5. Recognition 6. Salary 7. Achievement 8. Working conditions 9. Administrative policies 10. Advancement	20	Greatest importance or satisfaction to lowest importance or satisfaction	1–5	Split half internal consitency coefficient =.80.

Table I.2. (continued)

Source	Description/ purpose	Study design	Satisfaction measure used	Measurement domains	No. of Items	Response options	Item range	Reliability
Mullins, Nelson, Busciglia, & Weiner (1988)	A study of the influence of organizational structure and management power on job satisfaction.	Of 56 for-profit nursing homes, 46 facilities (88%) participated. Number of respondents ranged from 3 to 16. Respondents included, at minimum, the head of nursing, 1 RN, 1 LPN, and 1 aid.	Job Satisfaction Survey (JSS) (Spector, 1985).	1. Pay 2. Promotion 3. Supervision 4. Rewards / appreciation 5. Working conditions 6. Co-workers 7. Job requirements 8. Communication	36	Strongly disagree to strongly agree	1–5	Alpha coefficient for total measure was .91.
Waxman, Carner, & Berkenstock (1984)	A study of the relationship of turnover rate to job satisfaction and perceptions of environmental climate.	In groups, 234 day and evening shift nursing assistants in 7 proprietary nursing homes (3 urban, 4 suburban) completed a questionnaire that was distributed and orally administered by researchers. All aides approached completed the survey.	Minnesota Satisfaction Scale short form (Weiss, Davis, England, & Lofquist, 1967).	1. Intrinsic 2. Extrinsic	20	Very dissatisfied to very satisfied	1–5	Not reported, but prior studies found .80 or higher for both sub-scales (Price & Mueller, 1986).

REFERENCES

Astrom, S., Nilsson, M., Norberg, A., Sandman, P., & Winblad, B. (1991). Staff burnout in dementia care: Relations to empathy and attitudes. *International Journal of Nursing Studies, 28*(1), 65–75.

Astrom, S., Norberg, A., Nilsson, M., & Winblad, B. (1987). Tedium among personnel working with geriatric patients. *Scandinavian Journal of Caring Science, 1*(3–4), 125–132.

Brannon, D., Cohn, M. D., & Smyer, M. A. (1990). Caregiving as work: How nurse's aides rate it. *The Journal of Long-Term Care Administration, 18*(1), 10–14.

Colombotos, J., & Gorman, S. (1992). Psychological morale and job satisfaction among homecare workers who care for persons with AIDS. *Women and Health, 18*(1), 1–21.

Dunn, L., Rout, U., Carson, J., & Ritter, S. (1994). Occupational stress amongst care staff working in nursing homes: An empirical investigation. *Journal of Clinical Nursing, 3*, 177–183.

Grau, L., Chandler, B., Burton, B., & Kolditz, D. (1991). Institutional loyalty and job satisfaction among nurse aides in nursing homes. *Journal of Aging, 3*(1), 47–65.

Hackman, J. R., & Oldman, G. R. (1980). Work redesign. Reading, MA: Addison-Wesley.

Helmer, T., Olson, S., & Heim, R. (1993). Strategies for nurse aide satisfaction. *Journal of Long-Term Case Administration, 21*(2), 10–14.

Holtz, G. (1982). Nurses' aides in nursing homes: Why are they satisfied? *Journal of Gerontological Nursing, 8*(5), 265–271.

Insel, P. M., & Moos, R. H. (1974). *Work environment scale-form R*. Palo-Alto, CA Consulting Psychologists Press.

Mullins, L. C., Nelson, C. E., Busciglio, H., & Weiner, H. (1988). Job satisfaction among nursing home personnel: The impact of organizational structure and supervisory power. *Journal of Long-Term Care Administration, 6*(1), 12–19.

Pines, A., Aronson, E., & Kafry, D. (1981). Burnout from tedium to personal growth. New York: The Free Press.

Porter, L. W., Steers. R. M., Mowdy, R. J., & Boulieo, P. V. (1974). Organizational commitment, job satisfaction and turnover among psychiatric technicians. *Journal of Applied Psychology, 59*, 603–609.

Price, J. L., & Mueller, C. W. (1986). *Handbook of organizational measurement*. Cambridge, MA: Ballinger.

Sheridan, J. E., Vredenburgh, D. J., & Abelson, M. A. (1984). Contextual model of leadership influence in hospital units. *Academy of Management Journal, 27*, 57–58.

Spector, P. E. (1985). Measurement of human service staff satisfaction: Development of the job satisfaction survey. *American Journal of Community Psychology, 13*, 693–713.

Warr , P., Cook, J., & Wall, P. (1979). Scales for measurement of some work attitudes and aspects of psychological well-being. *Journal of Occupational Psychology, 52*, 129–145.

Waxman, H. M., Carner, E. A., & Berkenstock, G. (1984). Job turnover and job satisfaction among nursing home aides. *The Gerontologist, 24*(5), 503–509.

Weiss, D. J., Davis, R. V., England, G. W., & Lofquist, L. H. (1967). *Manual for the Minnesota satisfaction questionnaire.* Minneapolis: University of Minnestoa Press.

EXAMPLES OF SATISFACTION SURVEYS

RESIDENT AND FAMILY SATISFACTION SURVEYS

- Nursing Care Facility Resident Satisfaction Survey, National Research Corporation\Healthcare Research Systems
- Customer Satisfaction Instrument, K & K Research, 1994
- Selected portions of the "Long-Term Care Resident Evaluation Survey" (Norton, van Maris, Soberman, Murray, Tasa)
- Quality of Care Monitor Satisfaction Survey; Parkside Associates, Inc.
- Nursing Home Satisfaction Scale; Jean Kruzich
- Kethley House Family Satisfaction Survey; The Margaret Blenker Research Center, The Benjamin Rose Institute

STAFF SATISFACTION SURVEYS

- Strategies for Nurse Aide Satisfaction (Helmer, Olson, & Heim)

National Research Corporation

NURSING CARE FACILITY RESIDENT SATISFACTION SURVEY

Directions

Please mark the answer that best tells how you feel about the care and services you receive at our Nursing Care Facility.

Please answer the following questions based on *your own experience* as a resident in our facility. There may be some questions that do not apply to you or that refer to services that you have not used. We ask that you leave those questions blank.

Please be honest so that we may use the information received from these surveys to help improve the services that we offer. Individual responses for the surveys will be kept confidential by National Research Corporation who will be doing analysis of the information. Individual resident names will *not* be included in any of the reports so that the responses will remain confidential.

After you have completed the survey, please place it in the enclosed envelope addressed to National Research Corporation. The postage has been prepaid for your convenience.

Remember, please leave any questions blank that do not apply to you.

ADMISSION	Strongly Disagree	Disagree	Neutral	Agree	Strongly Agree
I felt welcomed by the other residents when I first moved in.	SD	D	N	A	SA
I felt welcomed by the staff when I first moved in.	SD	D	N	A	SA
I felt well-informed when I first moved into the nursing care facility about who to ask for help.	SD	D	N	A	SA

Comments:

ADMINISTRATION

	Strongly Disagree	Disagree	Neutral	Agree	Strongly Agree
I feel I am involved enough in making decisions about my life at the nursing care facility.	SD	D	N	A	SA
The administrative staff members are accessible.	SD	D	N	A	SA
The resident handbook is current and available to all residents.	SD	D	N	A	SA
This nursing care facility promotes resident independence.	SD	D	N	A	SA
Overall, I am satisfied with the administration of the nursing care facility.	SD	D	N	A	SA

Comments:

DINING SERVICES

	Strongly Disagree	Disagree	Neutral	Agree	Strongly Agree
Are you on a special or restricted diet? [circle one]	YES	NO			DON'T KNOW
The food tastes good.	SD	D	N	A	SA
The food is presented attractively.	SD	D	N	A	SA
The menu offers variety and choices that I like.	SD	D	N	A	SA
The food is served at the appropriate temperature.	SD	D	N	A	SA
The dining area is a pleasant place to eat.	SD	D	N	A	SA
I receive my meals at the same time every day.	SD	D	N	A	SA
I get assistance with my meal if I need it.	SD	D	N	A	SA
I can obtain between-meal snacks and beverages.	SD	D	N	A	SA
I have the opportunity to make suggestions about dining choices.	SD	D	N	A	SA

Comments:

DOCTOR AND OTHER MEDICAL PROFESSIONALS

	Strongly Disagree	Disagree	Neutral	Agree	Strongly Agree
My doctor provides adequate information to me concerning my medical condition.	SD	D	N	A	SA
Overall, I am satisfied with my doctor.	SD	D	N	A	SA
My dental, vision and hearing needs are being met.	SD	D	N	A	SA
Overall, I am satisfied with therapy services.	SD	D	N	A	SA

Comments:

ENVIRONMENT

	Strongly Disagree	Disagree	Neutral	Agree	Strongly Agree
The interior of this building is clean and well-maintained.	SD	D	N	A	SA
This facility's exterior and grounds are well-maintained.	SD	D	N	A	SA
This facility provides a home-like environment.	SD	D	N	A	SA
Personal storage space is adequate.	SD	D	N	A	SA
The laundry department always returns my clothes to me after they are laundered.	SD	D	N	A	SA
The housekeepers clean my room and bathroom thoroughly.	SD	D	N	A	SA
Evening noise levels are acceptable and allow an uninterrupted night's sleep.	SD	D	N	A	SA
In general, the maintenance staff responds promptly and satisfactorily to my requests for repairs.	SD	D	N	A	SA
I feel my personal belongings are safe.	SD	D	N	A	SA
I feel safe.	SD	D	N	A	SA
I have confidence in the staff's ability to handle emergency situations.	SD	D	N	A	SA

Comments:

NURSES

	Strongly Disagree	Disagree	Neutral	Agree	Strongly Agree
The nurses spend enough time when attending my needs.	SD	D	N	A	SA
The nurses respond promptly to my requests.	SD	D	N	A	SA
The nurses treat me with dignity and respect.	SD	D	N	A	SA
Overall, I am satisfied with the quality of care I receive from the nurses.	SD	D	N	A	SA

Comments:

NURSING ASSISTANTS

	Strongly Disagree	Disagree	Neutral	Agree	Strongly Agree
The nursing assistants spend enough time when attending my needs.	SD	D	N	A	SA
Nursing assistants respond promptly to my requests.	SD	D	N	A	SA
The nursing assistants treat me with dignity and respect.	SD	D	N	A	SA
I know who to go to if I have a problem with a nursing assistant.	SD	D	N	A	SA
Nursing assistants provide me the opportunity to do my own care without being rushed.	SD	D	N	A	SA
I receive assistance with grooming when I request it.	SD	D	N	A	SA
In general, the quality of nursing care I receive from the nursing assistants is excellent during the *night* shift.	SD	D	N	A	SA
In general, the quality of nursing care I receive from the nursing assistants is excellent during the *evening* shift.	SD	D	N	A	SA
In general, the quality of nursing care I receive from the nursing assistants is excellent during the *day* shift.	SD	D	N	A	SA
In general, the quality of nursing care I receive from the nursing assistants is excellent during the *weekdays*.	SD	D	N	A	SA
In general, the quality of nursing care I receive from the nursing assistants is excellent during the *weekends*.	SD	D	N	A	SA
Overall, I am satisfied with the quality of care I receive from the nursing assistants.	SD	D	N	A	SA

Comments:

SOCIAL

	Strongly Disagree	Disagree	Neutral	Agree	Strongly Agree
I am well-informed about the activities that are offered........	SD	D	N	A	SA
A variety of educational, creative, social and recreational activities is available.................	SD	D	N	A	SA
In general, the activities staff provides activities I enjoy........	SD	D	N	A	SA
I have the opportunity to participate in an exercise program.......	SD	D	N	A	SA
There are staff members available to help me get to the activity and program areas if I need assistance........	SD	D	N	A	SA
My needs for worship are being met........	SD	D	N	A	SA
I receive my mail unopened and in a timely manner........	SD	D	N	A	SA
I receive prompt assistance in obtaining personal items........	SD	D	N	A	SA
I am able to have private visits with family or friends........	SD	D	N	A	SA
Overall, I am satisfied with the barber/beauty shop........	SD	D	N	A	SA

Comments:

OVERALL

	DAILY	WEEKLY	MONTHLY	PERIODICALLY	
Family/friends visit me: [circle one]........	DAILY	WEEKLY	MONTHLY	PERIODICALLY	

	Strongly Disagree	Disagree	Neutral	Agree	Strongly Agree
My family/friends like visiting here........	SD	D	N	A	SA
Overall, I am satisfied with the nursing care facility........	SD	D	N	A	SA
I would recommend the nursing care facility to others........	SD	D	N	A	SA
Whose opinions are reflected in this survey? [circle one] .. RESIDENT	FAMILY MEMBER		OTHER		

Comments:

WE VALUE YOUR OPINION AT CUSTOMER SATISFACTION INSTRUMENT.

The target audience includes both residents and family members or guardians of residents.

We are interested in your opinions about the services provided at our nursing home. Please answer the following statements in a way that best describes your opinion. For example, if you "strongly agree" with a given statement, then circle the number 1 in the Strongly Agree column. If you have no particular opinion about a statement, circle the number 3 in the Neutral column.

In my opinion . . .	Strongly Agree	Agree	Neutral	Disagree	Strongly Disagree
1. The nurses are well trained.	1	2	3	4	5
2. The nursing staff understands how residents feel.	1	2	3	4	5
3. The aides know what they are going when caring for residents.	1	2	3	4	5
4. The aides like their jobs.	1	2	3	4	5
5. The staff members care about the residents.	1	2	3	4	5
6. The residents appear to be comfortable.	1	2	3	4	5
7. Most of the residents have adjusted to the nursing home.	1	2	3	4	5
8. The staff members communicate well with all concerned.	1	2	3	4	5
9. The staff members are patient.	1	2	3	4	5
10. The staff members deal honestly with the residents.	1	2	3	4	5
11. The staff members need to be more safety conscious.	1	2	3	4	5
12. The dietician is easy to talk with.	1	2	3	4	5
13. A variety of meals are provided.	1	2	3	4	5
14. The food is good tasting.	1	2	3	4	5
15. The food servers are pleasant.	1	2	3	4	5
16. The nursing home is clean.	1	2	3	4	5
17. The housekeeping department does a good job.	1	2	3	4	5
18. Housekeeping staff are pleasant to visit with.	1	2	3	4	5

	Strongly Agree	Agree	Neutral	Disagree	Strongly Disagree
19. There are activities available to encourage thinking.	1	2	3	4	5
20. The resident's property is often stolen and never recovered.	1	2	3	4	5
21. There is a bad odor in the nursing home.	1	2	3	4	5
22. The surroundings are uncomfortable.	1	2	3	4	5
23. The chapel services are not adequate.	1	2	3	4	5
24. The administration spends money wisely.	1	2	3	4	5
25. Residents will get a change in roommate if they request.	1	2	3	4	5
26. If requested, residents will get a change in care.	1	2	3	4	5
27. The staff is sensitive to the needs of the family/custodian.	1	2	3	4	5
28. Updated reports of the resident's condition are provided.	1	2	3	4	5
29. The staff communicates well with the family/custodian.	1	2	3	4	5
30. The staff members are honest and direct in their communication.	1	2	3	4	5

I am satisfied with . . .

	Strongly Agree	Agree	Neutral	Disagree	Strongly Disagree
31. the feeling in the home	1	2	3	4	5
32. the aides' service	1	2	3	4	5
33. the dietary service	1	2	3	4	5
34. the nursing service	1	2	3	4	5
35. the housekeeping service	1	2	3	4	5
36. the administration	1	2	3	4	5
37. I would recommend this home to a friend or relative	1	2	3	4	5
38. **In general**, I am satisfied with the home	1	2	3	4	5

Would you please provide us with the following information about yourself for statistical purposes? (Check one box for each item.)

39. What is your relationship with the nursing home resident? The resident is my:

☐ Mother
☐ Father
☐ Brother

☐ Sister
☐ Friend
☐ Other (please specify)

40. How long has it been since you last visited the nursing home?

☐ Within the last week
☐ Within the last month
☐ Within the last 3 months

☐ Within the last 6 months
☐ Within the last year
☐ Over a year ago

41. Length of time your family member or client has been in the nursing home.

☐ 0–6 months
☐ 6–12 months
☐ 1–3 years

☐ 3–6 years
☐ More than 6 years

42. What percent of the nursing care cost is provided by you?

☐ 0%
☐ 1–20%
☐ 21–50%

☐ 51–99%
☐ 100%
☐ don't know

43. Your sex

☐ Female
☐ Male

44. Your age

☐ 20–34 years
☐ 35–44 years
☐ 45–54 years

☐ 55–64 years
☐ 65–74 years
☐ Other (under 20 or over 74)

45. What is the highest level of education you have received?

☐ High School
☐ Attended College

☐ Graduated College
☐ Beyond College

46. What is your level of personal income?

☐ Below $10,000
☐ $10,000–$24,999
☐ $25,000–$39,999

☐ $40,000–$49,000
☐ $50,000–$74,999
☐ Over $75,000

Do you have other concerns about the home or information that we should know?

_____

_____

_____

_____

Thank you for taking your time to complete this questionnaire.

K & K Research © 1994.

Note. From "Perceptual Measures of Quality: A Tool to Improve Nursing Home Systems," by H. F. Koenig and I. K. Kleinsorge, 1994, *Hospital & Health Services Administration, 39,* 4.

The authors can be reached at College of Business, Oregon State University, Corvallis, OR 97331-2603.

SELECTED PORTIONS OF THE "LONG-TERM CARE RESIDENT EVALUATION SURVEY" DEVELOPED AT THE SUNNYBROOK HEALTH SCIENCE CENTRE (SHSC) IN TORONTO, CANADA

The domains from the questionnaire (Norton et al., 1996, p. 45) are as follows:
1. Autonomy
2. Living Area
3. Food
4. Activity
5. Staff
6. Dignity

Questions from the Living Area (Norton et al. 1996, p. 40) domain include:
- Is this place "homelike"?
- Do you have enough privacy?
- Are your personal belongings safe here?
- Could you injure yourself and staff wouldn't know?
- Does the noise around here bother you?
- Is the residence dreary?
- Does the smell in the residence bother you?
- Is the residence clean and tidy?
- Is your room how you would like it to be?
- Overall, how would you rate the living environment here at Sunnybrook?

A 5-point rating scale was used for the one overall rating question at the end of each domain:

Terrible	=1
Poor	=2
Fair	=3
Good	=4
Excellent	=5

Two global satisfaction questions were included (Norton et al. 1996, p. 40) at the end of the survey:
1. If long-term care were needed for another family or friend, would you recommend this facility to others? Would you say Yes, Maybe, or No?

2. Overall, how would you rate the quality of care and services you receive here at SHSC? [Answer on the 5-point scale]

© Soberman & Murray.
Note. From "Satisfaction of Residents and Families in Long-Term Care. Construction and Application of an Instrument," by P. G. Norton, B. van Maris, L. Soberman, and M. Murray, 1996, *Quality Management in Health Care,* 4(3), pp. 40–45.

Please contact Peter Norton, M.D. for permission to use.
Dept. of Family Medicine
University of Calgary
UCMC, Sunridge
3465-26 Ave. NE
Calgary, Alberta, Canada
T1Y 6L4
Phone: 403-219-6125
Fax: 403-219-6140
E-Mail: norton@ucalgary.ca
Satisfaction Surveys in Long-Term Care: Appendix II

SATISFACTION SURVEY

Below are a number of questions about our resident care and services. Please answer each question by checking the box that best indicates your opinion, or if a question doesn't apply to your situation, check "Don't Know" or "Does Not Apply." If the resident is able to assist in the completion of the survey, feel free to include his/her feedback. Your answers will help us to improve our services.

Please make marks inside boxes and avoid stray marks. Correct marks: ☒ ☑ ■   Incorrect ◌ ⊠

Overall ratings
What Is your overall opinion of:

	Poor	Fair	Good	Very Good	Excellent	Does Not Apply
The quality of care received?	☐	☐	☐	☐	☐	☐
Nursing care?	☐	☐	☐	☐	☐	☐
Physician care?	☐	☐	☐	☐	☐	☐
Social workers?	☐	☐	☐	☐	☐	☐
Housekeeping services?	☐	☐	☐	☐	☐	☐
Food service?	☐	☐	☐	☐	☐	☐
Administration?	☐	☐	☐	☐	☐	☐
Mail service?	☐	☐	☐	☐	☐	☐
Billing?	☐	☐	☐	☐	☐	☐

Facility Care & Services

	No	To Some Extent	Yes	Don't Know
Does the staff adequately explain the resident's condition and care plan?	☐	☐	☐	☐
Does the facility offer an adequate range of activities and recreation?	☐	☐	☐	☐
Is the resident given all of the care and services he/she needs?	☐	☐	☐	☐
Does the facility encourage appropriate family members' or friends' involvement with the resident's care?	☐	☐	☐	☐
Are the resident's preferences and choices respected by the staff?	☐	☐	☐	☐
When a physician is needed, can one be seen promptly?	☐	☐	☐	☐
Would you recommend this facility to your family and friends?	☐	☐	☐	☐

Comfort and Cleanliness

How would you rate the:

	Poor	Fair	Good	Very Good	Excellent	Don't Know
Cleanliness of the resident's room?	☐	☐	☐	☐	☐	☐
Temperature and ventilation of the resident's room?	☐	☐	☐	☐	☐	☐
Protection of personal property?	☐	☐	☐	☐	☐	☐
Comfort of the resident's room?	☐	☐	☐	☐	☐	☐
Cleanliness of the facility in general?	☐	☐	☐	☐	☐	☐
Ability to personalize the resident's room?	☐	☐	☐	☐	☐	☐
Scent within the facility?	☐	☐	☐	☐	☐	☐

Nursing Care

	Never	Rarely	Sometimes	Often	Always	Don't Know
Do the nurses call the resident by name?	☐	☐	☐	☐	☐	☐
Does the resident feel comfortable about sharing personal concerns with the nursing staff?	☐	☐	☐	☐	☐	☐
Do you feel the nursing staff treats the resident with respect and dignity?	☐	☐	☐	☐	☐	☐
Does the resident receive satisfactory answers to questions from the nursing staff?	☐☐	☐	☐	☐	☐	☐☐
Does the nursing staff seem to know what they are doing?	☐	☐	☐	☐	☐	☐
When there is a concern or problem, does the resident now who to go to for help?	☐	☐	☐	☐	☐☐	☐☐
Are medications given in a timely manner?	☐	☐	☐	☐	☐	☐
Does it appear there is an adequate number of staff available?	☐☐	☐	☐	☐	☐☐	☐☐
Is adequate attention given to personal grooming needs?						

Staff Courtesy

How would you rate the courtesy of the:

	Poor	Fair	Good	Very Good	Excellent	Don't Know
Nurses?	☐	☐	☐	☐	☐	☐
Activity and recreation personnel?	☐	☐	☐	☐	☐	☐
Food service staff?	☐	☐	☐	☐	☐	☐
Therapists?	☐	☐	☐	☐	☐	☐

Food Service

How would you rate the:	Poor	Fair	Good	Very Good	Excellent	Don't Know
Flavor of the food?	☐	☐	☐	☐	☐	☐
Temperature of the food?	☐	☐	☐	☐	☐	☐
Menu alternatives?	☐	☐	☐	☐	☐	☐

Restorative Care

	No	To Some Extent	Yes	Don't Know
Does the resident feel his/her condition has improved as much as expected?	☐	☐	☐	☐
Was the resident's therapy adequately explained to him/her?	☐	☐	☐	☐
Did the resident receive satisfactory answers to his/her questions from the therapy staff?	☐	☐	☐	☐
Was the resident's physician involved with his/her therapy process?	☐	☐	☐	☐
Were the follow-up medical instructions clear and understandable?	☐	☐	☐	☐
Overall, is the resident satisfied with the effectiveness of his/her therapy?	☐	☐	☐	☐

General Information

Why did you choose this facility? (Check all that apply)

- [ ] Physician's recommendation
- [ ] Friend's or relative's recommendation
- [ ] Other reason: _____
- [ ] Reputation of facility
- [ ] Location
- [ ] Hospital staff's recommendation
- [ ] Insurance requirements

What is the primary source of payment for the resident's care? (Check One)

- [ ] Blue Cross
- [ ] Commercial
- [ ] Medicare
- [ ] Medicaid
- [ ] HMO
- [ ] PPO
- [ ] Private Pay
- [ ] Other _____
- [ ] Unsure

Has the resident been at this facility for less than 1 year?

- [ ] Yes
- [ ] No

Your gender:
- [ ] Male
- [ ] Female

Resident's gender:
- [ ] Male
- [ ] Female

What is your relationship to the resident?

- [ ] Spouse
- [ ] Son or Daughter
- [ ] Brother or Sister
- [ ] Friend
- [ ] Other Relative
- [ ] Other _____

When was your most recent visit to the facility?

- [ ] Past week
- [ ] Past 2 weeks
- [ ] Past month
- [ ] Past 3 months
- [ ] Past 6 months
- [ ] Past year
- [ ] More than 1 year ago
- [ ] I have not been to the facility

How often do you visit the facility?

☐ Daily   ☐ Bi-weekly   ☐ A few times a year   ☐ Less than yearly
☐ Weekly   ☐ Monthly   ☐ Yearly   ☐ I have not been to the facility

☐ Please check here if the resident complete or helped complete this survey

Please Tell Us

What most impressed you? _____

_____

_____

How could we improve our service? _____

_____

_____

_____

Copyright 1996, Parkside Associate, Inc.
Please contact Parkside Associates for permission to use.
205 West Touhy Avenue, Suite 204
Park Ridge, Illinois 60068
www.ParksideAssociation.com
Mostyn, M., Seibert, J., Race, K. (in press). Quality assessment in nursing home facilities: Measuring customer satisfaction . American Journal of Medical Quality.

NURSING HOME SATISFACTION SCALE

For the next set of questions, I'm interested in knowing your impressions about this nursing home. There are no right or wrong answers to the questions. I would just like to know your thoughts and feelings. I am going to read some statements and I want to know if you agree or disagree.

Instructions to Interviewer: Display Response Cards. Check Neutral if respondent's response has elements of YES and NO, or YES — BUT.

(NEUTRAL is determined by the interviewer)

	AGREE (YES)	NEUTRAL	DISAGREE (NO)	IDK	NR
1. The food is good here.	1	2	3	4	5
2. Your room and surroundings are clean.	1	2	3	4	5
3. You can keep as many personal possessions in your room as you want.	1	2	3	4	5
4. You can see a doctor as often as you would like.	1	2	3	4	5
5. Most of the nurses and nursing assistants have the skills to provide the care you need.	1	2	3	4	5
6. At night you have a choice of going to bed when you want.	1	2	3	4	5
7. The amount of noise here bothers you.	1	2	3	4	5
8. When you need help, someone will come within a reasonable time.	1	2	3	4	5
9. You have enough privacy here.	1	2	3	4	5
10. This is a cheerful place.	1	2	3	4	5
11. You have a choice in deciding what clothing you will wear each day.	1	2	3	4	5
12. When you have a complaint, something is done about it.	1	2	3	4	5
13. Life is boring here.	1	2	3	4	5
14. Some of your personal belongings have disappeared.	1	2	3	4	5
15. Most of the nurses show a personal interest in you.	1	2	3	4	5
16. Most of the nursing assistants show a personal interest in you.	1	2	3	4	5
17. Life here is better than you expected when you first came here.	1	2	3	4	5

Jean Kruzich, Ph.D.

1997 KETHLEY HOUSE FAMILY SATISFACTION SURVEY

THE MARGARET BLENKNER RESEARCH CENTER
© 1995 THE BENJAMIN ROSE INSTITUTE

PLEASE CHECK THE BOX THAT INDICATES WHETHER IMPROVEMENT IS NEEDED WITH:	No Improvement Needed	Some Improvement Needed	Great deal of Improvement Needed	Not familiar With
1. ADMITTING PROCESS • Pre-admission planning/preparation • Opportunity for you to ask questions				
2. NURSING CARE • The quality of the care provided by Nurse Assistants • The amount of compassion and respect shown to the resident by Nurse Assistants • The quality of the care provided by Registered and Licensed Practical Nurses (RNs/LPNs) • The amount of compassion and respect shown to the resident by Registered and Licensed Practical Nurses (RNs/LPNs)				
3. SOCIAL SERVICES • Social Worker's follow-up and response to resident's concerns • Social Worker's follow-up and response to family's concerns • The amount of compassion and respect shown to the resident by the Social Worker				

PLEASE CHECK THE BOX THAT INDICATES WHETHER IMPROVEMENT IS NEEDED WITH:	No Improvement Needed	Some Improvement Needed	Great deal of Improvement Needed	Not familiar With
4. DIETARY SERVICES				
• The cheerfulness of the decor in the dining room				
• Dietary staff's follow-up and response to resident's food preferences				
• The tastiness of the food				
• The temperature of the food (hot foods are hot and cold foods are cold)				
5. LAUNDRY SERVICES				
• The handling of personal clothing (properly cleaned and returned without loss)				
• The timeliness with which personal laundry is returned				
6. THERAPY				
• The quality of the therapy (individualized / personalized) provided by Physical Therapist(s)				
• The quality of the therapy (individualized / personalized) provided by the Occupational Therapist(s)				
• The compassion and respect shown to the resident by the Physical Therapist(s)				
• The compassion and respect shown to the resident by the Occupational Therapist(s)				

PLEASE CHECK THE BOX THAT INDICATES WHETHER IMPROVEMENT IS NEEDED WITH:	No Improvement Needed	Some Improvement Needed	Great deal of Improvement Needed	Not familiar With
7. ACTIVITIES				
• The variety of activities available				
• The quality of activities (appropriate/stimulating) for residents				
• The amount of compassion and respect shown to the resident by the activity staff				
8. MEDICAL AND ANCILLARY SERVICES				
• The quality of care provided by lab and x-ray services				
• The quality of care provided by the physician				
• The compassion and respect shown to the resident by the physician				
9. OFFICE MANAGEMENT				
• The efficiency of Billing Department				
10. RECEPTIONIST				
• The timeliness with which the phone is answered by the receptionist				
• The courtesy with which calls are answered				
11. ADMINISTRATION				
• The willingness and availability to discuss problems with residents				
• The willingness and availability to discuss problems with families				
• Is responsive, takes action, gets back to you, is informative				

PLEASE CHECK THE BOX THAT INDICATES WHETHER IMPROVEMENT IS NEEDED WITH:	No Improvement Needed	Some Improvement Needed	Great deal of Improvement Needed	Not familiar With
12. ENVIRONMENT INSIDE THE HOME				
• The cleanliness of room and bathroom areas				
• Comfortable and non-glaring lighting				
• The availability and maintenance of equipment (wheelchair/walker)				
13. OVERALL ATMOSPHERE OF THE HOME				
• Peaceful and comforting environment				
• The odor within the facility				
• The noise level				
• The privacy available when you visit				

14. Overall, how satisfied are you with Kethley House?

15. Would you recommend Kethley House to other families or friends?

16. Please list any new activities you would like to see Kethley House provide for your relative:

_____

_____

17. Only if you would like a staff person to contact you for any reason, please write down your name and phone number:

Name _____ Phone number _____

18. Any additional comments you'd like to make about the services or staff ? (Use additional sheet if necessary)

_____

_____

_____

19. Form filled out by: _____ Spouse _____ Child _____ Grandchild _____ Niece/Nephew _____ Other (specify)

Note: If printed on legal size paper, this instrument is only two pages. When printed back-to-back on legal size paper, it is only one page. It is used in the latter format by The Benjamin Rose Institute.

The instrument is copyrighted and permission must be obtained to use the instrument or items from it from Dr. Linda Noelker, Associate Director, The Margaret Blenkner Research Center, The Benjamin Rose Institute, 850 Euclid Avenue, Suite 1100, Cleveland, OH 44114.

STAFF SATISFACTION SURVEY: QUESTIONS AND RESULTS FROM 246 STAFF MEMBERS

		(1,2) Disagree	(3) Neither	(4,5) Agree
1.	My present salary is satisfactory.	71%	16%	13%
2.	Most people do not appreciate the importance of nurse aide work in nursing homes.	29%	19%	52%
3.	I feel I am supervised more closely than is necessary.	52%	24%	24%
4.	I receive sufficient recognition ad appreciation for the work done here.	40%	23%	37%
5.	There is not enough opportunity for advancement or growth in my job.	26%	22%	52%
6.	I am satisfied with the types of activities I do on my job.	24%	23%	53%
7.	It makes me proud to talk to other people about my job.	15%	19%	66%
8.	Excluding myself, nurse aides at this facility are dissatisfied with pay.	26%	14%	60%
9.	I wish administrators and charge nurses would show more respect for nurse aides.	15%	14%	71%
10.	Management makes me feel "in" on things.	40%	24%	36%
11.	I am sometimes frustrated because all of my activities seem programmed for me.	44%	32%	24%
12.	There is too much paperwork required for nursing personnel.	56%	21%	23%
13.	I feel I have sufficient input into the program of care for each of my residents.	30%	18%	52%
14.	New employees are quickly made to feel at home on my unit.	17%	14%	69%
15.	My benefits and working conditions are reasonable.	38%	21%	41%
16.	I have sufficient time for direct resident care.	26%	21%	53%
17.	What I do on my job is really important.	3%	6%	91%

Note. From "Strategies for Nurse Aide Job Satisfaction," by F. T. Helmer, S. F. Olson, and R. I. Heim, 1993. *The Journal of Long-Term Care Administration,* 21(2), 10–14.

Please contact F. Theodore Helmer, Ph.D., for permission to use. Professor of Management, Northern Arizona University, Flagstaff, AZ. e-mail: Ted.Helmer@nau.edu

NORMS/BENCHMARKING: RESIDENT AND FAMILY SATISFACTION SURVEYS

RESIDENT EXPERIENCE AND ASSESSMENT OF LIFE (R.E.A.L.).,
Gwen C. Uman and Vital Research, LLC

FREQUENCY DISTRIBUTION, MEAN, AND STANDARD DEVIATION FOR ITEMS ON THE NURSING HOME SATISFACTION SCALE,
Jean Kruzich

SAMPLE REPORT PAGES FOR A HYPOTHETICAL FACILITY AGAINST THE NORMS FROM THE PARTNERS IN QUALITY ® LONG-TERM CARE SURVEY AT ANY FACILITY, ANY CITY, ANY STATE,
Parkside Association, Inc.

Table III.1 Resident Experience and Assessment of Life Resident Interview Guide

List of Questions by Consumer Requirement

HELP AND ASSISTANCE

	Benchmark	Standard
Do the people who work here help you put on your makeup or comb your hair? (women only)	89%	72%
Do the people who work here help you put on your clothes?	94%	80%
Do the people who work here help you go to the toilet?	91%	82%
Does somebody answer your call button right away?	57%	74%
Do the people who work here help you eat your food?	100%	82%
Is there somebody to talk to here if you have a problem?	84%	81%
Do you have to ask for something more than once?	63%	70%
Do the people who work here help you walk?	88%	81%
Do the people who work here help you get around in your wheelchair?	87%	80%
Do the people who work here help you change your wet (diaper, Attends, Pampers) as often as you want?	85%	81%
Do the people who work here help you brush your teeth or clean your dentures?	83%	77%
Do the people who work here help you shave (MEN ONLY)?	100%	78%
Does anybody here do something to lower your pain?	91%	86%

Table III.1 *(continued)*

COMMUNICATION		
	Benchmark	Standard
Do people come here from the outside (from the community) to do things with residents?	77%	59%
Do the people who work here spend time with you?	54%	72%
Do you understand the people who work here when they talk to you?	86%	84%
Are there new people working here all the time? (No)	30%	59%
Do the people who work here ever hold your hand or put their arm around you to show they care about you?	51%	77%
Do the people who work here talk with you?	71%	84%
Do the people who work here smile at you?	83%	86%
Do the people who work here listen to what you say?	81%	81%
Do the people who work here tell you about the daily schedule?	68%	75%

SAFETY AND SECURITY		
	Benchmark	Standard
Do the people who work here knock on your door before entering your room?	78%	82%
Do the people who work here ever get angry at you? (No)	84%	85%
Do you feel physically safe in _____ (FACILITY NAME)?	97%	89%
Do the people who work here handle you gently?	90%	87%
Are your personal belongings safe here?	81%	80%

Table III.1 *(continued)*

AUTONOMY AND CHOICE

	Benchmark	Standard
Can you decide when to get up in the morning?	58%	62%
Can you decide when to eat?	31%	59%
Can you decide what clothing to wear?	84%	73%
Can you decide when to _____ (SHOWER, BATHE)?	44%	66%
Does _____ (FACILITY) offer a variety of activities?	83%	75%
Do you go to the activities here?	49%	67%
Do the people who work here ever take you to places away from _____ (FACILITY)?	30%	60%
Do you ever go outdoors (OUTSIDE)?	63%	64%
Can you be alone here?	86%	74%
Can you decide when to go to bed?	80%	69%
Do you get as many _____ (SHOWERS, BATHS) as you want?	77%	62%

COMPANIONSHIP

	Benchmark	Standard
Are you friends with anybody who lives here?	67%	72%
Do you talk to other people who live here?	78%	73%
Are you alone too much? (No)	88%	67%
Are you friends with anybody who works here?	61%	53%

FOOD AND ENVIRONMENT

	Benchmark	Standard
Do you get fresh food here?	86%	80%
Do you get a variety of food here?	86%	81%
Is food served at the right temperature?	80%	79%
Do you have enough time to finish your meal?	95%	83%
Is it clean here?	100%	84%
Are you ever kept awake because of noise? (No)	70%	77%

Table III.1 *(continued)*

OVERALL SATISFACTION		
	Benchmark	Standard
Would you recommend _____ (FACILITY) to a friend?	91%	81%
Overall, are you satisfied with this place?	90%	80%

Benchmark: Represents the median score for 44 Nursing Homes in three regions of the U.S.
Standard: Represents the standard for minimum acceptable quality of life as defined by nine long term care experts.

The format for the Resident Interview Guide with required prompts, alternative wording, branching logic, response options, and order of items is not shown here. © 1998, Vital Research, LLC. For further information contact Dr. Gwen C. Uman, 8380 Melrose Avenue #309, Los Angeles, CA 90069, 323.753-7411, 323.653.0123 FAX, guman@vitalresearch.com.

Table III.2 Frequency Distribution, Mean, and Standard Deviation for Items on the Nursing Home Satisfaction Scale ($N = 289$)

Items	Disagree	Unsure Don't know	Agree	M	SD
1. The food is good here.	24%	22%	54%	2.30	.83
2. Your room and surroundings are clean.	1	2	97	2.95	.22
3. You can keep as many personal possessions in your room as you want.	21	9	69	2.48	.82
4. You can see a doctor as often as you would like.	17	13	70	2.53	.78
5. Most of the nurses and nursing assistants have the skills to provide the care you need.	8	12	80	2.70	.62
6. At night you have a choice of going to bed when you want.	14	2	84	2.70	.69
7. The amount of noise here bothers you.	21	10	70	2.48	.82
8. When you need help, someone will come within a reasonable time.	10	13	76	2.66	.66
9. You have enough privacy here.	8	4	88	2.79	.57
10. This is a cheerful place.	13	17	69	2.56	.72
11. You have a choice in deciding what clothing you will wear each day.	8	4	88	2.80	.56
12. When you have a complaint, something is done about it.	10	27	63	2.54	.66
13. Life is boring here.	60	13	27	2.40	.87
14. Some of your personal belongings have disappeared from your room.	47	3	50	1.97	.98
15. Most of the nurses show a personal interest in you.	11	13	75	2.65	.67
16. Most of the nursing assistants show a personal interest in you.	15	15	70	2.56	.73
17. Life here is better than you expected when you first came here.	21	28	50	2.30	.79

Note. From "Personal and Environmental Influences on Nursing Home Satisfaction," by J. M. Kruzich, J. F. Clinton, and S. T. Kelber, 1992. *The Gerontologist, 32*(3), 345. Copyright 1992 by The Gerontological Society of America. Reprinted with permission.

PARTNERS IN QUALITY ®

LONG-TERM CARE SURVEY

at
Any Facility
Any City, IL
Report #8

An Analysis of Respondents Surveyed
May XXXX

Prepared March 1999 by
Parkside Associates, Inc.
Park Ridge, Illinois

TABLE OF CONTENTS

GUIDE TO INTERPRETATION OF DATA

This report presents data on patients discharged from your facility compared to facilities in Parkside's norm database.

Graphs

The first graph presents your recent scores in the Composite Quality Scale. The next two graphs illustrate the overall quality of care rating and the willingness to recommend the facility. The last four graphs illustrate the results for the subscales that form the Composite Quality Scale (Comfort and Cleanliness, Nursing Care, Facility Care and Services and Food Service subscales). Each graph also includes a comparison to the scores observed at other facilities.

Tables

Each table displays results for specific survey items. Data for the current items, reasons for facility choice, and a demographic profile of the current report, three previous reports, and the norm database are shown, along with flags indicating consistency and differences from the norm.

Item Scores and Percentages

Tables with rating scale items display percentages for each response category as well as report an Item Score. The Item Score is calculated by assigning a numeric value to each of the response categories (e.g. Excellent, Yes, Always = 100 and Very Poor, No, Seldom/Never = 0) then summing these values across all respondents and dividing by the number of responses. The maximum Item Score = 100 and the minimum Item Score = 0.

Standard Deviation Flags

On tables I through 7, each report column is flagged as needing attention or recognition. Facilities are placed in one of five groupings:

A blank (no symbol) indicates that the facility is average (i.e. within plus or minus one standard deviation of the norm).

* indicates that the favorable response is below average (i.e. one to two standard deviations below the norm, in the bottom 2.3% to 16% of all facilities).

** indicates that the favorable response is well below average (i.e. two or more standard deviations below the norm, in the bottom 2.3% of all facilities).

+ indicates that the favorable response is above the average (i.e. one to two standard deviations above the norm, in the top 2.3% to 16% of all facilities).

++ indicates that the favorable response is well above average (i.e. two or more standard deviations above the norm, in the top 2.3% of all facilities).

Streak Flags (Consistency)

Tables I through 7 have a column on the extreme right entitled, "STREAK CONSISTENTLY ABOVE/BELOW NORM". Facilities are placed in one of three groupings:

A blank (no symbol) indicates that the facility's scores are neither consistently above nor consistently below the average.

>> indicates that the favorable responses are consistently above average (four reports at least 1% above the norm).

<<> indicates that the favorable responses are consistently below average (four reports at least 1% below the norm).

In future reports your facility may use the national norms or employ whatever other norm your facility feels may be more appropriate (based on region, chain affiliation, bed size, religious affiliation, etc.). See Appendix B.

RESPONDENTS IN CURRENT REPORT

Group Size	Sample Completed	Surveys Surveys	Undeliverable Rate	Response
ALL PATIENTS	200	127	5	65%
SITE 1	100	63	3	65%
SITE 2	100	64	2	65%

ANY FACILITY
GROUP IS ALL PATIENTS
COMPARED TO NATIONAL NORM

LONG-TERM CARE SURVEY
CURRENT REPORT PERIOD IS
MAY XXXX

GLOBAL SATISFACTION INDICATORS

| ■ ALL PATIENTS | — MEAN OF OTHER FACILITIES | ☐ RANGE OF OTHER FACILITIES |

COMPOSITE QUALITY SCALE
(A WEIGHTED AVERAGE OF FOUR SUBSCALES)

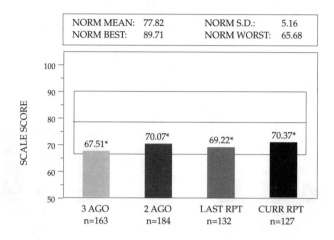

| NORM MEAN: | 77.82 | NORM S.D.: | 5.16 |
| NORM BEST: | 89.71 | NORM WORST: | 65.68 |

SCALE SCORE

3 AGO	2 AGO	LAST RPT	CURR RPT
67.51*	70.07*	69.22*	70.37*
n=163	n=184	n=132	n=127

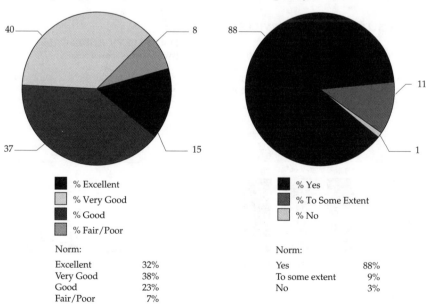

What is your overall opinion of the quality of care received?

40 — 8
37 — 15

- ■ % Excellent
- ☐ % Very Good
- ■ % Good
- ■ % Fair/Poor

Norm:

Excellent	32%
Very Good	38%
Good	23%
Fair/Poor	7%

What is your overall opinion of the quality of care received?

88 —
— 11
— 1

- ■ % Yes
- ■ % To Some Extent
- ☐ % No

Norm:

Yes	88%
To some extent	9%
No	3%

Standart Deviation Flags:
+ Above Average (1 Std Dev Above Mean)
* Below Average (1 Std Dev Below Mean)
++ Well Above Average (2+ Std Devs Above Mean)
** Well Below Average (2+ Std Devs Below Mean)

ANY FACILITY
GROUP IS ALL PATIENTS
COMPARED TO NATIONAL NORM

LONG-TERM CARE SURVEY
CURRENT REPORT PERIOD IS
MAY XXXX

GLOBAL SATISFACTION INDICATORS

■ ALL PATIENTS — MEAN OF OTHER FACILITIES ☐ RANGE OF OTHER FACILITIES

COMFORT AND CLEANLINESS
SUBSCALE
(Weight in Composite Scale = 0.33)

NORM MEAN:	69.08	NORM S.D.:	7.43
NORM BEST:	87.28	NORM WORST:	47.58

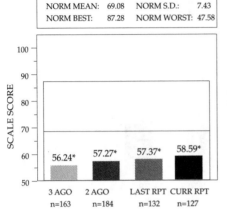

NURSING CARE SUBSCALE
(Weight in Composite Scale = 0.32)

NORM MEAN:	84.59	NORM S.D.:	4.09
NORM BEST:	93.79	NORM WORST:	73.53

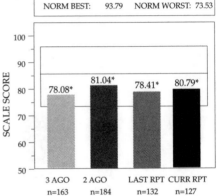

FACILITY CARE AND SERVICES
SUBSCALE
(Weight in Composite Scale = 0.25)

NORM MEAN:	86.19	NORM S.D.:	4.68
NORM BEST:	96.05	NORM WORST:	72.91

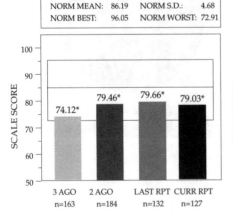

FOOD SERVICE SUBSCALE
(Weight in Composite Scale = 0.11)

NORM MEAN:	65.20	NORM S.D.:	7.42
NORM BEST:	83.69	NORM WORST:	48.99

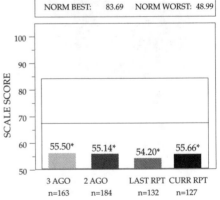

ANY FACILITY
GROUP IS ALL PATIENTS
COMPARED TO NATIONAL NORM

LONG-TERM CARE SURVEY
CURRENT REPORT PERIOD IS
MAY XXXX

TABLE 2: Comfort and Cleanliness Subscale Questions

QUESTION	RESPONSE CATEGORY	3 REPORTS AGO (n=163)	2 REPORTS AGO (n=184)	LAST REPORT (n=132)	CURRENT REPORT (n=127)	NORM	STREAK FLAG
1. What is your overall opinion of house-keeping services?	EXCELLENT	13%*	15%*	9%*	15%*	30%	<<
	VERY GOOD	29%	28%	31%	29%	34%	
	GOOD	37%	40%	35%	41 %	24%	
	FAIR/POOR	21%	17%	24%	15%	12%	
	Item Score	57*	59*	55*	60*	70	
	# of Responses	n=158	n=178	n=128	n=124		
2. How would you rate the cleanliness of the resident's room?	EXCELLENT	14%*	11%*	13%*	13%*	34%	<<
	VERY GOOD	31%	36%	33%	36%	35%	
	GOOD	36%	38%	36%	38%	22%	
	FAIR/POOR	20%	15%	17%	13%	9%	
	Item Score	59*	60*	59*	62*	73	
	# of Responses	n=160	n=183	n=129	n=127		
3. How would you rate the cleanliness of the facility in general?	EXCELLENT	16%*	13%*	20%*	14%*	38%	<<
	VERY GOOD	34%	41%	35%	43%	36%	
	GOOD	35%	38%	37%	36%	21%	
	FAIR/POOR	14%	9%	8%	7%	5%	
	Item Score	63*	64*	66*	66*	77	
	# of Responses	n=160	n=184	n=130	n=127		

TABLE 2: *(continued)*

QUESTION	RESPONSE CATEGORY	3 REPORTS AGO (n=163)	2 REPORTS AGO (n=184)	LAST REPORT (n=132)	CURRENT REPORT (n=127)	NORM	STREAK FLAG
4. How would you rate the comfort of the resident's room?	EXCELLENT	11%*	10%*	9%*	11%*	26%	
	VERY GOOD	20%	23%	24%	22%	35%	
	GOOD	45%	50%	47%	49%	29%	
	FAIR/POOR	24%	18%	19%	18%	10%	
	Item Score	53**	56*	55*	56*	69	<<
	# of Re.sponses	n=158	n=182	n=129	n=127		
5. How would you rate the temperature & ventilation of the resident's room?	EXCELLENT	9%*	7%*	8%*	9%*	24%	
	VERY GOOD	21%	25%	27%	24%	35%	
	GOOD	41%	43%	38%	45%	27%	
	FAIR/POOR	29%	25%	27%	22%	14%	
	Item Score	51*	53*	52*	54*	66	<<
	# of Responses	n=160	n=182	n=128	n=125		
6. How would rate the scent within the facility?	EXCELLENT	20%	12%*	15%	13%*	26%	
	VERY GOOD	19%	30%	27%	31%	30%	
	GOOD	39%	38%	38%	38 %	28%	
	FAIR/POOR	22%	20%	20%	18%	16%	
	Item Score	58	58	58	60	66	<<
	#of Responses	n=157	n=180	n=128	n=123		

TABLE 2: *(continued)*

QUESTION	RESPONSE CATEGORY	3 REPORTS AGO (n=163)	2 REPORTS AGO (n=184)	LAST REPORT (n=132)	CURRENT REPORT (n=127)	NORM	STREAK FLAG
7. How would you rate the protection of personal property?	EXCELLENT	7%*	5%*	7%*	7%*	21%	<<
	VERY GOOD	18%	22%	24%	22%	28%	
	GOOD	39%	35%	33%	33%	27%	
	FAIR/POOR	36%	39%	36%	39%	24%	
	Item Score	46*	45*	48*	46*	s9	
	# of Responses	n=154	n=179	n=125	n=123		
8. How would rate the ability to personalize the resident's room?	EXCELLENT	18%*	14%*	16%*	16%*	33%	<<
	VERY GOOD	29%	32%	39%	34%	35%	
	GOOD	38%	44%	39%	40%	24%	
	FAIR/POOR	15%	9%	7%	10%	8%	
	Item Score	62*	63*	66	64*	73	
	# of Responses	n=155	n=180	n=121	n=124		

Item Score Values: Minimum Item Score (Poor, Never, No)=0   Maximum Item Score (Excellent, Always, Yes)=100

Standard Deviation Flags: +Above Average (I Std Dev Above Mean)   ++Well Above Average (2+ Std Devs Above Mean)
*Below Average (I Std Dev Below Mean)   **Well Below Average (2+ Std Devs Below Mean)

Streak Flags: Consistently Above (>) Or Below (<<) Norm For Four Repons (By At Least I %)

ANY FACILITY
GROUP IS ALL PATIENTS
COMPARED TO NATIONAL NORM

LONG-TERM CARE SURVEY
CURRENT REPORT PERIOD IS
MAY XXXX

TABLE 3: NURSING CARE SUBSCALE QUESTIONS

QUESTION	RESPONSE CATEGORY	3 REPORTS AGO (n=163)	2 REPORTS AGO (n=184)	LAST REPORT (n=132)	CURRENT REPORT (n=127)	NORM	STREAK FLAG
1. What is your overall opinion of nursing care?	EXCELLENT	16%*	19%*	10%**	18%*	37%	<<
	VERY GOOD	33%	38%	50%	40%	37%	
	GOOD	37%	36%	29%	37%	21%	
	FAIR/POOR	14%	7%	11%	6%	6%	
	Item Score	62*	67*	65*	67*	76	
	# of Responses	n=159	n=178	n=127	n=124		
2. How would you rate courtesy of the nurses?	EXCELLENT	30%*	41%	38%*	44%	52%	<<
	VERY GOOD	36%	30%	28%	27%	32%	
	GOOD	28%	25%	28%	27%	13%	
	FAIR/POOR	6%	4%	6%	2 %	4%	
	Item Score	72*	77*	74*	78	83	
	# of Responses	n=159	n=180	n=130	n=124		
3. Does the nursing staff seem to know what they are doing?	ALWAYS	50%	58%	52%	56%	58%	
	OFTEN	34%	33%	35%	36%	37%	
	SOMETIMES	15%	8%	13%	8%	4%	
	RARELY/NEVER	1%	0%	0%	0%	0%	
	Item Score	83*	88	85	87	88	
	# of Responses	n=157	n=166	n=124	n=114		

TABLE 3: (continued)

QUESTION	RESPONSE CATEGORY	3 REPORTS AGO (n=163)	2 REPORTS AGO (n=184)	LAST REPORT (n=132)	CURRENT REPORT (n=127)	NORM	STREAK FLAG
4. Does the resident receive satisfactory answers to questions from the staff?	ALWAYS	43%	44%	39%	45%	51%	<<
	OFTEN	30%	35%	33%	32%	39%	
	SOMETIMES	24%	17%	24%	18%	8%	
	RARELY/NEVER	3%	4%	5%	4%	2%	
	Item Score	78*	80	76*	80	85	
	# of Responses	n=100	n=131	n=85	n=93		
5. Does the nursing staff treat the resident with dignity & respect?	ALWAYS	56%	63%	56%	64%	64%	<<
	OFTEN	34%	28%	36%	28%	31%	
	SOMETIMES	9%	9%	7%	8%	6%	
	RARELY/NEVER	1%	0%	1%	0%	1%	
	Item Score	87	88	87	89	89	
	# of Responses	n=156	n=162	n=125	n=112		
6. Are medications given in a timely manner?	ALWAYS	68%	66%	66%	68%	67%	<<
	OFTEN	23%	28%	23%	25%	29%	
	SOMETIMES	8%	6%	8%	7%	3%	
	RARELY/NEVER	1%	0%	3%	0%	1%	
	Item Score	90	90	88	90	91	
	# of Resoonses	n=122	n=137	n=99	n=96		

TABLE 3: *(continued)*

QUESTION	RESPONSE CATEGORY	3 REPORTS AGO (n=163)	2 REPORTS AGO (n=184)	LAST REPORT (n=132)	CURRENT REPORT (n=127)	NORM	STREAK FLAG
7. Does the resident feel comfortable sharing personal concerns w/ staff?	ALWAYS	27%*	44%	32%*	42%	46%	<<
	OFTEN	34%	25%	31%	23%	36%	
	SOMETIMES	30%	28%	30%	33%	13%	
	RARELY/NEVER	10%	2%	7%	2%	4%	
	Item Score	69*	78	72*	76	80	
	# of Responses	n=101	n=130	n=87	n=91		
8. When there is a problem or concern, does resident know where to find help?	ALWAYS	39%	54%	35%*	54%	49%	<<
	OFTEN	19%	22%	26%	22%	37%	
	SOMETIMES	26%	18%	25%	18%	10%	
	RARELY/NEVER	16%	6%	13%	6%	4%	
	Item Score	69**	80	68**	80	82	
	# of Responses	n=106	n=138	n=91	n=93		
9. Do the nurses call the resident by name?	ALWAYS	69%	65%	69%	63%	69%	<<
	OFTEN	25%	28%	30%	27%	27%	
	SOMETIMES	6%	6%	1%	8%	3%	
	RARELY/NEVER	1%	1%	0%	2%	1%	
	Item Score	90	89	92	88	90	
	# of Responses	n=156	n=176	n=127	n=121		

Item Score Values: Minimum Item Score (Poor, Never, No)=0   Maximum Item Score (Excellent, Always, Yes)=100

Standard Deviation Flags: +Above Average (I Std Dev Above Mean)   ++Well Above Average (2+ Std Devs Above Mean)

*Below Average (I Std Dev Below Mean)   **Well Below Average (2+ Std Devs Below Mean)

Streak Flags: Consistently Above (>) Or Below (<<) Norm For Four Repons (By At Least I %)

Sampling Error Estimates for Individual Questions

The sampling error estimates for the favorable responses (usually "Yes" or "Excellent") of the national norm data are negligible (less than 1 percentage point for all questions). However, there will always be some sampling error in an individual hospital's data which will vary with the percentage of favorable responses to each item and the number of patients in the report period and the size of the patient population. The following table can be used to estimate the sampling error and associated confidence interval (i.e., 95% and 99%) for an individual item based on patients in a given period or combination of periods:

Estimated Standard Error of Proportions For Various Patient Sample Sizes

Percentage of Favorable Responses	Number of patients providing retinas					
	50	100	150	200	250	300
10% or 90%	±4.2%	±3.0%	±2.4%	±2.1%	±1.9%	±1.7%
20% or 80%	±5.6%	±4.0%	±3.3%	±2.8%	±2.5%	±2.3%
30% or 70%	±6.5%	±4.6%	±3.7%	±3.3%	±2.9%	±2.7%
40% or 60%	±6.9%	±4.9%	±4.0%	±3.5%	±3.1%	±2.8%
50%	±7.0%	±5.0%	±4.1%	±3.5%	±3.2%	±2.9%

Sampling error will be at a minimum when the percentages in the favorable response category for consecutive periods are averaged and the total number of patients in multiple report periods are used as the base number. Sampling error estimates are multiplied by 1.96 for the 95% confidence level and 2.58 for the 99% confidence level.

Correction Factor for Small Population

When the sample represents a large percentage (i.e. over 20%) of the total population, the sampling error is reduced by multiplying the estimated error by the following correction factor:

$$\sqrt{1 - \frac{\text{NUMBER OF PATIENTS PROVIDING RATINGS}}{\text{TOTAL POPULATION}}}$$

For example, if the sample represents 40% of the total population, the correction factor would be 0.77 x (estimated error in the above table.)

DATABASE PROFILE OF LONG-TERM CARE FACILITIES
(Total =200)

Census Region	Number	Percent
Northeast	40	20%
Middle Atlantic (NJ, NY, PA)		
New England (CT, ME, MA, NH, RI, VT)		
Midwest	92	46%
East North Central (IL, IN, MI, OH, WI)		
West North Central (IA, KS, MN, MO, NE ND, SD)		
South	34	17%
East South Central (AL, KY, MS, TN)		
South Atlantic (DE, DC, FL, GA, MD, NC, SC, VA, WV)		
West South Central (AR, LA, OK, TX)		
West	34	17%
Mountain (AZ, CO, ID, MT, NV, NM, UT. WY)		
Pacific (AK, CA, HI, OR, WA)		
Ownership Status		
Non-Profit	109	55%
For Profit	61	31%
Not Reported	30	15%
Chain Affiliated		
Yes	45	23 %
No	122	61%
Not Reported	33	17%
Religious Affiliations		
Catholic	22	11%
Protestant	16	8%
Jewish	5	3%
Other religions	10	5%
Non religious	110	55%
Not reported	37	19%
Hospital Owned		
Yes	58	29%
No	108	54%
Not reported	34	17%
Total Number of Residents		
75 or less	40	20%
76–150	46	23%
151–225	19	10%
226 & Up	17	9%
Not reported	78	39%

*This database profile is reflective of self-reported demographic information about participating facilities.

EXAMPLES OF SUPPORTING MATERIAL

EXAMPLE OF A COVER LETTER TO FAMILIES,
Farida K. Ejaz, The Benjamin Rose Institute

**EXAMPLE OF A SUMMARY OF
OPEN-ENDED RESPONSES,**
Farida K. Ejaz,
The Benjamin
Rose Institute

EXAMPLE OF A REPORT,
Farida K. Ejaz,
The Benjamin Rose Institute

**CHECKLIST FOR COMPARING SATISFACTION
SURVEY INSTRUMENTS,**
Jiska Cohen-Mansfield

ADDITIONAL RESOURCES

EXAMPLE OF COVER LETTER TO FAMILIES

(DATE)

Dear Family Member,

I am asking for your help to fill out the annual Family Satisfaction Survey for family members of the long-term care residents at (NAME OF FACILITY). Since a resident's family is often the best judge of services provided to a relative, we believe that your input will help us improve our services and care. Although we are mailing the survey to only one family member per resident, please feel free to discuss the survey with other family members and give us your opinions of the services and care received by your family member at (NAME OF FACILITY).

The survey was developed by the (RESEARCH CENTER/ ORGANIZATION). It is very comprehensive and covers a wide range of services provided at (NAME OF FACILITY). It also includes areas in which you can write personal comments. I encourage you to note positive and negative comments about the facility, its staff and services.

The research center staff will analyze the results and prepare a report for (NAME OF FACILITY) staff. All responses will be summarized and no names will be mentioned in the report. Therefore, it is not necessary for us to have your name on the form. All responses will be treated as highly confidential and data will be presented in aggregate form (using percentages and averages). If however, you would like to be contacted by a staff person, please write your name and phone number (QUESTION #) on the survey form. We welcome open discussion of your opinions.

Your participation in filling out this survey is strictly voluntary. If you decide not to participate, the care received by your relative at (NAME OF FACILITY) will not be compromised in any way. However, I urge you to make your opinions known so that we can achieve our goal of high quality services and thus better meet the needs of residents at (NAME OF FACILITY). Please help us achieve our goals by returning the survey in the enclosed self-addressed stamped envelope by *(DATE)*. Thank you.

Sincerely,

(EXECUTIVE/ RESEARCH DIRECTOR)

SUMMARY OF OPEN-ENDED COMMENTS

OVERALL COMMENTS

POSITIVE COMMENTS		NEGATIVE COMMENTS	

GENERAL

POSITIVE COMMENTS		NEGATIVE COMMENTS	
• Staff prompt in assisting with concerns.	1	• 4th floor care uneven, very poor/understaffed.	2
• Treatment rendered is super.		• Too many "part-timers"	3
• Very pleased with everything.			

NURSING

• Always courteous and reassuring; very pleased with care; some are great; treated Mom with a lot of love and care; paid special attention to Dad.	7	• Understaffed: staff too busy, always writing notes; lack of personal attention to residents.	3
		• Turnover too frequent. New head nurse twice in the year.	3

NURSING ASSISTANTS (NAs)

• Most are efficient, pleasant.	4	• Understaffed: Not enough NAs on 4th floor.	3
		• More needed to help with toileting.	1

ENVIRONMENT

• Like the room, comfortable.	5	• Rooms should be cleaner, bathrooms cleaned daily; wheelchairs should be cleaned.	3

LAUNDRY

• Clothes returned clean and pressed.	2	• Clothes missing and mixed with other laundry, poorly handled.	6

DIETARY

• Food is wholesome and tasty.	3	• Food needs much improvement—cold , poorly cooked, concerned with quality.	2
		• Need more help with feeding patients.	1

Please note: These data are fictious and do not belong to any facility. The data are merely made up to reflect how open-ended response can be categorized.

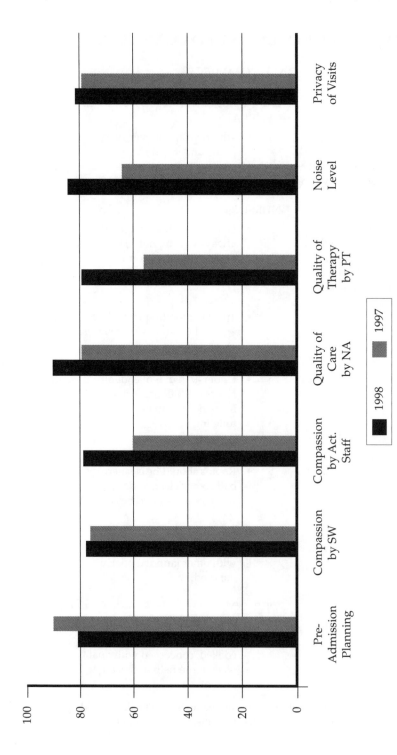

Family Satisfaction Survey: Areas of Excellence
Comparison with 1997 Responses (*n* = 54)

75% or More of Respondents Report No Improvement Needed in 1998
*NOTE: The data used in this chart is fictitious.

Table IV.D Checklist for Comparing Among Survey Instruments

Content
- Topics/domains covered
- Length: Number of items
- Clarity of:
  - Items
  - Scale
  - Appropriateness of scale to items
  - Organization of items within questionnaire
- Items:
  - Open/closed ended
  - Statements/questions
  - Lack of bias
  - Each item should not include more than one topic
  - Item vs. group of items per topic
  - Focused vs. general
- Scales: range of scales used
- User friendliness:
  - Quality of introduction, statement of purpose
  - Space for comments
  - Ease to follow
- Options /flexibility in :
  - Customizing survey for institution's needs
  - Including specific personal input
  - Customizing different questionnaires by respondent: by type of care, by department
  - Other criteria
  - Reliability—which type
  - Validity—which type, against which criteria
  - Norms—for service industry in general, for LTC
  - Cost
  - Do the instrument's format and attributes fit the goals?

Table IV.E Additional Resources

For more information on the surveys in the appendix, please contact the following sources:

- Nursing Care Facility Resident Satisfaction Survey
  National Research Corporation
  Please contact Kris Benson at (402) 475-2525 for permission to use.
- Customer Satisfaction Instrument
  K & K Research
  The authors can be reached at College of Business, Oregon State University, Corvallis, OR 97331-2603.
- 1997 Kethley House Family Satisfaction Survey
  Dr. Linda Noelker
  Associate Director
  The Margaret Blenker Research Center
  The Benjamin Rose Institute
  850 Euclid Avenue, Suite 1100
  Cleveland, OH 44114
- Resident Experience and Assessment of Life (R.E.A.L.)
  Dr. Gwen C. Uman
  Vital Research, LLC
  8380 Melrose Avenue
  Los Angeles, CA 90069
  tel. 323-753-7441 fax 323-653-0123
  guman@vitalresearch.com
- Quality of Care Monitor Satisfaction Survey and Sample report pages for a hypothetical facility against the norms from the Partners in Quality® long-term care survey at any facility any city, any state
  Parkside Associates
  205 West Touhy Avenue, Suite 204
  Park Ridge, Illinois 60068
- AHCA provides customer satisfaction measurement instruments for use in long term care facilities at no charge. The six Satisfaction Assessment Questionnaires available include the following:
  - Cognitively intact nursing facility residents
  - Family members of cognitively intact nursing facility residents
  - Family members of mild dementia nursing facility residents
  - Assisted Living residents
  - Medically complex subacute facility residents
  - Rehabilitation subacute facility residents
  For information, please contact:
  American Health Care Association (AHCA)
  1201 L Street, NW
  Washington, DC 20005-4014
  202-842-4444

Table IV.E *(continued)*

- Staff Satisfaction Survey
  F. Theodore Helmer, Ph.D.
  Professor of Management, Northern Arizona University,
  Flagstaff, AZ
  e-mail: Ted.Helmer@nau.edu

- Long Term Care Resident Evaluation Survey
  Peter Norton, Ph.D.
  Professor and Head
  Dept. of Family Medicine
  University of Calgary
  UCMC, Sunridge
  3465-26 Ave. NE
  Calgary, Alberta, Canada
  T1Y 6L4
  Phone: 403-219-6125
  Fax: 403-219-6140
  E-Mail: norton@ucalgary.ca

- Nursing Home Resident Satisfaction Scale
  Jacqueline Zinn, Ph.D.
  Associate Professor
  Risk, Insurance, and Health Care Management
  Speakman 201
  Fox School of Business Management
  Temple University
  Philadelphia, PA 19122
  Phone: 215-204-1648
  Fax: 215-204-3851

INDEX

('i' indicates an illustration; 't' indicates a table)